T

How
Set U
Run Your Own
Business

SIXTEENTH
EDITION

Helen Kogan

Lincoln

KOGAN
PAGE

Yes – but is the house ready for you?

By Martin Ashton

For anyone considering the option of working from home – an option which is becoming more and more viable today with the increasing choice of communication systems available down a telephone line – one of the most important but least obvious considerations is the house itself and its ability to cope with the ever-increasing range of modern communication systems.

There are usually two choices for someone approaching the decision to change their place of work to their home – conversion of an existing room, or construction of a totally new office.

If you intend to take over an existing room in your home for an office for the next few years, you must obviously give serious consideration to your communication needs during that time. The connection facilities you will need include:

1) Sufficient power points for computer, scanner, monitor, fax machines, VCR, mobile telephone charger, etc. It is not safe to use just one double socket with countless adaptors – preferable by far is to install upto 6 separate sockets for today's modern business needs. In addition, of course, the computer should be protected from current fluctuations by a surge protector – a relatively cheap device which simply interfaces between the computer and your mains power supply.

2) Sufficient telephone points for current and future needs. You may decide, on grounds of cost-saving, to start with just one business line for all external communication facilities – telephone, fax and Internet. However, you will soon find as the business grows that there is an increasing need to be on the phone and on the Internet at the same time – or maybe you want to send an urgent fax while reading some other vital e-mail. You can overcome this by ensuring in advance that the existing line to your home is upgraded to ISDN standards, enabling you to use the fax and Internet at the same time, or by adding an extra one or two additional lines. At the moment, many suppliers are providing quite large cost-saving deals on additional phone lines to domestic premises, and if you go down this route you will be assured of log-jam free external communications for the future.

If there is any chance of expanding your at-home business into other parts of the building, the problems of internal communication become as important as those of external communications outlined above. Consider, for instance, what would happen if, in a couple of years, you decide you need some part-time administrative help. Is there room in your existing office for another person? If not, where will they be located? Are there sufficient power and telephone points to support a second person? Will you have networking links between the two computers?

At this point, it would become an expensive and highly disruptive operation to upgrade the telephone, electric and communications systems within the structure of the building – so perhaps it would be more sensible to consider our second option – to design your new office building from scratch.

Construction from new

Whether you decide to go ahead with building a new office as an extension to your home or as a new stand-alone building, or whether you intend to move to a new home which is able to carry both your domestic and business needs, then all the principles outlined above must be considered.

In addition, the speed at which new advances in communication technology are coming on line makes it imperative that your future office is built to a sufficiently high standard that it will be able to accept modern technological improvements such as UMTS – Universal Mobile Telecommunications Systems. UMTS allows high-speed Internet access, video-conferencing, e-mail and a range of other information services to be transmitted to mobile phone handsets. This third-generation system will enable you to contact your home from your mobile telephone and operate appliances – turn on the central heating, check security by linking up with the security cameras, even draw the curtains and switch some lights on. Brilliant in concept, certainly – but what use is UMTS if your house cannot respond?

Ortronics International is a global organization based in Newbury, Berkshire, that has come up with the perfect answer to this and countless other similar internal and external communication needs. Developed in the USA, the Ortronics *In-House* system has been designed to provide an impressive range of benefits when it is incorporated into a home or small office – preferably at the build stage.

In-House is a complete structured cabling system that supports audio, video, data, voice, computer networking, Internet access and security monitoring systems throughout the whole of the building. The *In-House* system uses a central Control Cabinet as the hub of the communication system which can be equipped with any number of modules – comparable in some ways to building blocks – which in turn provide links to the audio, voice, data or video systems. The Cabinet itself can be located anywhere in the house – under the stairs, at the back of a built-in wardrobe – but not in areas of high humidity such as utility rooms housing washing machines, tumble driers, etc.

The Control Box, hub of the Ortronics In-House system

For a building equipped with a full structured cable system, the modules can be added as and when needed – initially, perhaps, to provide audio around the building so that you can be playing your favourite CD or keeping an eye on the kids playing in the garden while you work. You want coffee – so as you go into the kitchen you simply turn up the music in the kitchen speakers (and in the hall or any other rooms on the way) or switch the monitors over to the CCTV system. The flexibility in life-style that an *In-House* system can bring is almost unbelievable – the full range of computer, telephone and television services accessible in every room, the ability to see what your security or baby-monitoring cameras are seeing whenever you want, wherever you are, internal computer networking, and a lot, lot more.

And for someone considering working from home, the benefits are even greater – no more having to dedicate a family room or spare bedroom specially for an office. The Ortronics system allows you to work wherever you want in the building, with full and instant access to your computer and all external communication systems. So no more working from a cramped back bedroom or converted loft, you can work in whichever room you want, wherever you want with immediate and uninterrupted communication facilities to your family, colleagues and friends always available.

There is no doubt this is going to be the environment for the standard-setting home business of the future – but the future has already arrived, for Midas Homes are currently in the final stages of the development of over 50 new homes, every one of which incorporates an Ortronics *In-House*

system. Each home has been wired up to provide an average of 40 data outlets, 8 TV outlets, CCTV facilities at the front and rear, wall or ceiling speakers wherever required (yes, before you ask – even in the bathroom if required!) and sufficient integral wiring to cope with all immediate and long-term future needs.

A modern executive home which has been built to the highest IT standards, including fully the Ortronics In-House system.

Even if it's not primarily used for work, the *In-House* system is perfect for today's modern family as it keeps pace with the benefits that technology can bring to their home – and the home in question can be anything from an apartment to a castle, for the *In-House* system is perfect for any building, no matter how big or small.

So the house of the future is now available in the UK – and if you don't want to move to keep up with the latest in-home technology, you must at least move on to consider the *In-House* concept – a building that is fully wired-up for the future, even if you're not.

Martin Ashton,
UK Vice President,
Ortronics International Ltd

<u>v</u>

The start is just the beginning
A cautionary tale for the would-be self-employed

At the last count, more than three million people in this country were self-employed*. Now representing around 13% of the UK's workforce, their numbers have increased by more than half since the beginning of the last decade.

But what is the attraction of being self-employed? For most people starting out, it's the thought of independence – making your own choices and reaping your own rewards. But even with luck on your side, success in your venture will only come with planning. It may be a cliché, but it's sadly still true to say that: We never plan to fail, we simply fail to plan'.

Planning doesn't only require an appreciation of the physical aspects of your future business. It's clearly important to identify basic necessities such as suppliers, premises, equipment needs and perhaps most importantly of all, customers. But as with all plans, it's also important to take steps to protect your business should the unforeseen happen.

Insurance is vital to any business plan. In addition to the sort of cover which most of us already have, to protect our car, office or the family home, there are also all manner of statutory requirements to think about. For example, if you're planning to employ someone, you'll need employer's liability insurance to cover them against accidents at work. And depending on the type of business you have, you may need public liability insurance or professional indemnity cover.

The need for protection doesn't stop there. Being self-employed puts you at the very cornerstone of your business. But despite this, even those who are well used to working for themselves often fail to consider the implications to being unable to work. And yet this can have important repercussions for not only their business, but also themselves and their families.

According to a poll carried out by Continental Research, almost two thirds of the self-employed do not have any form of cover to provide a replacement income during periods of longer term illness. Yet going it alone means sacrificing the support of a sympathetic employer and accepting the prospect of only minimal support from the state. What's more, while being unable to work may prevent you from earning an income, it won't put a stop to the fixed costs which your business will continue to incur.

Remember, being your own boss brings independence in all things – not only managing but also protecting the future of your business. So Lincoln recommends that you find an adviser who is able to suggest ways of protecting your most important asset – you.

Wayne Taylor,
Marketing Projects Manager,
Lincoln Financial Group

Lincoln is a marketing group regulated by the Personal Investment Authority providing life assurance, pensions, unit trusts and ISAs. Any regulated advice offered will relate only to the products of Lincoln.

*National Statistical Office, Social Trends

Investments?

I've got more

important

things to

worry about.

True. There are more pressing issues on your mind than where to put your money. But perhaps we can offer a little sound financial advice. And leave you with more time for the things matter most.

For further information or to arrange an appointment, please telephone **free** on

0800 783 0222

Clear solutions in a complex world

Lincoln Financial Group®

The Daily Telegraph

Guide to Lump Sum Investment
Twelfth edition
Liz Walkington

Whether you have won the lottery, received a redundancy payment or inherited a lump sum, you will want to know how to invest the money to make it grow.

This new edition of this comprehensive guide describes the various short- and long-term investment possibilities, whether they are best for capital growth or income, how easy it is to withdraw money, the costs, the most efficient investments for different situations, how safe the money is, likely rates of return and so on. Topics covered in detail include:

- Fixed capital investments
- Gilts
- Equities
- Unit trusts and offshore funds
- Investment trusts
- ISAs
- Life insurance-linked investments
- Pension planning
- Tangible investments
- Charitable giving
- Where to go for advice.

£12.99 • Paperback • ISBN 07494 3311 6 • 320 pages • 2000

KOGAN PAGE
120 Pentonville Road, London N1 9JN
Tel: 020 7278 0433 • Fax: 020 7837 6348 • w w w . k o g a n - p a g e . c o . u k

First published in 1983

Thirteenth edition 1997
Fourteenth edition 1998
Fifteenth edition 1999
Sixteenth edition 2000

Published by Kogan Page Limited for The Telegraph plc,
1 Canada Square, Canary Wharf, London E14 5DT

Kogan Page Limited
120 Pentonville Road
London N1 9JN

British Library Cataloguing in Publication Data
A CIP record for this book is available from the British Library.
ISBN 0 7494 3308 6

Typeset by Saxon Graphics Ltd, Derby
Printed and bound in Great Britain by Thanet Press Ltd, Margate

Contents

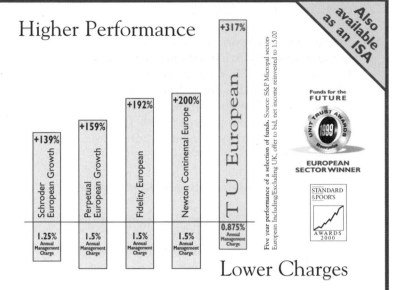

Contents _____

THE CONTRIBUTORS

The publishers would like to express their appreciation of the help given by the following contributors in the preparation of earlier editions of this book: Hugh Aldous, John Anisworth, Henry Ballantyne, Carol Barrie, Roger Bennett, John Blundell, Norman Boakes, Michael J Brookes, Geoffrey Burcher, David Byrne, Roy Chapman, The Charterhouse Group, Heather Coath, Colin Davis, Henry Deschampsneufs, Robert Fleeman, Andrew Hamilton, Charles Hodder, Keith Jones, Jim Kerevan, Michael Killingley, Richard Lee, David Marcelline, Graham Mott, Bill Packer, David Philip, Max Pullen, Michael Reader, Frank Rounthwaite, Royal Institute of Chartered Surveyors, Pradesh Shah, Tony Timberlake, Michael Tomlinson, Frank Walker, Rodney Westhead, Ken White, David Wise, H H Yates and David Young.

The publishers are indebted to:

Department of Trade and Industry

Brian Finch

Maurice Hine

Michael Malone

Dave Patten

for their help with updating the sixteenth edition of this book.

NOTE

Masculine pronouns have been used throughout this book. This stems from a desire to avoid ugly and cumbersome language, and no discrimination, prejudice or bias is intended.

PITNEY BOWES LAUNCHES UNIQUE MAILING PRODUCT FOR HOMEWORKERS AND SOHO BUSINESSES

Pitney Bowes launched a new desktop digital mailing system aimed at SoHo businesses and homeworkers. The small device, called PersonalPost™, applies a postal frank impression to all sizes of envelope or parcel at a rate of up to ten items per minute. The product is currently the only one of its kind to be developed specifically for the mailing requirements of small businesses and home workers.

The PersonalPost? product automates many of the administrative processes associated with handling mail. Rather than having to make trips out of the home or office for stamps, PersonalPost? allows users to download postage over a telephone line within 30 seconds.

The system, which weighs just over 2.5 kilograms (under six pounds), comes with a set of postal scales to help users avoid overstamping (where excess postage is applied to individual mail items). The device also provides comprehensive accounting facilities for accurate postal record keeping.

Pitney Bowes' PersonalPost? includes a facility for automatic mail dating – usually only available on more expensive systems – to prevent improperly dated mail from being returned.

New MORI research for Pitney Bowes indicates that two-thirds (66%) of SoHo businesses feel franked mail looks more professional than stamped mail. The new product enables small businesses and home workers to frank even small volumes of mail and still post it into standard Royal Mail post boxes. Pitney Bowes has targeted the SoHo user with its new pricing. PersonalPost? is available for £595 (+VAT) to buy, or £19.95 (+VAT) per month to rent.

In addition to a frank postal mark, SoHo businesses can use any of the eight pre-loaded advertising slogans within PersonalPost? to improve the appearance of their mail. Alternatively, they can design and install their own company logo or special message.

"The SoHo sector encompasses the overwhelming majority of Britain's businesses and the sector's performance will continue to have a major impact on the country's economic well-being," commented Steve Hornsey, vice president Marketing & Office Direct, Pitney Bowes. "However, it's now clear that smaller organisations are failing to recognise the hidden financial impact of time spent on their own admin. Greater office automation has an obvious role to play in helping these companies grow."

He continued: "Pitney Bowes is the first supplier to produce a product for the SoHo market that has a significant role to play in improving the cost-effectiveness of SoHo business communications. Convenience has also been considered and as a result, PersonalPost? can be purchased on-line from the Pitney Bowes website."

About Pitney Bowes

Pitney Bowes is the world's leading provider of mailing and messaging products for organisations and businesses of all sizes. The company offers a full range of mailing equipment and related financial services and is actively developing new communications products and technologies.

The company is currently introducing a range of digital franking machines, all of which enjoy the advantages of being recredited on line. The 'third generation' in franking machines, these digital machines are software-driven. This means they can be easily upgraded, integrated with computer networks, and provide businesses with comprehensive management information about the mailing operation.

Pitney Bowes has a growing portfolio of Internet-enabled mail and messaging solutions, including internet-based metering technology. These systems, which will allow users to download postage from the Internet were invented by Pitney Bowes. Pitney Bowes also has the ability to manage the electronic delivery of documents from iSend which provides secure e-mail transmission over public networks, to Digital Document Delivery or D3, which allows firms to deliver employee and customer communications such as bill in either electronic or paper formats.

Pitney Bowes' vision is to draw upon its heritage in mailing systems by becoming a complete provider of messaging management services ? to add value to a company's total messaging throughput, encompassing both electronic and paper-based communications.

Since the establishment of the company in 1920, Pitney Bowes has grown to become a global business with a turnover of four billion euros (US$4.4 billion) and in 1999 achieved a significant climb in the FT500 survey of the world's leading companies. Pitney Bowes Inc. is listed on the New York Stock Exchange (NYSE: PBI) and can be seen on the Internet at www.pitney-bowes.co.uk

The Daily Telegraph

Guide to Funerals and Bereavement

Sam Weller

Funerals are probably one of the largest yet most unexpected costs that we have to face, yet arranging a funeral usually takes place when the bereaved are at their most vulnerable. Unfortunately, the funeral directing trade is not licensed or regulated and there is concern about the level of pricing and standards. Relatives do not wish to appear mean where their loved ones are concerned so often end up paying more than they can afford.

> The Daily Telegraph
> LIFEPLANNER
>
> Guide to
> Funerals and Bereavement
>
> Sam Weller

In this practical book Sam Weller examines the entire 'death care industry'. He provides clear information on arranging a funeral, cremation, burial and memorialization, and the costs involved. He takes a holistic view of death and its aftermath. The book spans:

- **planning for a funeral and what to do when someone dies**

- **memorialization**

- **ownership and inheritance of grave plots**

- **rights and responsibilities in cemeteries and churchyards.**

£8.99 • Paperback • ISBN 0 7494 3057 5 • 208 pages • 1999

KOGAN PAGE
120 Pentonville Road, London N1 9JN
Tel: 020 7278 0433 • Fax: 020 7837 6348 • w w w . k o g a n - p a g e . c o . u k

Would you like free Internet calls 24 hours a day, 7 days a week?

Yes   **No**

Do you spend £5 or more on phone calls every month?

Yes   **No**

If you answered 'yes', you're in luck.

With LineOne there are no Internet call charges 24 hours a day, 7 days a week and no monthly subscription fees. In fact, you can even save up to 60% on national and international phone calls*.

All you have to do to access the Internet completely free of charge is spend £5 or more a month on national or international phone calls with Quip! - the new low cost phone company. There is no need to change your current phone line or number, simply pay a one off charge of £20 for a telephone adapter that plugs into your existing phone socket.

Call **0800 111 210** now or register at **www.lineone.net/freeinternet**

www.lineone.net

TOTALLY FREE INTERNET!
Free Internet calls
*24 hours a day, 7 days a week!**

WHATEVER your experience of the Internet already, if you haven't yet tried LineOne, you haven't discovered just how much more LineOne can offer compared to other ISP offerings in the market.

LineOne really knocks the spots off the competition. It's fast, reliable and provides a great Internet service in terms of broad and superb exclusive content. Originally a paid-for Internet service, LineOne has maintained it's high level of quality service and product offerings since going free last year, providing many time-saving tools and unique features that put other services well and truly in the shade. Plus — as well as free Internet access – members can now get free Internet calls, 24 hours a day, 7 days a week.

As well as the usual forms of Internet communication like email, instant messaging and chat, LineOne offers RocketTalk. With RocketTalk you can send and receive voice messages via your PC. It's quick, easy and reliable but, best of all, there's no special software or downloads needed to hear the messages and your recipients don't have to be a RocketTalk member.

Talking about things audio — and visual for that matter — where other services offer a diet of the usual news, sport, weather, etc, with LineOne you can not only read the latest news headlines but you also have the choice to **listen** to the latest ITN headlines or **watch** video clips of all the top stories. You can even have the latest news emailed to your inbox every morning with eNews. And you can listen to all the top UK radio stations currently available live on the Net.

The sense of community is very strong on LineOne too. You can make new friends with other members who share your interests in the many chat rooms, or you can debate and swap advice in the many forums (otherwise known as message boards) ranging from education, computing and business to sport, food, lifestyle and even pets! You're sure to find several to suit your tastes.

As well as many features like those mentioned above, LineOne has over a *million* pages of highly impressive UK content.

Take LineOne's Business section for example. Thinking of starting your own business but don't know quite where to start? You'll find all the

information you need to get you started and turn your business ideas into a reality. There's help with marketing and business plans from KeyNotes and LineOne, plus the latest business news and business banking rates, company and market reports, up-to-the-minute share prices and stock indices and hints and tips to make your life a little easier! LineOne also provides links to other organisations which you may want to access information from, such as Business Link, The Princes Trust and DTI sites.

In the one-stop Travel section, for example, you can access an excellent range of travel information and special offers 24 hours a day. There are discounts on over a million flights and thousands of hotels, car hire and holiday packages — all bookable online or by phone. Undoubtedly one of the best travel sites on the net.

In LineOne Shopping, you can get some fantastic offers and member discounts. And to make your online shopping experience quick and safe, LineOne has set up its own Shopping Charter to offer an additional level of excellence in online customer service.

Need to keep the kids happily occupied on a wet day? LineOne is crammed with exciting and safe things for the young 'uns to do. Need help with homework or academic study? LineOne has a wide array of educational resources in Learning. Then there's help with personal money management, hugely popular online games, support for people running a business, adult-only areas, lots of

places to chat and meet friends, and much much more.

It's no wonder LineOne has rapidly become the second largest free Internet Service Provider in the UK, with over 950,000 members and growing fast. Get more from the Net with LineOne.

**Call 0800 111 210
for your free start-up pack or
join online now
www.lineone.net**

1 | What Kind of Business?

This book is a basic introduction to the world of the self-employed and the small businessman. It has been written on the assumption that you have spent your working life to date as an employee, and that your knowledge of value added tax (VAT), National Insurance (NI), controlling a business and such matters is limited.

There are over three million people in business on their own today. Two and a quarter million are self-employed, and the remainder are directors of their own limited companies. Large numbers of people every month are setting up in business. Some 96 per cent of all firms are small businesses, accounting for 20 per cent of our gross national product.

So what do these small business people do? By far the most popular is the retail sector, followed by the building industry. Indeed, of the 2.3 million enterprises with no employees, 25 per cent are in the construction sector. Wherever there is a gap in the market, you are likely to find self-employed people trying to satisfy the demand for goods and services. From the shopkeeper, the builder and the farmer to the Internet start-ups selling specialist goods – you name it, the self-employed are doing it.

HAVE YOU A VIABLE PROPOSITION?

Two essential elements in a viable business proposition are the product (or service) and the people involved. Until the marketability of the product has been established, there is little point in proceeding further, but given a commercial product and a good management team, it will then be necessary to look carefully at the premises, equipment and financial resources necessary to start the business.

It is tempting to think that a novel idea has better prospects than a proven product; in practice it is not as simple as that. Key questions to ask are:

☐ If you plan to sell your product or service to an established market, are you sure that your sales projections are realistic for a business starting from scratch?

☐ You need to consider the size of the total market, whether it is expanding or contracting, the number of competitors active in it already and how the market is divided among them.

☐ Ask yourself what proportion of the market the new enterprise aims to capture in the first year, the second year and so on, and why people should buy from you instead of from someone else.

☐ How sensitive are your projections to the impacts of a fairly small variation in the market share achievements?

☐ Finally, in reviewing your product, make sure that you have the legal right to produce and sell it. Legal advice may be necessary in order to safeguard the future of your project.

WHAT KIND OF BUSINESS?

Let us begin by looking at the initial stages of starting a business. Deciding on the structure of your business will be the first decision you will have to make. If you are setting up as a sole trader, say a freelance consultant, with a turnover below the VAT threshold, no premises and no staff, and you are trading under your own name, then virtually all you have to do is tell the Inland Revenue and the Department of Social Security (DSS) of your change in status, and then begin to trade. However, once you reach the VAT threshold, use separate business premises, take on staff and trade perhaps as a limited company, the picture is very different. Your choice of business structure will ultimately determine your legal and financial responsibility and should be given serious thought.

THE SOLE TRADER

The simplest way of going into business is to trade on your own and under your own name. The main point to bear in mind is that you are personally liable for all debts since you have no limited liability.

However, you may feel that your name is not the most striking, or the most easily remembered, so you may decide to trade under a name other than your own. In this case, as the name is not your own and therefore ownership of the business is not immediately apparent, it is necessary to show in three places your name and an address within Great Britain at which the service of documents will be effective. This must appear on all letters, orders, invoices, receipts and written demands for payments, and must be prominently displayed at all places in which the business is conducted, and to which customers and suppliers have access. You have what is known as a general statutory duty to divulge ownership of the business and an effective address within Great Britain at which a document may be served upon you. This you may have to do on demand, in writing. Even though you are trading under a name which is not your own, you are still personally liable for all debts.

To set up as a sole trader you simply need to:

- [ ] carry your name and address on your stationery;
- [ ] make legal checks on any trading name that is different from your own;
- [ ] inform the Inland Revenue;
- [ ] consider whether or not you are liable for VAT;
- [ ] check with the local planning office that your premises are suitable for work.

While personal liability may be considered to be a risk of running a business as a sole trader, if well advised, considerable tax advantages are offered from being self-employed and coming under Schedule D. There is also the additional benefit of lower national insurance contributions. However, this, in turn can be outweighed by the necessary precaution of investing in a personal pension and other safety nets to cover ill health and the spectre of business failure. Further advantages and disadvantages are weighed up by Philip Treleaven:

Sole Trader

Pros:	*Cons:*
Start trading immediately	Unlimited personal liability
No registration: minimal formalities	Low business status
No set-up costs (e.g. lawyers)	Limited access to investment capital
No annual audit or audit fees	Higher tax rates than a limited company
No disclosure of trading information	Limits on pension contribution

Source: *Start-ups.co.uk*, Philip Treleaven, Barclays/Kogan Page.

GOING INTO PARTNERSHIP

The same basic rules apply to a partnership as to the sole trader, the main difference being that you are working with someone else and not by yourself. It is also worth remembering that should your partner amass business debts, unknown to you, then in all likelihood you will be responsible for those debts (other than debts relating to purely personal matters) if your partner disappears.

Procedures to follow in setting up a partnership are:

☐ display names and business address on the stationery;
☐ check any made-up business name under which you trade is legally acceptable;
☐ draw up a legally binding partnership agreement;
☐ take out life insurance on each partner to protect the partnership;
☐ inform the Inland Revenue you are self-employed;
☐ check with the local planning office your place of work is suitable;
☐ consider whether you need to register for VAT;
☐ consider whether to form a limited (liability) partnership.

You are strongly advised to have a partnership agreement drawn up by a solicitor in order to prevent difficulties arising from any future break-up of the partnership. This agreement needs to cover the basis on which the partners intend to work together, and should among other stipulations include:

1. The partnership name and address and the nature of the business.
2. The date you start and end the partnership.
3. The amount of capital contributions.
4. The bank account.
5. How profits are to be calculated and divided.
6. Provision requiring regular accounts.
7. An arbitration clause.
8. A clause permitting arrangements to be made with creditors through the courts if there are cash flow problems.
9. Dissolution.

Source: _Law For the Small Business_, Patricia Clayton.

Limits on financial commitments can be made but it is necessary that at least one partner has unlimited liability for business debts. Along with the reduction in risk the limited partner's involvement is also diminished and has less say in the running of the business and is really viewed as a lender to the company. The Registrar of Joint Stock companies should be informed of a limited partner status.

If you are going into a partnership or starting up as a sole trader, remember that the statutory benefits to the self-employed, sickness benefit, for example, are considerably less than those for the employed. Permanent Health Insurance (PHI) policies, pensions, etc all need to be considered. Ask your insurance broker to submit a number of quotes from different insurance companies.

Partnership

Pros	_Cons_
Start trading immediately	Unlimited personal liability on partners
No registration, minimal formalities	Limited access to investment capital
Minimal set-up costs	
Optional annual audit	Partnership agreements can be costly
No disclosure of trading information	Partnership ceases on death of a partner

Source: _start-ups.co.uk_, Philip Treleaven.

THE LIMITED COMPANY

The main difference between trading as a company and trading as a partnership is the limited liability factor. The directors of a company are not personally liable for debts incurred by the company except for non-payment of NI contributions. Everyone's circumstances are different and there are different schools of thought; if you are thinking of going into business and of forming a limited company, get advice from an accountant or solicitor first. Do not rush into it without thought and good reasons.

The creation of a business into a legal entity is achieved through the process of incorporation. This provides a legal structure and shifts the issues of liability from the individual to the company. It also allows for expansion and outside investments. There are two methods of incorporation. The first is to register a new business with Companies House (see below) which can take some time for the paperwork to be put in place. The second is to buy a company from Companies House that already exists. This is quite a normal procedure in which a company name can be changed easily and in which the previous shareholders resign.

Additionally, there are four main matters to be dealt with in forming a company (in some instances your solicitor will be able to help):

- [ ] choosing a name;
- [ ] defining the business purpose of the company (its 'objects');
- [ ] settling its contribution and procedural rules (the company's Memorandum and Articles of Association);
- [ ] filing particulars with the Registrar of Companies, Companies House, Crown Way, Maindy, Cardiff CF4 3UZ (you can ask your solicitor to deal with this for you; details required are the company's registered office, particulars of shareholders, directors and company secretary).

The Memorandum and Articles of Association set out shareholders' liabilities, rights and obligations. The company's Memorandum sets out the limits of authority within which directors and shareholders should stay and as such provides security of personal liability against creditors' claims.

The Memorandum of Association should state:

1. The company's name.
2. Where the company's registered office is, ie England, Scotland, Wales.
3. The objects for which the company is formed.
4. That the liability of shareholders is limited by their shares.
5. The amount of initial normal capital and how it is divided into shares.
6. The names of subscribers (signatories) to the memorandum and that they agree to take out at least one share each.

Source: *Law For the Small Business*, Patricia Clayton

The organisation of the company and shareholders is set out in the Articles of Association. It also identifies the powers and responsibilities of directors. The Stationery Office provides a standard form of Articles. Limited companies must also present accounts in a set way and have an annual audit. Furthermore, limited companies must file accounts and annual returns with the Companies Registrar.

Limited Company

Pros	*Cons*
High business status	Company has to be formally
Company carries liability	registered
Access to investment capital	Professional annual audit
Possible flotation on stock	required
market	Public disclosure of trading
Business life independent	information
of founders	Directors' duties and
Lower tax rates	obligations

Source: *Start-ups.co.uk*, Philip Treleaven.

Other forms of business

Although the three business structures already discussed are the most common, there are several other alternatives to choose from. For example, if there are more than seven people starting the business you might consider becoming a co-operative. This would allow for the business to be jointly owned by all its members. The registration of a co-operative is statutory and is a complicated procedure. Advice can be sought from the Co-operative Development Agency, 21 Panton Street, London SW1 4DR.

Another option for those starting educational, artistic or religious businesses might be to consider applying for charitable status. Exemption from some forms of taxes would benefit trustees but charities are not able to make profits.

WORKING WITH FAMILY

Research undertaken by the Stoy Centre for Family Business has found that family businesses account for over 76 per cent of all UK businesses and that 50 per cent of the workforce in the private sector is employed in such companies. However, if your business opportunity is also a means to work alongside loved ones it is worth taking a long, hard, look at some of the complexities and problems presented by family businesses.

As with working in a partnership, working with family will mean that any weaknesses in business skills and financial liabilities will have to be borne by the company. However, unlike choosing a business partner, a family member's skills and business acumen may not be scrutinised in the same way. The tough but necessary question of 'Would I go into business with my wife/husband/son/daughter, etc if they were not family members?' is essential. Many individuals set up their own company with the prime motive of wanting to work with their family members. However, business criteria must be the first and dominant driving force behind any new company if it is to be successful. Business failure and family bust-ups might well be the result of not being objective about the aims of the new company.

A recent report by business advisers Grant Thornton, *The Family Business Report*, identified some of the problems facing family-run businesses including a failure to monitor key performance indicators and early warning signals such as debtors, stock levels or outstanding orders. Andrew Godfrey, Head of Growth and Development Services at Grant Thornton, believes that this could be a result of the overall workload of those running start-ups: 'It could be that owner–managers are so wound up in the day-to-day running of the business that they believe they have no time to spend on monitoring.' He also advises that family businesses should be 'professionalized at all levels' and advises on some key steps to achieve this:

- ☐ adequately documented shareholder agreements;
- ☐ agreement on goals and objectives for the business;
- ☐ growth rates;
- ☐ acceptability of risk levels;
- ☐ expected returns on investment;
- ☐ timely and accurate accounting information to facilitate planning, operational decision-making and performance review;
- ☐ a sufficiently skilled and integrated management team.

Source: _Family Businesses_, Institute of Directors.

There are many examples of successfully run family businesses. However, for every success there is a tale of failure and feud. The best advice is to think through the issues objectively before you jump in.

WHAT MAKES AN ENTREPRENEUR?

So what sort of qualities do self-employed people need? They have to be healthy, persevering, enterprising, hard-working, unflappable, motivated, confident and independent. If you are going to be self-employed you have to be the sort of person who can cope with a bank manager ringing up in the morning telling you that you have gone over your overdraft limit again. You have to be able to handle irate customers and cope with the VAT or planning officer coming in and bothering you at the same time, and be able to get on and do your business as well. David Hall identifies the three tasks of entrepreneurship in _In the Company of Heroes_ as:

1. Spotting, creating, or seizing opportunities where others often see only chaos and confusion.
2. Marshalling the resources that others may own, in order to take up the opportunity.

3. Building the capability within the business to translate the opportunity into something of value.

If you feel that you will not be able to cope with such stress, then self-employment is not for you. The first qualities noted in the list above was health. As mentioned earlier, the DSS and National Insurance are none too generous as far as self-employed people go, and so good health is essential. Government statistics show that for every ten days the typical employed person is ill, a self-employed person is ill for only three days. If you are self-employed, you will probably work much longer hours in much tougher circumstances. If you are the sort of person who is not very healthy, with a long record of sickness then perhaps opening a shop every morning at 8 am and staying open until 6 pm is not for you.

Being self-employed is a risky business and nine out of ten people who set up in business this week will not be running that same business in five years' time. That does not mean that 90 per cent will have gone bankrupt. There are hundreds of reasons – from emigration to death – to explain why a business will not be running in five years' time. There might be the odd business that is obviously going to run into deficit and so is closed down before its owner goes bankrupt. But people do end up losing the roof over their heads with their houses being put up for sale to pay off their debts, so think very carefully before risking everything in business. If you are still determined, despite all the warnings and potential hazards, then you are advised to do all your homework first so that you go into business with your eyes wide open.

Checklist: What kind of business?

☐ Have you assessed the size of the total market and how it is divided amongst your competitors?

☐ Are your sales projections realistic and can they cope with variations in the market?

☐ Seek out advice to make sure that you have the legal right to produce and sell your product.

☐ If you are operating as a sole trader, but not under your own name, have you displayed the ownership of your business on three places, ie receipts, letters and invoices?

☐ Have you had a partnership agreement drawn up by a solicitor?

☐ Consider new insurance policies to cover you for ill health and obtain a number of quotes from your broker.

☐ If you are considering setting up a limited company seek out advice from your solicitor to help draw up the legal documentation.

☐ If you are planning to work with a member of your family think through the issues and draw up any agreements as you would with non-family members.

☐ Consider your health and whether you are able to withstand long working hours associated with working for yourself.

2 | What Types of Capital are There?

This chapter is not only about types of capital, but also about some of the principal factors you need to take into consideration in deciding how to finance your business. The following chapter on 'Presenting your case' will guide you through some tried and tested routes.

In financing a small business or raising capital for a new one, you will encounter contrasting viewpoints. Ambitious entrepreneurs need the courage of their convictions, and one of those convictions may well be the infallibility of their idea or project. In other words: 'The banks and other lending establishments should put their money where *my* idea is!'

Those who are in the business of lending money will shake their heads, knowing that in practice the failure rate is high and that most entrepreneurs underestimate the amount of money they will need in order to develop their business – and fail to learn by their mistakes as they do so. The banks will ask:

☐   Who bears the initial risk?
☐   Are you going to put your money alongside our money?
☐   And if your business goes wrong, how far will you be committed personally?
☐   What security can you offer?

It is worth understanding these two points of view before studying the capital structure of new businesses and the types of capital and their sources. This is because central to the growth of any business will be the support of a lending banker. The lending banker has a relatively uncomplicated ambition: to get the original loan back at the end of its term, while receiving the current market rate of interest on it in the meantime. This does not mean that the loan is risk-free. The banks will share some risk, but will seek to ensure that the risks of a business are fairly shared between its proprietors and its financial backers.

It is not possible to cover in one chapter all types of capital for all types of business. It would take a whole book just to cover sole traders, partnerships and limited companies, and then consider capital for new businesses, development capital for growing existing businesses, and public capital for successful businesses.

GETTING THE RIGHT CAPITAL

The most crucial consideration for financing a new business is getting the capital structure right at the beginning. There will doubtless be plenty of other crises as a business develops, without starting out with the kind of finance that cannot sustain the inevitable financial setbacks. Chapter 3 is all about assessing and presenting the case to the banks and explains the projections which you should undertake. Those projections should enable bankers and venture capitalists to assess possible ways in which the business may progress, and to judge whether the initial capital is sufficient.

One of the venture capital companies has done some research on the problems of new businesses. Apart from highlighting hopeless management, this research suggests that new manufacturing companies, growing steadily, need cash resources of maybe 25 per cent to 30 per cent of the value of their growing sales in order to finance stocks, debtors (less creditors) and other working capital requirements. If you add to that the capital equipment needed, the initial start-up losses from funding overheads and the product development costs, you may get a severe cash requirement over maybe two or three years. If sufficient capital can be raised in one form or another for the assets of the business, even allowing for initial losses, to be twice the amount which the new business borrows, then that will be more than enough to make sure that further temporary facilities can be arranged to cover any hiccups and delays in cash receipts. The business will then be financially stable.

The problem which faces many small businesses at the outset is under-capitalisation; many lose the confidence of their bankers at their first crisis. It is not the lending banker's job to gamble money on a business which only pays a market rate of interest on the uncertain outcome of a new venture. Those small businesses are the first ones to fail. Having more capital at the outset gives you some insurance against unforeseen setbacks.

PROPRIETOR'S CAPITAL

Any business should make sure that it starts life with an adequate base of risk capital. A significant part of that will be the proprietor's capital. Backers, whatever form they take, are more inclined to lend money when they know that the proprietor is doing the same.

There are three sources, at least, for that risk capital:

☐ the management – you, the one who wants to start or develop your own business;
☐ external investors (friends, relatives, associates and trading partners);
☐ venture capital companies. The role of private individuals such as business acquaintances who invest in new companies is often overlooked but many enterprises are financed in this way. Such investors are called 'business angels'. There are also some sources of quasi-capital: money which is totally at risk and which will only be paid off if the venture is successful (some government project finance is like that).

The Enterprise Investment Scheme (EIS), successor to the Business Expansion Scheme (BES), is likely to be of more interest now that the Chancellor has added to 20 per cent income tax relief the ability to roll over capital gains tax due from the sale of a previous business or any other business asset. An individual can invest up to £150,000 per year in new shares. With 60 per cent tax relief from these sources, entrepreneurs who have made money in other businesses have a big incentive to invest in new ones. Investment through EIS also makes the sale of shares that have been held for five years free of capital gains tax.

The rules relating to eligibility for EIS are complex and professional advice should be sought. Be particularly careful about remuneration for investing directors, and about mixed loan and equity investment. EIS or tax roll-over relief can be lost if errors are made.

The individual can borrow capital, and will usually get tax relief on the interest. Consequently, if they really believe in their venture, it must be rare for the managing individuals to be unable to raise even a modicum of capital as equity share capital.

Then there are the venture capital companies. Each major clearing bank has connections with some of these companies, if it is not connected with one entirely of its own. This form of capital embraces a wide range of potential investments which are not just for high technology companies. The British Venture Capital Association (BVCA), which is based in London, provides a free list of venture capital companies. Venture Capital Report (VCR; see Appendix III) publish a guide to venture capital in the United Kingdom and Europe and also publish a monthly report which details relevant information on small businesses (between five and fifteen per report) who are seeking venture capital. However, it is worth remembering that venture capital is only for businesses which have been incorporated into limited companies.

What venture capital companies will consider doing is financing your business partly with share capital of various types, and partly with loans. If they do a good job they will offset sufficient of the risk which they bear by taking on completely new ventures with the prospect of gain on the few businesses which are successful. This will enable them to offer a high proportion of loan money, and this loan money should be for a sufficiently long term so that the business not only has some financial security for its early years but is still free to finance temporary needs by overdrafts. Sometimes entrepreneurs look on these finance packages as requiring them to 'give away' some of their equity. That seems an unreasonable view since the investment is not just lending, it is sharing considerable risk. The statistics show that most new businesses fail yet few entrepreneurs accept that, as far as the bank or venture capitalist is concerned, theirs could be one of them.

If you structure the finance of a business properly, and are prepared to 'cut in' others, it will have a greater chance of enabling you to share in most of the prosperity brought by success rather than being left – along with the creditors – with 100 per cent of failure.

A venture capital company will probably draw up a shareholders' agreement which will further ensure that the business is managed in its interests and that it shares in any profits.

DIFFERENT KINDS OF SHARES

The equity in the business may be composed of various types of shares.

Ordinary shares

In the UK, shares have a notional or 'par' value. This is not really material since one can pay £1 for a 1p share. This is typical for each share: one equal amount subscribed, one vote, one equal right to any declared dividend or to the capital of the business. There are all sorts of variations on such ordinary shares. The management's ordinary shares might have dividend rights deferred until a certain participation in profit has gone to the other shares. All those other shares, owned by the venture capitalist, might have a right to a special dividend if profits exceed a certain level.

As the company's worth increases, so does the value of each share held. It is worth noting, however, that should the business fail, borrowed money will have priority for repayment, and both the Inland Revenue and HM Customs and Excise will take what is owed to them before shareholders have a chance of getting anything back.

These are all 'sweeteners' to persuade the investor to provide finance with less of a stake in the equity than if his equity stake had only the same rights as everyone else's. Although this seems quite a good idea, to avoid the feeling of 'giving away' too much of the equity, be careful: if the business is a success it is going to be quite expensive to buy back these shares from the investor who has special profit-sharing rights – even though they did enable the business to get started in the first place.

In businesses where there are sole traders or partnerships, the equity represents any capital introduced plus profits still held in the business.

Preference shares

Preference shares usually carry a fixed cumulative dividend that is paid before ordinary shareholders receive dividends, hence the term 'preference'. However, they usually have restricted voting rights and may not participate in the capital growth of the business. They may be redeemable at some time in the future. The rights attached to them may vary widely, and so some financiers will view them as debt and others as part of the equity capital of the business. For a lending bank, the key question is whether the dividends have to be paid, like interest on a loan. Since preference shares are unsecured, ranking behind debt, a lender will usually view them as equity as long as payment of dividends depends upon the ability of the business to afford them.

WHERE TO LOOK FOR LOANS

There are three types of loan, best described by the length of time they are available: long-, medium- and short-term loans.

Long-term loans

Generally speaking, long-term loans (ten years or more), for use as equity capital, are not provided by the clearing banks but are available from other institutions or some subsidiaries of the clearing banks. Banking prudence, and the principle of matching their sources of funds with their assets, mean that clearing banks very rarely lend longer than ten years, unless under a special contract – five to seven years is more usual.

Long-term loans are more likely to be provided by insurance companies, pension funds, building societies, 3i (Investors in Industry) and the institutions which provide industrial property mortgages, many of whom are also connected with insurance companies. These lenders are looking for a high running yield (high return) on the funds, either because they need that income to meet payments – as the pension funds do – or because that matches the type of finance which they have raised. They require a debenture to secure their loans. If you have a proven track record in running your business it might be possible to negotiate with the lending institution on the matter of how that debenture ranks against the bank, that is, who gets paid first if your enterprise fails. An understanding institution that is prepared to consider a package of loan and equity capital in which the loan is subordinate to an element of bank lending can be a marvellous support to a growing business, but do not expect such support if you have not yet proved yourself.

Contractual term loans are formalised by a specific agreement to cover a specific purpose, period and repayment programme – which might match a cash flow of a project.

Medium-term loans

Medium-term loans are much more home ground for the banks. Every bank has some form of development loan scheme providing five- or seven-year money. Most have some sort of start-up loan scheme by which they will lend money to new businesses, and hope to recover their money and make some sort of extra gain from those which are successful. Most banks also have asset loan schemes for specific purchases.

The cost of schemes, if they involve equity options or royalties, may be difficult to quantify, although in general the banks will want to charge the equivalent of between 3 and 5 per cent above base rates on the money lent.

The cost of more conventional medium-term finance may be slightly less, and the banks will generally look for security in the form of a fixed or floating charge over the company's assets. A commitment fee is usually charged and the borrower is required to pay any costs.

External shareholders, who have a stake in the capital of the business will often provide loan capital as well, possibly linked to a right to acquire more shares in the business.

Instalment credit (hire purchase, in colloquial terms) and leasing have a major application in financing the fixed assets of businesses. Leasing will be the more effective method if taxable profits are not yet anticipated. Instalment credit has now been extended to cover stocking finance for certain industries where the stock items are identifiable. Most leasing companies will demand personal guarantees from directors of new businesses unless the asset that is leased provides very strong security.

When doing your cash flow calculations, remember that leasing companies often charge three months rental as a deposit. There are also items, such as software, that they may decline to finance. Most of the banks have their own leasing companies.

Short-term loans

Factoring provides sales accounting and debt collection services, and sometimes an element of protection against bad debts; usually some 80 per cent of the debts due to the business is receivable immediately and the balance, less charges, is paid when the debt is recovered. There is a range of other discounting services which may not involve managing the sales accounting. They tend to be a little expensive but can relieve the business of time and trouble. They can also, by chasing your debts for you, reduce your administrative costs and your cash tied up by debtors.

If you are embarking on an export programme (see Chapter 11), then letters of credit, or bills of exchange, can be accepted on the London markets and your bank will be able to do this for you.

Revolving credits are rather like household budget accounts, but for companies.

The cheapest form of borrowing is often by the simple overdraft. 'Blue chip' companies have frequently enjoyed overdrafts at a margin of 1 per cent above the bank's base rate. Smaller companies usually bear a margin of 2 to 3 per cent, with new companies being charged up to 4 per cent. Do not blindly accept 4 per cent if another bank will offer you 3.5 per cent – change your bank if necessary. Remember, competition between banks also works to your advantage.

Your bank manager may offer you a loan at a fixed rate of interest: if interest rates rise above the rate charged, you are fortunate. However, the reverse can happen. Think very carefully before accepting a fixed rate option.

Interest rates are an emotive subject. Do not devote all your attention to the rate of interest and ignore bank charges. These should be agreed at the same time since they can swamp loan interest and are equally negotiable. Some industry associations have negotiated special terms with banks on behalf of their members. This may provide sufficient reason to join an association. Always ask about 'arrangement fees' and any other charges, such as legal or security fees. They can be substantial so try to reduce them too.

Many bank managers will have nursed along a new small business on nothing more than an overdraft facility supported by personal guarantees. As a minimum consideration, the overdraft facility should be protected by making sure that 'hard core' overdraft borrowing – that is, the lowest level of borrowing beneath which the overdraft does not go at any time in the course of a year – should be financed in some other way. One of the most common mistakes made in financing small business, after getting the overall gearing (ratio of loans and leasing to equity) too high, is relying too heavily on short-term credit. This pushes up the overdraft and extends creditors to such a level that all flexibility is lost.

Remember that an overdraft is 'on call': the bank can withdraw it at any time without having to give a reason.

Try to avoid giving personal guarantees. Start by saying 'No' when these are demanded. As well as putting your home at risk they make it harder to switch to another bank if you are dissatisfied.

GOVERNMENT SCHEMES

Government grants tend to be associated with assisted areas, areas of economic deprivation and so on. 'Why go to the middle of nowhere when you can come to the middle of London?', asks the London Docklands Development Corporation.

The whole emphasis of government aid for industry changes from time to time, so it cannot be predicted year to year. Also, its scale is not always appreciated. The latest changes favour 'high-quality, knowledge-based projects that provide skilled jobs' over and above simple job creation, which used to be the prime objective.

Assisted areas are now in three tiers, with different state-aid ceilings applying to each. However, at the time of writing, the map of these areas, although submitted by the UK government, has not been approved by the EU. The areas proposed for Tier 1, which gets the maximum level of state aid, are; Cornwall, Merseyside, South Yorkshire, West Wales and the Valleys and the Highlands & Islands Enterprise Area. Tier 2 is a more complex listing. Within Tiers 1 and 2, Regional Selective Assistance will operate. If you feel you may be in or near to an area that might benefit from such grants it is worthwhile telephoning the DTI, Scottish or Welsh Offices (see Appendix III for addresses, telephone numbers and the Web site). Grants are not automatic but are negotiated between the company and the operating department.

Regional Selective Assistance has a defined geographical coverage, is a one-off grant up to £75,000 and is limited to 15 per cent of capital expenditure on a project – so a total project cost up to £500,000 may qualify. However, the grant is reduced to 7.5 per cent for 'medium-sized enterprises', as defined by EU rules, outside the Assisted Areas. Small enterprises employ up to 50 people, while up to 250 employees classify a business as medium sized.

Enterprise grants will provide assistance within the first two tiers and also to a wider third tier area and will be available for businesses employing up to 250 people. Those areas qualifying will be local authority districts suffering high unemployment, coalfield areas and Rural Development Areas.

Don't worry if you are finding this confusing. If contemplating a major project or starting a business it must be worthwhile calling the DTI to see whether there may be assistance you can apply for, even if it means moving your business a few miles down the road. It may be surprising but even around London and the southern counties there are areas that qualify. The DTI Web site (www.dti.gov.uk/assistedareas) can provide more information.

At the other end of the scale there is the Business Start-up Scheme, details of which are available from the Training and Enterprise Councils in England and Wales, and the Local Enterprise Companies in Scotland, through Jobcentres. It is directed to individuals: the main requirements are that you have been unemployed, that you are in receipt of unemployment benefit, and that you have some start-up capital to put into the company, partnership, co-operative or as a sole trader. Under the old scheme (Enterprise Allowance) an allowance of £40 per week was payable for up to 52 weeks to supplement the income of a new business. Now, however, the size and duration of the allowance is more closely tied to each particular enterprise. The sum can range from £20 to £90 a week and be given over a period varying from 26 to 66 weeks. But before you decide whether to apply, go and talk to your tax consultant, as certain tax disadvantages might be brought out regarding your own particular situation should you be a sole trader or in a partnership. The Training and Enterprise Councils also administer funds that may help with staff training or even business planning for new and established companies. Since each of the TECs has different schemes and levels of funding available, it is important to check what your local TEC has to offer.

The Enterprise Fund, which was introduced in December 1998, also makes provision for public and private sector financing to small and medium-sized firms. The four elements of the fund are:

☐ small-firms Loan Guarantee Scheme;
☐ venture capital support for high-tech business;
☐ support for small equity investments (those up to £0.25 million);
☐ the Department of Trade and Industry's 'challenge' to finance industry to come forward with innovative proposals.

The main method of delivery assistance through the Enterprise Fund is via the Loan Guarantee Scheme.

This is a form of selective assistance whereby the government guarantees loans to encourage banks and other financial institutions to lend to small firms that lack security or track record. For new business, or start-ups, the guarantee is 70 per cent on loans of between £5,000 and £100,000. For firms which have been established for two years or more the guarantee is 85 per cent on a maximum loan of £250,000. The borrower has to pay the government a premium of 1.5 per cent on variable interest rate loans and 0.5 per cent on fixed interest rate loans.

Before offering a Loan Guarantee Scheme loan, lenders must satisfy themselves that they _would_ have offered conventional finance but for lack of security. They should establish that all available assets have been used for conventional loans. No personal assets or personal guarantees can be taken as security for the loan. _It is the lender's decision whether or not personal assets are available to be used for conventional lending._ However, the borrower may be required to pledge premises, machinery and other possessions in connection with the businesses as security for the guaranteed loan. The lender will usually take a fixed or floating charge over such assets.

Another government scheme, available through the Department of Trade and Industry, is that of part-contribution towards the cost of export market research. For companies, the contribution can be up to 50 per cent of either eligible costs of the companies' own in-house research or consultancy fees, up to a maximum contribution of £20,000; for trade associations the contribution can be up to 75 per cent of costs incurred on the first application, then a reducing percentage for subsequent applications.

Only companies employing fewer than 200 people may apply for grants for export market research and they must not have made three or more successful applications since 1 January 1986.

The scheme is administered by the Association of British Chambers of Commerce (address in Appendix III).

Another source of finance can be obtained at interest rates well below those of the market. These loans are available from some high street banks, using funds provided by the European Coal and Steel Community (ECSC). Primarily, these loans are for existing manufacturing companies although certain service businesses may also qualify. The aim of the project is to create jobs in areas where high unemployment has occurred in the steel and coal industry. The loans must be secured by a bank guarantee or equivalent security. An ECSC loan can represent up to 50 per cent of the fixed asset element of the project. There is an upper limit per project of £5 million. Loans are usually for periods of five to eight years and the commencement of repayments can often be deferred. When applying to them, the banks ask for a full business plan – including five years' historic accounts – together with profit and cash flow forecasts.

OTHER GRANTS

Some local authorities provide grants to assist established businesses. While this does not directly assist a start-up, the finance may all be part of taking the business through its early development. It is worth contacting your local authority to find out what help might be available for marketing or business development. In addition, funding is available through local Training and Enterprise Councils for training. Contact your local TEC directly or your local Business Link. The Business Link organisations co-ordinate the provision of information on grants and other assistance. They can, themselves, often provide subsidised training.

IT START-UPS

For Internet start-ups there are various schemes from the telephone companies and equipment suppliers that may reduce costs or delay payments. These change frequently and it is worth making enquiries about what is available. Barclays Bank has produced a useful guide for businesses in this area called 'start-ups.co.uk'.

CAPITAL STRUCTURE

There is a plethora of types of capital for small businesses, and all too often the wrong approach is used in the search for finance – to attempt to raise as much loan finance as possible with minimal personal commitment. The banks and the institutions know by experience that a high proportion of new businesses fail quickly and that most businesses will need more funds than the entrepreneur asks for. It is therefore wise to set out to find the right capital structure. Once you have decided upon the right type of capital which is available to meet your requirements, the next chapter shows you how to present your case to obtain it. Having received some form of finance, we will then show you the sort of records you need to keep and how to monitor and control your business.

Checklist: What types of capital?

☐ Have you identified how much of your own money you are able to invest in the company and if you are prepared to risk it if the business goes wrong?

☐ Consider sources of risk capital and make realistic projections of how much your business will need to get going.

☐ Get advice on the capital structure that is appropriate for you.

☐ Identify what type of loan is suitable for your business and what type of organisation should be approached ie: banks, insurance companies, factors.

☐ Contact the Department of Trade and Industry for information on government support.

---

3 Presenting Your Case for Raising Capital

There are many reasons why you may be wanting to raise capital. Your business may be starting-up or has just started; you may need development finance for expansion or to buy another business, seek export finance, trade credit or a government grant. After early setbacks you may need more money to keep going. In all these examples you will need to make a presentation to persuade people who have the money you want, to invest it in your ideas. Whatever your specific case, this chapter covers the general principles you need to know for making a presentation about your company.

HOW MUCH CAPITAL IS REQUIRED?

A healthy profit forecast does not necessarily mean that little capital will be required. Some of the biggest demands on capital are:

- launching and other preliminary expenses;
- the cost of equipment and premises (sometimes including a premium on leasehold premises);
- the cost of financing stock, work-in-progress and debtors, after allowing for credit granted by suppliers ('working capital');
- sales falling significantly short of expectations, and other deviations from the original plan.

A word of warning when preparing the budget. There is always the risk that sales will be slow to reach expectations, or even that they will not reach them at all: costs may be higher than anticipated. It is therefore important to make sure that adequate capital is available to cover any reasonable shortfall in profits, and it is strongly recommended that profit and cash projections are prepared to reflect the worst envisaged sales income as well as the most likely sales income. An increase in your sales also has to be financed as it means, for example, that you will have to purchase more raw material; you may also have an increased wage bill, as well as other extra costs. These higher costs will generally have to be paid before your customers pay you, leaving a period when you will have to finance the extra costs. When businesses grow faster than they are able to finance this timing difference it is called 'over-trading' and can lead to the bankruptcy of profitable enterprises.

In your cash forecast you should include all items where sums for goods or services are received or paid for at the time of receipt or when the payment occurs. It is different from the trading and profit/loss account which does not deal with any investment you may make and which assumes all is paid in and paid out for a year's business irrespective of the exact timing. In the cash forecast 'capital' items such as equipment and lease premiums as well as pre-trading expenditure must be included. Listed below are some items which have a significant impact on cash forecasts and should therefore be borne in mind:

- ☐ the proportion of sales on credit and the expected credit period;
- ☐ the terms of credit, affecting both purchases and sales;
- ☐ staffing levels and the timing of changes;
- ☐ upgrading accommodation or equipment as the business expands;
- ☐ the nature of timing of capital injections.

The cash forecast should cover the same period as the profit projection, showing projected monthly movements for the first year. It will give you an indication of:

- ☐ the maximum capital requirement (before allowing for interest, which will be dictated by the type of financing deal eventually negotiated);
- ☐ the month in which the maximum requirement will arise;

☐ the pattern of the capital requirement (useful to establish the timing of injections and repayments of capital, and the form of finance most suitable);

☐ the impact on the capital requirement of slower than expected sales progress.

Remember that the exact timing of receipts and payments is crucial for a new business. If receipts are a week late and payments are demanded a week early, life can become very uncomfortable. Factors such as precisely when VAT or NI becomes payable or when the rates bills arise can be very important to get right.

What is the capital required for?

If the evidence gained from your forecasts suggests that much of the capital will be invested in assets on a medium- to long-term basis (say, for at least two years), then short-term sources of capital such as a bank overdraft or a temporary loan should not be considered. The components of the capital requirement should be analysed to establish what the fund will be used for and therefore the timescale of the financing required. As a general rule it is best to consider longer-term capital unless dealing with, for example, a business requiring virtually no investment in fixed assets (i.e. equipment and premises), and only modest finance for working capital which fluctuates and can be financed by an overdraft.

Your end objective: a bankable proposition

Most businesses ultimately survive, or not, on the strength of the continuing confidence of their bankers. All other financial dealings must result in a bankable balance sheet. If you insist on proceeding against the better judgement of your bank manager, you will risk edging your business that much closer to the appointment of a receiver.

The funding of the business should be sufficient and stable enough to enable it to survive a conceivable period of misfortune. Until that position is reached the business will be fragile, and investors and bankers are likely to take a cautious view. Expansion will certainly require finance for more working capital; so will misfortune. Without an adequate equity base you may have no leeway.

SEEING IT FROM THE OTHER SIDE

This is all about seeing ourselves as others, such as bankers and investors, see us. It is often extremely difficult for smaller entrepreneurs to look at their position critically; they are sure they are right – and very often they are – but nobody will be convinced by assertions. This is where your accountant comes in, who can help you to get an objective view of yourself and your business and should be the person who understands what you are currently engaged in. *Present your business as others want to see it.* To do that you are going to have to anticipate your needs: *anticipation* and *control* should be the two themes of your presentation. A banker wants to see an application which anticipates what might happen, both the worst and the best, and what you plan to do about it, the information you gather and how you use it and how you demonstrate your ability to control the business. Your anticipation and contingency planning feed through into the financial picture the report paints and reflects your management ability. A potential backer will also need full details of the business, from machinery to personnel to sales potential. Make sure that all this information is in a readable form. Your story is exciting – make sure you bring that out and don't make it sound dull.

Many small businesses fall into the trap of being wildly optimistic with their sales projections while forgetting whole areas of cost, leading them to raise too little money for too short a term. Professional advice can be a very good investment.

HAVE YOU GOT A BALANCED MANAGEMENT STRUCTURE?

Before we discuss the finance of your prospective business in detail, we need to take a look at the management, i.e. you and your partners. The question to ask yourself is whether you and/ or your partners or fellow directors have the necessary management expertise for running a business of the kind you hope to start. Take a good look at the experience you can offer between you, and ask yourself whether it is relevant to your proposal. Remember, others will ask these questions about you.

MAKING AN EFFECTIVE PROPOSAL

The picture you must present is of the whole business, warts and all. The points which need to be included in any proposal are listed below:

☐ description: physical factors, a broad picture of its operation, factors which might strain, limit or influence operations (e.g. space, plant and machinery, trained personnel);
☐ the product, its market and its place in that market, even for a corner shop;
☐ competitors and your advantages over them;
☐ its base maintainable performance: the level of activity above which you hope to rise but below which there is a very limited danger that you will fall;
☐ its track record: trading, not statutory, accounts;
☐ what factors affect trading, and how;
☐ management's ability and credentials.

Put the detail in schedules or appendices so that the opening is brief, and simply portrays the present business. Always remember to set out just the important factors at the beginning. These two maxims are worth remembering: first, *attention starts to wander after four pages*, and secondly, *you may not be there in person to add your explanations*. Your proposal may have to live and fight alone at some area office or bank committee meeting. If you discover that your bank manager will be passing on your proposal to someone else to deal with, find out who it will go to and send it to him yourself.

Sound business

Your banker is going to want to know some very simple things, such as – is the business sound? It is, therefore, important that you really substantiate your base maintainable profit.

Present your case as others will want to see it, and unless you have financial training and are skilled at financial presentations, turn to your accountant to present an objective case. Take a critical look at your business and its future, just as the banker will do. How much? How long? What if? How do I get it back? These are the questions to be answered. Your presentation should be lucid, logical and frank.

Making assumptions for the future

You should follow your description of the proposition with a careful analysis of the assumptions for the future. Your case is made or broken on the validity of your assumptions and their root in practical business probability. It is vital to get a grip on the essential assumptions about your business, and then put the essence of them across succinctly to your bankers. If they do not understand from your presentation what it is that is crucial to the success or failure of your proposal, and why and how that success or failure comes about, then you will have failed. 'When in doubt do nowt' is a banker's motto. Do not blame the bank manager – blame your presentation.

One can say, cynically, that your crucial assumptions will be those very reasons you will give as excuses when the project collapses: continuing economic recession, poor market launch, high rates of interest, high wage inflation, lack of skilled labour, cheap imports. All the things which made it not your fault that the project collapsed are the things which should have been properly tackled in your initial assumptions. Some areas for assumptions are:

- [ ] the economy of the country;
- [ ] volume of trade: your market;
- [ ] seasonality;
- [ ] personnel;
- [ ] fixed assets and capacity;
- [ ] inflation;
- [ ] the competition;
- [ ] pricing;
- [ ] conclusions from market research;
- [ ] interest rates.

Volume of trade is very important. If you want to start a corner shop it is almost impossible to know how many people are going to come in and buy Mars bars. If you are setting up a new factory, it is very difficult to say what the volume of business going through the factory will be. But in both cases you can make a reasonable attempt. You need not go for full-blown market research, but you can estimate the size of the market you can reach, how much you can sell against the competition, set it against how much you can produce, and then make some hard judgements. You will probably find some useful statistics in the public reference library: use trade associations, key suppliers, newspaper articles, industry 'experts', etc. If you take professional advice, make sure you choose an adviser who is experienced in marketing at your level of business, such as a business counsellor or a consultant. Bankers are all too familiar with volume predictions of the type that say 'one item will be sold in the first month, two in the second', and so on. Be realistic; you understand your business and you must convey that confidence and knowledge to the bank.

YOUR FORECASTS

The working schedules at the back of your presentation are its engine-room. Here you will have to set out three essential schedules with supporting working papers, which stretch forward over the duration (recommended two- to three-year period) of the required finance:

1. Profit and loss: split between the composition of trading gross profit and overheads.
2. Cash flow: showing as a separate line the contribution from trading before finance and capital items.
3. Balance sheets: including leased assets and leasing liabilities.

Make it clear how the forecasts were arrived at. The assumptions should flow naturally into the profit projections. Some further analysis will help your lender with the answer to 'What if?' Any reader of your presentation should be able to import an assumption of their own and form a view of the impact of that on your business – where, how and with what consequence.

_____

KNOWING YOUR BUSINESS

It is worth pausing here to see what it is that the banker or investor is expecting from the presentation that you have prepared so far. They want to understand your business, but they also want to see that *you understand your business*. In preparing your plan, always consider what could go wrong and what you would do about it. Answer the reader's concerns before they are raised. Your lender will also be looking for evidence of competent financial control – evidence that you are where you are knowingly. Many firms believe that any form of planning is a waste of time, but cash forecasting and the discipline of matching plans to resources do not have to be elaborate and have often proved vital. Finally, your lender will be interested in three particular banking concepts: matching finance to its use, gearing and security. All three should be considered together.

Matching finance

When putting together a presentation it is very important not to be tempted to leave the business that you know about and start playing in the business of money. The most common mistake is to attempt to finance long-term assets with short-term money, and to argue on the hope that increasing property values are going to make an otherwise not very sensible level of borrowing turn into a profitable venture for you.

Any good, small business accountant keeps in touch with the banks and the lending institutions and has a feel for the way they are thinking. One of the things that your accountant should do, apart from converting your 'back of the envelope' ideas into an effective presentation, is to insist that your presentation brings out the financial stability which follows from your proposals. Broadly speaking, this means that long-term investment should be funded with long-term money, and readily leasable assets can often be leased at attractive interest rates and over most of their useful lives. Finance for a particular project or asset should be repaid out of the proceeds generated by the business on that project or asset. Do not try to finance one project by the proceeds of another; the road to ruin is paved with plans for cross-funding. Overdrafts should be limited to working capital requirements, and should be self-liquidating as part of the trading cycle. The cash-flow and profitability projection should be carried forward so that it can be demonstrated that debt finance is repaid out of cash generated by the project. If that cannot be done, then you probably ought to look for longer-term institutional money.

Gearing

The banker will be interested in three forms of gearing. The first concern is the gearing that emerges from your balance sheet. In the past a banker's norm has been one-to-one capital gearing; in other words, the bank puts in a pound for every pound you either put in originally or have retained in the business. (Bankers will often say that they prefer this 1:1 gearing ratio; a climb past a 2:1 ratio is often indicative of a banker's concern, in direct proportion to the extent of the climb.) The ideal approach is to demonstrate that even a higher level of gearing initially will correct itself back to a comfortable norm, without relying on crocks of gold.

The second concern is income gearing. It shows to what extent the cash flow of the business (generally, profits plus depreciation – that is, cash from trading) covers the repayment of finance, interest and leasing costs.

Finally there is operational gearing, which relates to the proportion of fixed costs in the business. If this is high then only a small drop in sales can turn large profits into large losses.

Security

The banker is also interested in security, but is much more interested in minimising the risk than in realising security. Trying to realise a second charge or second mortgage is fraught with problems. No banker wants this type of situation to arise. They are much more interested in the proposition which indicates that there is very little risk; after all, bankers do not like putting receivers in or ending up with fleets of tankers or corner shops.

AND

TAKING HOME SECURITY AND HOMEBASED BUSINESSES INTO A NEW ERA

Trends

Perhaps the most important aspect of starting your own small business or working for yourself is timing. Finding the right product or service at the right time for the market place in a pioneering phase of a product or service's growth has propelled many start up businesses to enormous success. Identifying a growth trend or trends is critical to all business success. Trends are not short lived fads such as "Yo Yo's" that create short term wealth for a few, but waves that build up and up over decades like the plastics industry in the 1960's, the Electronics Industries in the seventies, and the IT industries in the eighties and nineties. Trends can also be socio-economic developments influenced by people's desires, concerns, dissatisfactions or age demographics of the population. A single trend can create millions of opportunities for new businesses, as well as existing corporations. It is, however, in pioneering new product's or services in new industries influenced by people's desires where the greatest opportunity lies in working for yourself. It is widely agreed that what happens in the U.S.A., in terms of growth trends, transfers to the UK, Europe and the rest of the World four to five years after it starts there.

ADT Fire and Security, part of the $22 Billion turnover Tyco International, and Homesafe Intelligent Systems offer any individual looking to start their own homebased business the unique opportunity of pioneering a product and service and a business system that is on track with multiple trends. It is also backed up by a track record of phenomenal growth rates and proven success In the USA.

On Trend

Perhaps the biggest socio-economic trend is people's desire for financial freedom and time freedom. Dissatisfaction working for someone else, due to longer hours, commuting nightmares and job insecurity make the UK workers, according to a recent survey, the most miserable in industrialised Europe with 70% of workers stressed and dissatisfied. This situation is fuelling an enormous wave of growth into homebased businesses. In the USA it is estimated that more than 20 million people are running their own part time (with aims of transferring to full time once the income is high enough) or full time homebased businesses.

Another major sociological trend is the acceptance and power of the personal recommendation from one satisfied customer to another, rather than the reliance on the seduction of multi-million pound advertising campaigns. Consumer power is here to stay. Look at the growth in consumer advocacy programmes and organisations. The people want quality, service, value and honesty from companies. This has led to a fast growing sector of distribution where a company takes it's products and services directly to the consumer based on recommendation and referral marketing, one satisfied customer to another.

But probably the most worrying trend in modern society today, (driven by huge media publicity), is the fear of crime and the fundamental desire for security of themselves, their families and their possessions.

The Market Place

Being burgled is everyone's nightmare come true. The intrusion into people's lives and their belongings being stolen or damaged can cause extreme physical and emotional distress. Over one million homes were burgled in the UK last year. It is widely believed that the market place for Intelligent Security is poised on the edge of an enormous growth curve. This enormous growth will be specifically in the demand and requirement for monitored and maintained intelligent alarm systems, which provide 24 hour, 365 days per year protection and qualify for police response.

In the UK, as in other countries, the market place for security products has been set back to day one by the recent directive from the Association of Chief Police Officers (ACPO), which stated that the police would no longer respond to any "unverified" alarm activations. Currently less than 1% of UK and European households have a protection system that qualifies for police response to an alarm activation. Experts are predicting that within ten years more than 5 million homes in the UK will have a recognised and approved intelligent monitored and maintained protection system that qualifies for a police issued unique reference number (URN) and therefore Level 1 Police response. In America over 100,000 monitored and maintained systems are being connected per month!!

The Ultimate Protection. The Ultimate Companies

ADT, part of Tyco International, is the biggest Security Company in the world and has been serving the UK for over 100 years. Now in conjunction with Homesafe Intelligent Systems, who have specialised in the UK Domestic market for twenty years, they are seeking a network of Associates to pioneer their state of the art Intelligent products throughout the UK and on into Europe. The product is professionally installed by security screened engineers. It is approved by NACOSS, BSIA or SSAIB (The Major Industry Associations) and recognised by ACPO (The Association of Chief Police Officers). When activated, the system, which costs from £299.00 fully installed and inclusive of VAT with moni-

toring and maintenance at less than 99 pence per day, communicates instantly via the telephone line all relevant details and what is happening in your home. The 24 hour alarm receiving centre and the 24 hour security staff directly linked to your home initiate a response procedure in seconds informing the Emergency Services utilising the police issued unique reference number.

The Ultimate Business Opportunity

No prior experience, nor investment is necessary to become a Homesafe Associate and a full and free training programme is provided in the initial stages and on an ongoing basis. The business is run from your own home on a part time or full time basis with no requirements for premises, employees, equipment or stock holding. There is both immediate money, rapid profits and monthly recurring revenue from every single customer creating a monthly residual income that could create financial freedom. The income stream is so flexible that the Homesafe business could be used to supplement your existing income by £200 to £300 per week or it could become a national or international business with no limit to the income potential.

As Homesafe's Chief Executive, Paul Dodds comments: "We have the right product at the right price at the right time. Using recommendation, the most ethical way of distributing products or services, and our unique proven customer generation system, you are able to offer to an untapped marketplace, 24 hour protection with police response 365 days a year. A service of tremendous value and something you can really feel proud of.

This is an opportunity where anyone, regardless of their background or experience, can achieve tremendous satisfaction coupled with the highest part time or full time incomes. All your success requires is a little vision, some commitment and effort and a good work ethic."

Homesafe Tel No: 0870 443 5000
Website: www.homesafeintelligent.com
EMail: info@homesafeintelligent.com

Forecasting for the future

Here you have a choice: you can forecast in 'current-year' pounds, or you can forecast in 'inflated' pounds. If you use the former method – which is preferred by some people working on very large projects – you have a series of inflation differentials that are shown in a curious way, since they are real rate differences expressed in today's money. If you choose the latter method, you take inflation as one of your assumptions and take a view of wage increases and cost increases, and set all these out quite clearly.

A more complex matter is how you predict interest rates. It is wise not to base a business case on any assumption that interest rates will fall in the future.

Finally, it is amazing how many people put forward projections in which they have wholly overlooked some physical bottleneck or some manual or executive difficulty in actually getting that volume of activity within the timescale. Negotiations either with labour forces or with central or local government are in the forefront of such problems.

FINDING THE RIGHT FINANCE

Chapter 2 has guided you through some of the different types of capital available, and this section aims to emphasise the importance of selecting the right kind of finance, and to help you to do this successfully.

For the smaller business, directors' guarantees – usually supported by a charge over personal assets – are generally called for. While efforts to resist this are worthwhile, you may not succeed. The banks consider such guarantees necessary because the directors have all the assets under their effective control and the bank wishes to see that the management is totally committed. As to the security offered by the business, you might find that you can borrow up to 80 per cent of property valuations – depending on the location and the economic climate. Debtors can be factored, but a bank may go most of the way to meeting working capital. However, their security valuation of your stocks and debtors will depend on your specific business.

The longer the term of finance you require, the more expansive the presentation. This is because the medium-term assumptions become more and more important and there is more to build on any established track record.

It is worth stressing here that a viable project with good management does not necessarily succeed in raising finance. It is a widely held view of entrepreneurs that the trouble with this country is that the banks are too unimaginative and our financial institutions too rigid and dominated by security for business proposals to get off the ground. However, considerable finance is available and is keenly seeking good and clearly explained projects, acquisitions, ventures and buy-outs in which to invest.

This section is by no means definitive as there are other ways of raising capital. As we have stressed many times before, unless you are familiar with financial arrangement and control, get yourself a good accountant. After all, he or she is not only qualified to deal with such matters, but should also be fully aware of the opportunities which are available.

SHOPPING AROUND

In the case of long-term finance you are bound to find that not only will you have to talk about your proposal several times, but that it is also a good idea to arrange a tour of your operation and management for prospective financial backers. If substantial development capital is required, you may well find that the lender, who is effectively becoming the investor, would like some say in the management of your business, usually by representation on the board. Then, of course, you really must shop around. Money is available just like any other commodity. Different people place different prices on the money they have to offer – dramatically so, when looking for leasing quotes. You must shop around not only among lenders of the same type of finance but also between different types of capital. It is nearly always worth getting an opinion from one of the clearing banks – from a lively, enterprising manager local to your business. Sometimes you can go the whole way with a clearing bank; sometimes you will need to move on to a development capital house, venture capital or various institutions. You should not overlook government sources of finance – either from central government or from Europe, or, increasingly, from local government.

So there are seven vital factors for small businesses to remember:

- [ ] prove the volume of business;
- [ ] present the case for others to understand;
- [ ] concentrate on your assumptions;
- [ ] work through a profit and loss and cash-flow forecast;
- [ ] provide a series of projected balance sheets;
- [ ] match the assets and finance you are seeking;
- [ ] show you can monitor and control your business.

KEEPING INFORMED

Although not strictly part of any discussion about raising capital, installing and regularly reviewing your financial and management information system is not only important for running a business competently, it is also an important aspect of raising capital. Any banker will be delighted to find that you have a management information system which will regularly produce monthly accounts comparing your actual performance with your budgeted performance. Your bank manager will be very interested in a simple monthly package. This can readily be handled on a personal computer (PC), but shop around for a good computer package. Choose a proven system which many accountants are familiar with, rather than looking for the newest, cleverest package. Banks often ask for monthly accounts. You may give them abbreviated information or you may feel that this is too much trouble and simply give them what you have got.

Cash crises

It is relatively rare that one can be relaxed about cash crises, and these crises can happen whenever a business is thinly capitalised and expanding quickly. There is only a thin line between expansion and over-trading, and over-trading in a business with narrow margins during a time of high interest rates can sometimes tip the scales on a thinly capitalised operation towards a crisis.

It is important to realise that cash crises often have nothing to do with profitability. It is a not uncommon mistake for entrepreneurs to wave their internal accounts demonstrating that production is profitable, while simultaneously failing to see that a lot of the profit is going into stock and that the business is not generating cash.

There is, of course, no substitute for anticipation, so your management information system must be cash-sensitive. That should, in turn, imply that your operations are analysed by product, or outlet, or whatever other flow makes up your business, so that you can identify where the money is made or lost and what it is that contributes most to your costs. It is surprising how few businesses know which decisions involving allocation of resources generate cash and which lose cash. It is, however, a medium-term problem to get decision making right. The short-term solutions are usually to restrict stocks, to work vigorously on debtors, and to defer maintenance and asset purchase either by leasing or renting, or just by ceasing to buy plant and vehicles. Such an organised reduction in the level of activity needs to be handled very carefully. With skill, it can sometimes be achieved with judicious pricing-up. A slightly expensive but perhaps effective proposition might be to factor debts.

Whatever you do, do not tackle the problem of a cash crisis in a piecemeal fashion. It is just as important to present to yourself, to your fellow managers and, maybe inevitably, to your existing or new financial backers, a well-reasoned plan, another presentation if you like, of the agreed action that you intend to take and of the expected results, and then to monitor its achievement.

Some of the most rewarding work for accountants (and for managers and bankers) arises from 'intensive care work' where, through sitting with the company's management, sometimes over a long period, the accountants regain for them the trust and confidence of their bankers, help them pull the company round and nurse it back to health.

Fudged accounts

All too often accountants investigating a company for a client or an investing organisation come across the statement: 'Of course, we are much more profitable than our accounts show us to be. The directors take out £X0,000 in ways other than remuneration. There are lots of assets worth more than is stated in the accounts.'

It is very difficult to sell or finance a business on numbers that cannot be seen and the same applies when trying to impress a potential supplier or customer. Misleading accounts strike at your credibility and general honesty and when you *do* need money you will have to rebuild that credibility and trust.

QUOTATION

Finally, you may have long-term plans for allowing your shares to be traded, either outside the Stock Exchange through Ofex, or the Alternative Investment Market or through a full listing. You cannot prepare too early if your proposed course includes anything like a prospectus. Your presentation will then start with an accountant's investigation, known as a 'long-form report'. This will review the history of the business, past accounts and accounting policies, and will include a profit forecast and an examination of working capital needs. These investigations are rigorous, and your sponsors will rely on them.

SHOWING COMMITMENT

Make sure that you have a brief synopsis of the age, education and experience of yourself and your partners to prove that you are capable of running the business, and remember that in most cases you will not be present when the final decision is made. Make sure too that the investment and commitment you and your partners have made are clearly shown. Investors and bankers are keen to have security to ensure their money will not be lost. They also seek assurance of the commitment of management to protect a shared investment. Give brief details of your business, the product, its market and the competition. Explain why you are different and why you will succeed. If you are already in business, then show the latest accounts with up-to-date profit and loss as well as borrowing history. Give details of your key personnel, their functions and qualifications, and supply a list of the principal shareholders. Do explain fully the purpose of the business and the market-place in which its products are competing; your presentation will not be complete with just the financial information. Profit projections must be broken down to show costings, project sales, orders held, legal and audit fees. Be factual and state precisely the amount of finance required and what it will be used for, and make sure that your projections include repayments in the cash flow.

Be prepared, and before deciding whom to approach for financial backing, go along and talk it through with your accountant who will be in the best position to advise you on the different types of finance available and, more importantly, the kind of finance best suited to your needs. Be quite clear as to what your proposal will include and what assets are available for security purposes. Finally, it is worth noting that, depending on your own background, a presentation supported by a reputable professional intermediary such as a financial consultant or accountant may be considered in a more favourable light by potential backers, since they will have carried out some investigation. Not least, their experience may help in presenting a better case.

Checklist: Preparing finances

- ☐ Are your health, training, enthusiasm adequate? Have your family and friends agreed to compensate for your weaknesses?
- ☐ Have you drawn up a profit-and-loss type budget?
- ☐ Have you drawn up a cash-flow plan?
- ☐ Have you a business plan set out in writing?
- ☐ Is your potential profit worth all your effort?
- ☐ Is it possible to test the market further before final commitment?
- ☐ Have you checked on sources, quantities, costs, and reliability of material and stock supply?
- ☐ Is your budgeted profitability realistic?
- ☐ Have you registered as a sole trader/partnership or formed a company?
- ☐ Have you had business stationery printed to facilitate purchasing, negotiation, etc and did you receive a number of different quotes for its printing?
- ☐ What minimum accommodation will you need?
- ☐ Have you prepared a sketch of your layout plan?
- ☐ Have you arranged enough capital?
- ☐ Have you any further reserves (property, cars or other items)?

If you buy an existing business
- ☐ What will you pay for goodwill, fittings, plant, etc?
- ☐ How will you check the stock, debtors, tax debts, redundancy payments, etc are claimed?
- ☐ Will you insist upon seeing at least three years' audited accounts?

Reproduced by kind permission of the Department for Education and Employment from the Small Firms Service booklet, *Running Your Own Business*.

4 | Finding the Right Premises

'There are three things important in property: location, location and location.' For years this has been the golden rule in considering property and indeed, it is as true today as it has always been. However, in recent years occupiers have come to realise more and more the importance of the suitability of a property to their precise requirements in improving work processes, efficiency and profitability. When looking for accommodation, the main thing is to plan as far as possible in advance. It may be that you have certain timescales laid down for you; your lease on existing premises may be coming to an end, or you may have a certain piece of plant on order for which there is a delivery date for installation in your new property. Dealing with property is a complex subject and not all the factors will be under your control, so you need to avoid a mad panic in the last few weeks. Whatever business you are starting and whatever your needs, whether it is a corner shop, an office or a factory, do list precisely what your requirements are before starting your search.

WHAT SORT OF PREMISES DO YOU NEED?

Many questions need to be asked when considering potential properties for occupation and while many will be common to all types of occupier, you will need to consider your own specific requirements as well. However, some of the more general questions that need answering include:

- ☐ How reliant are you on passing trade?
- ☐ Are you going to lease or purchase and what price can you afford?

☐ Are irregular shapes acceptable, or must it be rectangular or square?

☐ Are precise dimensions of the property, including height, of prime importance? (eg for accommodating a racking system in a warehouse).

☐ Can you accept pillars or do you need a clear span?

☐ Are you going to have your offices and factory in the same complex?

☐ Is there sufficient capacity of gas, water, electricity and drainage for your needs?

☐ How secure should the property be in order to meet your insurance requirements?

☐ Do you want (and can you afford) a prominent or prestigious building or situation?

☐ How essential is accessibility for your suppliers and your own transport?

☐ If you do have your own transport, are you heavily reliant upon it, and what provisions for parking do you need to make? If not, how accessible are modes of transport such as train services?

☐ Are there adequate waste disposal facilities?

☐ Do you have any other special requirements specifically relating to your business?

☐ Does the prospective property have the necessary planning permission for your use?

☐ Is there likely to be a need for additional floor space in the foreseeable future?

These then are some of the common questions of a general nature that you will need to consider when choosing your premises.

Clearly, where applicable you will want to ensure that transport costs are kept to an absolute minimum. Therefore, it may well be that by siting your property so that access to essential motorways, main roads, airports etc, is convenient you can considerably improve the efficiency and profitability of your company, both in terms of accessibility to markets and in respect of fewer man hours lost by workers stuck in congestion.

If you are starting from scratch, you will obviously want to ensure you can obtain the right skills in your chosen locality. If you require advice in this direction, then the Department for Education and Employment will be able to provide a great deal of information about the skills available in your area. However, if you are moving an existing business, you will want to be sure that all your workers are willing and able to move to your new location if necessary. Ensure also that the move will not hinder future sales.

Town planning requirements are particularly important, because the property must have planning permission for the use to which you are going to put it. Look very carefully at any conditions that are attached to the planning permission; for example, there may be noise restrictions or restrictions on working hours, which could present very serious drawbacks. If the property does not have planning permission for your purpose, discuss the matter with the local town planning officer. If you do not make any progress, seek professional advice on how to proceed.

If you are a retailer, then clearly you must determine how reliant you are on passing trade. Obviously prime locations attract significantly higher rents which could be out of range for new retailers. In this case you may have to seek the next best thing; a secondary area where the levels of rents are within your grasp, but which is still in an acceptable trading location.

Many new small businesses will be owner occupied. Although not necessarily an investment – the primary concern is running a business – if you buy a property, then you commit a considerable amount of effort and money, and therefore it is wise to ensure when you do come to sell you are able to recoup a large amount of the investment, if not all of it.

The position of competitors will also need to be considered. Many firms, particularly retailers, obviously feel that their turnover will be all the better for a lack of competition in the immediate area. However, many businesses, often of a specialist nature, such as antiques shops, feel that there are benefits to be gained from being situated together as they will jointly benefit from the combined 'pull' of customers. Either way you clearly need to be fully aware of the location of any competition before you move.

The occupation of property incurs several additional costs which can vary significantly depending on the size and nature of your property. For instance, the payment of non-domestic rates is set upon the rental value at 1 April 1998. Rates are a significant cost of occupation and you will need to ensure that you are able to meet this liability. Similarly, unless you have an internal repairing lease you are likely to find yourself liable for maintaining the property in a good state of repair. Again financial allowances need to be made to accommodate this as indeed you will have to do so to ensure that the building is fully insured.

If you have, or are thinking of, setting up a high-tech business, there are a great number of Science or Business Parks being built throughout the country. These Parks are a relatively new inclusion in Britain and the units are specially designed to assist new small business, treating it as an embryo unit. Common facilities, such as managerial assistance, administration and secretarial work are usually included in the package. In addition to time sharing facilities there are other benefits such as published research, technological expertise and shared expenses on expensive equipment. Information on Science Parks can be found on the Web. Another form of help for start-ups comes from Incubation Parks.

Finally, before you decide to move into your new premises – having already calculated in advance the cost of agency fees, as well as solicitors' and other professional fees, petrol, telephoning, removal, time, etc – look around you. Have you considered equipment? How are you going to pay for the furniture and stationery? Have you thought of the cost of getting your letterheads printed? Though you will be able to claim tax allowances for many of these items, make sure that you have planned for these extra costs in your budgets.

BUYING OR LEASING?

There are three types of property ownership in the main: freehold, leasehold and ground lease.

Freehold

Owning the freehold interest in your property means that provided you stay within the statutory law, you can do with it basically what you will. The problem with buying is having to raise the purchase money. For new businesses, commercial mortgages can prove difficult to obtain and therefore close consideration needs to be given to this matter. This is very much the case at present as lenders, wary of having had their fingers burnt as a result of the crash in values in recent years, are very stringent in their vetting of potential borrowers. Additionally, at present mainstream commercial lenders will usually only give advances of up to circa 70 per cent of the purchase price and so a considerable amount of money will be required from other sources if a purchase is to go ahead. You will also have to be sure that your business can generate enough profit to pay the interest on the loan and it is quite likely that the risk capital that you have will give a much greater return if it is employed in the business rather than invested in the property. The level of return expected on premises in the long term is generally much lower than that expected if capital is invested within the business.

If you have been established in business for some time and if you buy a sound property at the right price, it could become a good capital investment over the years. In the past when you decided to realise your money from the sale of a commercial property, you found that it had been an excellent hedge against inflation. However, the dramatic fall in freehold values since the start of the decade means that, in many localities throughout the UK, this is no longer the case.

Leasehold

One advantage of leasing is that there is little capital outlay in acquiring occupation of the building. In many cases, it is just a question of fitting out – which you would have to do anyway with a purchased building. The principle of Section II of the Landlord & Tenant Act 1954, together with subsequent amending legislation, is that when your lease comes to an end you have the right to remain in occupation under the terms of a new lease. There are two exceptions to this rule. If you have been a bad tenant, then obviously there are means by which the landlord can get you out. What is slightly more important so far as the tenant is concerned is that if the landlord wants to occupy his own premises for his own purposes, or wants to redevelop, then he can, under certain circumstances, take possession against you. Normally, he will have to pay you compensation on a statutory basis, and this is related to the rateable value and the time that you have been in possession.

If you lease a building, you will sign a tenancy agreement with your landlord in which he ensures to the best of his ability that you are covenanted to look after the property and not to make any alterations or change its use without his approval. There will be other restrictions on what you can actually do to the property, subject to the landlord's consent, accompanied by regular rent reviews. Furthermore, you will not build up any equity in the property; in other words, when you come to dispose of your interest you will, at best, get only a nominal value for it unless a clause in your lease permits you to sell your outstanding lease to another.

Do not consider leasing a space larger than is required for your business, with the intention of sub-letting the extra space. There are strong restrictions on sub-letting and there is the added risk that (in many areas) you may not be able to find a sub-tenant for the extra space and you will still have to pay rent, rates, insurance and maintenance on it until such time as you are successful in doing so.

Always make sure that you know precisely how much you are paying and what you are getting for that amount; this applies particularly to the service charge.

While the landlord has by law to meet statutory requirements when leasing the property, it is the lessee's responsibility to ensure that the premises comply with the Health and Safety at Work Act.

Ground lease

If you are an established business looking to expand, or moving to premises purpose built for your use and processes, then this course of action may be viable. The prospective tenant effectively rents the site on a long-term basis from the landlord at a nominal rent and then builds the factory or other premises as required thereon. Clearly this can be a costly operation although it should be noted that at the present time construction costs remain relatively low.

For new businesses, commercial mortgages and other forms of funding may be difficult to obtain and therefore close consideration needs to be given to this matter.

NEW OR EXISTING PREMISES?

Whether you decide to go with new or existing premises will depend upon several factors and once again many of the considerations will be very specific to your own proposed use. For instance, your business may be such that the image it portrays is of key importance, in which case a more modern, clean looking, efficient property may be suitable. On the other hand, if you renovate or store machinery, then something less impressive may suffice.

One advantage of new premises is lower repair and maintenance costs. If the building has been designed correctly and built to the proper standard, then it will require very little attention – certainly for the first five or ten years or so. A new building is more likely to meet modern requirements in terms of thermal insulation, traffic circulation, car parking provisions and so on.

If the building is specifically designed for your purposes it can incorporate your exact requirements, and still leave room for expansion. Furthermore, by the time you have gone through planning permission and had the building designed and built, you can easily find that some 12 months or so has passed, even for the most modest scheme – and considerably longer for something more ambitious. If you are in a hurry, this sort of timescale may not be acceptable.

Another disadvantage of a new building is the high cost of purchasing or renting. In addition, the rateable value of a new building may be relatively higher than older premises.

An advantage of existing buildings is their availability. The number of new buildings on the market at any one time will obviously be far fewer than the number of existing buildings, and therefore there is a much greater choice. Existing buildings are also cheaper although they will have higher maintenance and running costs. It should be remembered that adaptation costs can be surprisingly high if the building has to be altered to suit your business needs – even the most minor work can cost several thousand pounds. Also many older buildings are ill suited for the installation of complex machinery, networked computer systems, air conditioning, three-phase power etc. Moreover, a building that was put up in the 1950s almost certainly will not have thermal insulation to speak of, and so your heating bills are going to be higher than in a modern building.

Most modern industrial buildings are single storey constructions which are more flexible in accommodating manufacturing processes and plant and machinery, but older buildings may not be. Consideration of the floor loading is particularly important to the industrial user and warehouseman and, in view of the new types of office equipment now available, the loading factor is also becoming important for office users. In older buildings this may present a problem which cannot be economically remedied.

Is there sufficient capacity of gas, water, electricity and drainage for your needs? For example, if the building has only a 29 gas supply and you have ordered a new industrial oven that requires a capacity, say, of 49 supply, then obviously you must calculate the cost of putting in the new gas main before you decide to buy the property. Take a look at the condition of the external services, especially in an older building.

Fire officers, the Health and Safety Executive and factory inspectors are becoming stricter all the time, particularly with regard to past construction methods and materials employed therein such as high alumina cement and asbestos. What was acceptable ten years ago will not necessarily be passed today, and you may well be advised to carry out certain improvements. There is also the disadvantage that, if the building is old or in a poor location, it may not hold its value as an investment and may be difficult to sell when you move to a more modern or larger property. It is therefore wise to seek professional advice.

FINDING YOUR PROPERTY

Chartered surveyors and estate agents

Your first port of call should be to contact either a chartered surveyor or a commercial estate agent. There are a number of firms, both large and small, in most towns and cities which deal with the acquisition, sale and leasing of commercial and industrial property, offices and shop premises; you will find them listed in the local directories or, alternatively, you can contact the Royal Institution of Chartered Surveyors (RICS) (Telephone: 020 7222 7000) for further advice and help in finding one. The RICS also produce a helpful publication, _The Business Property Handbook_, at only £5.95.

Furthermore you may feel that you need professional assistance and representation in acquiring a suitable property and again the chartered surveyor or commercial estate agent can perform this role. Find out what service each one can offer and under what terms. Take advice from colleagues with a personal knowledge of the various firms or seek the advice of the RICS before choosing the surveyor or agent who is best suited to your purposes. Brief him about the type of property you require and your price range. He will know what is available in the market and at what price.

As he is acting on your behalf it will be your representative's job to negotiate the best terms for you. However, it is as well to keep yourself informed as to how matters are progressing. Town planning matters, rating and insurance valuations are also dealt with by him and, if you are leasing property, then the surveyor can prepare a schedule of condition prior to occupation, if required. If you are considering development, then planning permission is required and Building Regulations approval needs to be gained, and your representative can again assist you in this.

If you have an existing property to sell, the chartered surveyor or estate agent can advise you on the best method of marketing it, the price to ask, and he can also put it on the market and negotiate the sale. In any case it is advisable to get an independent opinion from a surveyor when purchasing or leasing your chosen property. Your solicitor will scrutinise the terms of the lease or purchase before you sign.

Other sources of information

The vast majority of properties on the market are advertised, so the columns of your local newspaper will also give you a good idea of what is available, as will a number of specialist business space publications, along with property supplements appearing in a number of quality national newspapers. If nothing suitable is apparent, it may be worthwhile placing your own advertisement in a 'Premises Wanted' column. Increasing numbers of chartered surveyors are getting up Internet Web sites which carry details of properties available.

Additionally you may wish to contact the employment promotion units run by local authorities and government agencies. You will find them in the local telephone directory and they are extremely helpful in giving details of premises. Other government authorities will also be very helpful. If you seek a rural location, speak to the Rural Development Commission or a chartered surveyor in a rural practice.

Finally, drive around the desired areas and see what you can find. Not only will this be useful from the point of view of looking for suitable property and getting a feel for the general character of the area, but also to see if any of your competitors are in the immediate area.

WORKING FROM HOME

The advent of new information and communication technologies has positively encouraged the growth in the number of start-ups and small businesses that are run from home. If you do not need warehousing and storage space, or a frequent customer interface, this option might well be worth considering. Indeed, figures from Barclays Bank estimate that the average start-up costs for small businesses operating from home is £5000 compared to £13,000 for those operating from a separate premises. Furthermore, those working from home report that they work on average 11 hours less each week than those working from separate premises. However, the attraction of a reduction in start-up costs and time spent travelling might easily be outweighed by some of the disadvantages of working from home. For example, ask yourself the following simple questions:

☐ Would your business suffer if your three-year-old had the habit of picking up the telephone and answering calls from clients?

☐   Is your home suitable for business visitors (can you clear passageways of personal possessions and overeager pets)?
☐   Would you be happy to start your working day in the boxroom or on the kitchen table?

The questions might appear to be flippant but in fact they are good indicators as to whether or not your home can accommodate your business and if your domestic situation lends itself to providing the physical and psychological requirements of an income-generating environment. Indeed, you also have to ask yourself if you would really be happy working in isolation with the possibility of no daily face-to-face contact with colleagues.

Physical requirements

Obviously much of the decision to work from home depends on the type of business. Occupations as diverse as journalism, catering, child minding and counselling are conducted from home offices. Occupations that require storage, distribution and a customer interface are not generally well suited to home working. Many sole traders, however, find it to be the cheapest and easiest option.

Ideally, if you choose to work from home you should be able to identify a dedicated room or space to your business. As much as the practical issues of keeping paperwork and business documents in order, there is the psychological impact of having a separate space to 'go to work to' – even if it is in the next room.

Your space should provide a quiet and well-ventilated area. If your business involves close work, such as in art and design, it is worth paying attention to the quality of light in your chosen room. This is also true for computer-based occupations. Being able to place your screen against a source of natural light will reduce glare and protect your eyesight. Storage is another issue that is worth considering and paperwork will need to be filed in a coherent and accessible way.

Businesses that have a lot of customer and client interface might find that working from home is inappropriate. However, most businesses will have to have some contact with clients. Meetings can be held in hotels, at member organisations such as the Institute of Directors, or at the client's own premises. But there might still be some occasions when meeting at your home office becomes unavoidable. In this instance it is worth paying attention to the image presented to them. Passageways should be kept clear and a comfortable environment provided for their meetings.

Security of your home office should also be considered. Marking equipment with special markers and ensuring that you have adequate locks fitted is essential. Likewise, fitting a burglar alarm is also a good deterrent and security companies will often offer advice on how best to protect your property.

Informing authorities

Your first port of call should be to check any documents you have in relation to your home such as your mortgage agreement, or tenancy agreement. It is wise to inform your mortgage company of the change of use in your premises. However, there is not usually a problem with such a request if a dedicated room in a home is used without any major changes to the house. However, major alterations to your home – such as building an extension – to accommodate your work must be verified with your local authority to ensure that you comply with planning law. Furthermore, planning permission will be required if you intend to start a manufacturing process that produces noise, fumes or smells. Leases must also be checked for any restrictive clauses.

Bear in mind the effects of your business on your neighbours; an increase in noise or traffic might impact on their lives and, in such a case, they will have the right to complain to your local authority. Furthermore, compliance with health and safety regulations and environmental law is required, particularly if you intend to employ staff. The Health and Safety Executive has a range of literature on offer to small businesses and can give advice on these issues.

You should also inform your accountant of your intention to work from home. The advantage in this is that you can claim tax relief for business expenses and may even claim some of your rent or mortgage. However, it is important to discuss this with your adviser, as you might be liable for Capital Gains Tax should you decide to sell the property in the future.

Finally, it is essential that you insure your home and equipment adequately. Contact your insurers to inform them of your intention. Many domestic policies do not cover work-related equipment and it is important to clarify your situation from the start. It is also possible that by having business visitors to your home you will negate your domestic policy as well. Contact small-business organisations such as The Federation of Small Businesses for advice on this matter as well as your insurance company.

The psychology of home working

Keeping your motivation going is another issue to consider when working from home and Peter Chatterton's book *Your Home Office* (Kogan Page) provides good advice on how to keep your head down and to avoid getting distracted with domestic issues. Here are some of the points he makes:

- □ once you have got up in the morning, go to your office as soon as it is practical and start work;
- □ don't leave the office until your next break;
- □ make a daily list of things you want to get done and tick them off as you go;
- □ prioritise;
- □ accept that some days are good and others bad and if you are having trouble with one task find an easier one first;
- □ if you are working late into the night and not succeeding, leave it and sleep on it;
- □ even when things are not going well, keep to your set of rules and routines and be tough on yourself.

Working from home involves a complete change of lifestyle. You will have to create your own structures and routines. Certainly there is more flexibility in home working, however it shouldn't be underestimated how much it might impinge on your home life. The urge to work late at night or at weekends becomes harder to resist when your office is in the next room. This flexibility suits many people but it does create changes in both work and personal routines. Keeping in contact with other people is also important and it is worth thinking about how this can be maintained. Joining a local chamber of commerce or branch of your trade association could be one way of meeting people on a regular basis with similar business interests.

Choosing your premises

Whether you decide to opt for separate premises or a home-office, to buy or to lease, your work environment must be chosen because it suits your needs. You are likely to spend more hours than ever before at work when starting your own business and your environment should be conducive to enable good productivity and efficiency. Assess your needs carefully and make sure that you comply with any statutory requirements for your occupation. Furthermore, bear in mind that your needs might change and be prepared to move with them.

Checklist: Finding premises

- ☐ Do you know how much space will suffice for, say, three years?
- ☐ Will you commission an estate agent to help you locate premises for purchase or rental?
- ☐ Does a building to your requirements exist or will alterations need to be made?
- ☐ Have you allowed for good access, adequate height, easy loading, sound ventilation, drainage, etc?
- ☐ Who must you contact about alterations to buildings?
- ☐ Have you sought consent or advice on planning, licensing, health, trade, etc?
- ☐ Have you obtained full and thorough plant and equipment installation details?
- ☐ Have you considered the extent of open, secure or bonded storage?
- ☐ Will you require any special services (three-phase or high voltage electricity, gas, air, etc)?
- ☐ Are waste disposal facilities adequate?
- ☐ Are covenants within a lease likely to prove restrictive?
- ☐ What else should be considered in your case?
- ☐ When is the next rent review? How much is the service charge? How much is the Uniform Business Rate?
- ☐ Is there insurance due on top of a service charge?
- ☐ Who is responsible for repairs and maintenance?
- ☐ Is the rent still due if the property burns down? Are you properly insured and what would you do to continue trading?

Working from home

- ☐ Is your home able to accommodate your needs?
- ☐ Will your work impact negatively on your neighbours?
- ☐ Have you informed your mortgage lenders, lease holder and insurer of your intention to work from home?

5 Marketing and Sales

WHAT IS MARKETING?

This may come as a disappointment, but there is more to marketing than setting up your own Web page – much more. While this accelerating phenomenon will theoretically place your name within the reach of much of the educated globe, few as yet claim to be making profits out of the opportunity. A consultant's report in January 2000 claimed that new Internet retailers in the UK lost £75m on increased sales of £200m. Remember that turnover is vanity, profit is sanity. In the same way that the arrival of the office PC was going to produce a paperless office (it hasn't) and CD ROMs would kill off the book (more titles last year than ever before), the Internet is just another marketing tool that has to be supported by a strategy, research, customer care and value for money.

A sound appreciation of marketing principles will pave the way for long-term survival and growth. Much of it is common sense, once you stop and think about it, and that is the main hurdle for many new starters. Few plan ahead or realise the vital importance of working out where future sales are going to come from and how they are going to be achieved. Marketing costs invariably exceed first estimates, and results take longer to appear. You have to accept that an investment in a new brochure or series of adverts is just as important as a new truck or bit of plant. Marketing has to come first.

The accelerating pace of business life and consumer whims can be a worrying factor. Global marketing and media exposure can launch a new trend almost overnight. New products can be designed and sourced from Taiwan (or more likely China) in weeks. No one today can afford to be complacent or regard innovation as the province of just Mr Gates. This is the age of specialisation and where small firms can still winkle out a market; for it is your ability to change and react speedily to demand that should maintain an edge over your larger but more cumbersome competitors.

Get your marketing right and the rest of your business should be relatively straightforward. With a healthy, profitable order book you can approach lenders with more confidence, organise staff and output and sleep easy at night. Marketing is more than just selling: marketing is knowing where you want to go, selling is getting there. It encompasses research, advertising and promotion, public relations (PR), direct mail, packaging and presentation. It is a mixture of management experience, art, common sense, gut feel – and flair. An interest in psychology and motivation helps. Think of all the well-known successful businesses and if they are marketing or production led. Marks & Spencer have declined because they lost touch with their market, while Dyson successfully launched a vacuum cleaner three times as expensive as any other because it offered more benefits.

WORK OUT A STRATEGY

Before committing time and resources you need to think and plan where to direct your efforts. You need an overall marketing strategy that will include:

- [ ] whether you are targeting business or the public;
- [ ] an identifiable market niche (exploit a gap, don't follow the herd);
- [ ] a growth sector with good margins – what are the trends?
- [ ] basic simple research to identify a need and to determine at what price level and potential volume;
- [ ] a target sales forecast for the short- and medium-term;
- [ ] how you intend to research that market (direct sales, agents, advertising off the page, etc).

The strategy will set out some realistic targets in a given timescale and should act as a discipline to prevent you veering off on fruitless chases. The early days will inevitably be a toe-dipping exercise with each venture done in stages before committing yourself to a definite line. Don't be afraid to trial and test while all the while remembering that *profit,* not turnover, should be your goal. It is easy to be a busy fool.

PRODUCT OR SERVICE?

Products are usually easier to market than intangibles (such as providing a service), yet new service businesses outnumber manufacturers (and that includes crafts) by ten to one, probably because less capital is required to start. A product can be handled, loaned on trial and measured against known standards, whereas services are largely taken on reputation and promise. The personal element is all important and the way you approach and handle prospects can make or mar your business. Garages, hairdressers, travel agents, insurance salesmen are all there to spread confidence and knowledge in a highly competitive market. They all want repeat business.

It is important that you sell a service with belief, warmth and integrity: in reality you are selling yourself. What you really have to offer is almost of secondary importance. With no product, your marketing efforts should be directed towards cultivating a thoroughly professional image: stationery, signs, staff training, furnishings – the total environment in which you operate. Judicious use of PR (both internal and external) is needed to maintain a high and confident image. Customer care is of the utmost importance and must include a complete after sales service. Your best advertisement is through word of mouth. You need to develop a style and a personality for the way you run your business that fits your position in the market place.

FIRST DO THE RESEARCH

A common error with new businesses is to set up, replicate and undercut existing competition with little thought on how to survive on a lower price structure. A professional marketing approach will try and _differentiate_ your business from the competition – not attack it head on. So market research is needed to first identify:

- [ ] What are the gaps in current supply?
- [ ] Where is the competition?
- [ ] What are consumers looking for?
- [ ] How can you fulfil that demand profitably?
- [ ] How can you economically promote to that target audience?
- [ ] Is the market growing or shrinking?
- [ ] What will you need to increase your share of the market?
- [ ] What is the likely profile of your average customer?
- [ ] Where in the market should you position your product?

The last question may need some explanation as it is central to all your marketing. If you just think about shopping habits, you can divide this nation into those who shop at Sainsbury's and those who swear by the Co-op. Newspaper readers are often fiercely loyal to _The Daily Telegraph_ or _The Guardian_ and no amount of price manipulation will shift that loyalty, as recent price wars have shown. There is more to buying a product than just price. These papers have each positioned themselves to attract a certain type of reader who has a different outlook on life, spends their salary in different ways – and of course votes for a different party.

Your product should be no different. Positioning governs the tone of voice with which you advertise, package and price; even the quality of letter-heading that you use. It is the total image with which you speak to the public and this must be borne in mind throughout all your marketing decisions.

BUSINESS OR CONSUMER?

Your own background and experience may well decide whether you deal purely with business or the public. In some cases it is easier to deal solely with the trade – less paperwork, fewer and larger accounts and probably easier identification of the users. Companies tend to be more stable and can be tracked down by the multitude of sources including _Yellow Pages_, trade directories and magazines, exhibitions and mailing lists. Be careful not to become too dependent on one outlet and watch your credit control. If you supply the trade and the public, establish a price structure that differentiates the two or you will upset the trade and lose business.

FIND THE SEGMENT

Probably the main peril of the Internet has been to alert consumers to price differentials, driving down prices of branded goods. The cheapest supplier tends to hold the aces – until they disappear. It is therefore most important – for the small firm with limited buying power – to target areas where price is not the main reason for purchase.

Small businesses survive by selling to a selected part of the market, not by trying to cover the whole. The traditional grocer has disappeared into the clutches of the supermarkets but a delicatessen may survive if it stocks exotic or ethnic foods and is in the right location – it services a distinct sector of the market. Few garages now sell tyres and exhausts – that need has been picked up by the 'quick-fit' service centres. Mail order lends itself well to the specialist segment, from say jazz CDs to cigarette cards, provided that enough prospects can be identified.

Once you've found a segment (or niche in the market) then demand tends to be governed by expertise, product knowledge and availability rather than low price. Committed buyers will return and more importantly pass recommendations. Your task then is to find more products or expand the service into that widening customer base and to develop a loyal following.

KEEPING THE CUSTOMER HAPPY

Other than competing on price – which is not normally the road to riches – you must find a niche in the market where others are falling down or not meeting demand. As the world shrinks and the Internet becomes more common, the consumer is getting more sophisticated and demands better service and a wider range of products. Take travel agents. Every high street has offices of the national chains but you will soon discover that most are owned by the tour operators who are pushing their own wares. There is a restricted choice. The market is getting more sophisticated with a slackening of demand for crowded package resorts and a growing interest in more exotic places and for independent travel. This demand is met by small independent operators who cannot get a toe in the high street and have to sell 'off the page' in the Sunday papers.

The growth will come from specialist highly knowledgeable travel operators who can offer activity or educational packages to the over 60s who have the money, time and health to see more of the world. Price is not a relevant factor; high quality, immaculate customer care and destinations not reached by Thomas Cook will be in demand.

The retail book trade is currently in some turmoil with Amazon.com and English imitators, but even they have yet to show a profit. There is scope for a specialist who stocks in depth. One bookshop in London stocks _nothing_ but computer books – and does very well. People will travel a long way, or order by post, knowing that there is a very good chance that their demand will be stocked. It is the _service_, not the price, that is paramount. Richer Sounds, the hi-fi chain, has been built up entirely by obsessive attention to service to where it is now in the _Guinness Book of Records_ as the shop with the highest turnover per square foot in the world. They sell all branded goods that are obtainable at many other places, but they have succeeded by understanding the customer and by valuing their staff.

Big firms are bureaucratic and slow to change. Small firms should be quicker on their feet and better able to spot trends and fashion. Innovation should be your watchword. New ideas, new product lines, new offers and gimmicks keep your customers interested and alert. It stops _you_ getting bored or stale. The firm that stands still declines. Not all of your ideas will work, but try a sample run and change things in stages, taking stock at each step. Monitor enquiries and sales and learn as you go along. New ideas come from reading your trade or technical press (every sector has at least one publication) and visiting your trade show at the NEC or in London. Those publications not found on the bookstall can be tracked down by reference to *BRAD* (British Rate and Data) or *Willings Press Guide* (both can be found in a reference library). Details of forthcoming exhibitions (public as well as trade) can be found in *Exhibition Bulletin*, a monthly periodical in your local library. New ideas are often launched at these venues to test reaction, and because hiring space is so expensive the top people are there to button-hole. Make use of the opportunity.

NEEDS AND BENEFITS

Nobody buys anything without having a need, and all your marketing should be directed at isolating what the consumer needs and matching that with the benefits of ownership. For example, you could argue that drill salesmen are not selling bits but holes, Kodak not films but memories. Computer people have a habit of describing features and not the benefits. '64Mb of superfast RAM plus 512k pipeline cache' instead of 'a big memory avoids computer crashes'. All your promotional material should be written from the point-of-view of the user not the seller. Try and place yourself in the mind of the target audience.

ADVERTISING

Most businesses will have to advertise but the medium selected will of course depend on the market you are trying to attract. It is very easy to spend a lot of money with little reward so bear in mind that:

- ☐ the key is to identify your target audience;
- ☐ you need to decide how to reach most of them at the lowest cost.

Don't be misled by large circulation or readership. Wastage may be enormous and more expensive than running a small ad in a precisely targeted magazine under the right heading. The mainstream opportunities to advertise include:

- ☐ local papers, local radio – freesheets tend to be thrown away quicker than papers that are paid for;
- ☐ your own vehicles and premises signs – make the most of your location;
- ☐ handbills, leaflets, brochures;
- ☐ specialist magazines from _Autocar_ to _Exchange & Mart;_
- ☐ _Yellow Pages_, directories and year books;
- ☐ point of sales stickers, hangers, calendars, diaries.

Most printed papers and magazines work off what is called a rate card that sets out the standard sizes and advertising rates in mono and colour. The price will vary enormously. All newspapers offer classified small ads but some magazines only offer more expensive display adverts. Display ads can often be bought at knock down rates at the last minute, so always haggle. Within the rate card will be extravagant claims over readership (not to be confused with circulation – always far less – and is invariably ABC audited). Readership profiles on age, sex, and occupation will be listed but common sense and your own knowledge of the market should be observed.

The local press will be important to you as many areas enjoy very high readership. Don't overlook the small ads, as many people seem to read the classifieds from cover to cover. Be aware that there are limitations on what will reproduce: the paper used is generally poor, so don't expect fine type or pictures to print very well.

Design

You can either leave the design of the advert to the magazine or newspaper, though they will still want a rough, or produce it all yourself. With most papers containing hundreds of adverts your first task is to grab attention. This can be done by a headline or illustration. Put this at the top – not your name. An advert is a selling medium, so make sure you promise a benefit, and answer the selfish but realistic question, 'What's in it for me?'. You then expand on the headline in the text, not forgetting the essentials like price, ordering mechanism, shop hours if appropriate, guarantees and any other persuasive arguments, as long as space permits. Reversed type (white on black) is all right for large simple typefaces, but often becomes illegible when used for text. Make it difficult for the reader and they won't bother, so stick to simple messages with instant appeal which concentrate on why your reader should buy your product or service. An equally hard task for any advert is to promote action. You want readers to act – not discard the paper.

Be different

Try not to design 'me-too' advertising but differentiate the message and appeal. Make your ads distinctive and arresting so they are remembered and acted upon. That may mean becoming a little quirky but why not buck the trend for boring uninformative ads? You can achieve this by using unexpected items in your ad ('Double Glazing found in 16th Century Cottages' – Everest), bold headlines ('Smell the East with Small Party Travel'), tempting headlines ('Remember when fuel was just £1.59 a gallon? It still is' – Jet LPG).

Budget your advertising as part of your overall marketing strategy. Costing will be very important. However, bear in mind that whether you use an agency or place advertisements yourself, you get a reduction in price for block booking a number of advertisements. Monitor the level of response to your advertisements, noting not only how many respond but how many actually purchase. *Yellow Pages* (*YP*) is probably the most widely used advertising medium amongst small firms, but you need to adopt some common sense. In my experience, *YP* adverts work for those purchases where the buyer does not have a regular supplier. We are all creatures of habit and tend to stick to those we know. The real problem arises for those congested areas like kitchen installation, double glazing and builders. How is your small budget ad going to stand out amongst the whole page extravagance of national purveyors? There is little point in shouting 'We're the best' or 'We're the cheapest'. You have to differentiate your offering by your *locality* (all things being equal, people tend to travel to their nearest supplier), your stock range, specialised knowledge or some attribute (USP: Unique Selling Proposition) that only you can claim.

PUBLIC RELATIONS

PR is the least used marketing tool of small firms, yet the principles and methods are relatively easy to grasp. While PR has many facets – charity work, open days, sponsorship, newsletters, amongst many others – it is publicity direct to the media that should be your main thrust. With a little guidance most publicity can be undertaken on a local level by any competent businessman. It means studying the papers and specialist journals that fit your target segment and picking out what makes news. What is commonplace to you, because you do it every week, may be of newsworthy interest to some readers and, more importantly, the editor. Every firm tries to get in the national papers and mass circulation magazines, so unless you have some very riveting story, don't bother.

Distressingly, trivia stands a good chance of getting in the papers, particularly if you can tie it in with animals, babies, royalty, crime, local personalities and, unfortunately sex. For example, a Somerset basketmaking firm made a new dog basket for the Queen's corgis and the story and contrived photo made page 3 of _The Sun_, most of the national press – and Radio Montreal did a live broadcast in French. News content minimal; value to firm enormous.

When writing a press release it is worth bearing in mind the following points:

- □ print the words 'press release' at the top of the sheet;
- □ use a short headline to identify the story;
- □ use wide margins for printer's corrections;
- □ have a news slant to the press release rather than an advert for your business;
- □ customise it for different media and write for the readership: jargon and detail for the trade, more simply for the general public;
- □ open with the main point of the story, don't develop the news like a novel;
- □ most stories can be told in three paragraphs, if the sub editors like the story they will come back for more;
- □ remember to include your contact details;

☐　photos that are included must be of a professional standard;
☐　include local TV and radio stations.

An effective public relations campaign can do your firm a lot of good, but don't expect instant results. PR should be treated as a long-term strategy to raise the profile and image of your business. Journalists in your chosen sector should be cultivated and regularly fed with interesting stories so that eventually, they will come to you for news.

DIRECT MAIL

Direct mail has trebled in volume over the last ten years, but it is no easy task to avoid the label 'junk mail' and generate a profitable response.
　Successful direct mail relies on four factors:

1.　the quality of the mailing list: the target fit and accuracy;
2.　the message: perceived benefits and relevance to the reader;
3.　overall costs of the promotion;
4.　response rate.

You should devote most time, thought and money to compiling the list, not designing the sales message. Many firms only think of the target audience at the last moment. You can start to collect your own circulation list from market research, existing clients and advertising responses; or, if you wish to go about it more quickly, you can rent or buy a compiled list from a list broker. The Institute of Direct Marketing, 1 Park Road, Teddington, Middlesex TW11 0AR, tel 020 8977 5705, will send you a list of brokers. List brokers will sell – or more likely rent – you lists of everything from wealthy people in Mayfair to buyers of stretch covers. The cost will vary from £95 per thousand names to perhaps £250 per thousand depending on the quality and exclusivity of the list. Most have a minimum charge of around £300. Rental lists are for one time use only and will have concealed 'sleepers' of friends or employees to pick up unauthorised successive mailings.
　Careful selection of your list is very important as it directly affects your response rate. The national average for direct mail is

usually considered to be two per cent, but there can be wild fluctuations on this, including nil. The great advantage of direct mail over other forms of promotion is that you can try and test different offers, and learn the results very quickly, certainly within a week. It is statistically irrelevant to mail less than a thousand, but providing the remainder of your mailing list matches the test roll, then you can proceed on the results with greater confidence.

It is important to address the letter to the specifier, the decision maker, ideally by name or at least by job title if you are mailing to the trade. Consumer mailings, which tend to be far less rewarding for the small firm, should never be addressed to 'The Occupier' or 'Dear Sir/Madam'.

Below are seven further points to bear in mind:

1. You have no more than two seconds from starting the letter to convince the reader to continue, otherwise it will be junked. Your first headline and sentence are crucial.
2. Avoid putting too much text down, as you want to keep the reader's attention. You are not writing a story, you are selling your product.
3. You need to send at least four items. The sales letter, brochure, order form and reply envelope. If feasible, samples are helpful. Faxback forms are probably more likely to produce a response from business than a reply paid envelope.
4. Try to send each mailing in a white envelope rather than a brown one. The presentation has a better appearance although it is more expensive. Remember, the envelope can also be used as part of the overall campaign.
5. Make sure that your mailer makes it easy for potential clients to reply. Special offers and free samples can be used.
6. Depending on the volume and on whether you can afford the cost, try to use at least two-colour printing for the brochure.
7. Don't mail an unproven product. The returns could cripple you. Surprisingly fragile products can be posted, but the costs of packaging could kill the profit. Test, test, test.

When you receive your replies, assess your response rate and monitor the sales. If necessary, the copy can then be amended to attract other clients on subsequent mail shots; make sure each different mailer is coded so that monitoring is easy and effective.

Upon receipt of replies, do ensure that each one is dealt with swiftly and professionally by either your sales team or by the relevant customer service person. If further details are required then these must be sent out promptly. There is no point in initiating a response if your service is slow off the mark or non-existent.

THE INTERNET

Most pundits see the Third Millennium as when the Internet takes over our lives. From automatic re-ordering from the supermarket every time you take a pack of butter from the fridge, to the demise of the High Street as we know it. Certainly the theoretical opportunity is there for a small firm to reach a global market at relatively little cost, all day, everyday.

The difficulty of course is that it has been described as the world's biggest library but without a catalogue or index. For

example, a small Somerset firm markets an anti-radiation mobile phone case but a search on 'health scares linked to mobile phones' recently revealed well over a million references to that topic, much of it garbage. Just because it is on the Web, doesn't guarantee authenticity.

Broadly speaking, the Web is used for two reasons: information and purchasing, and from the small firms' profit viewpoint, it therefore makes sense to combine the two to ensure that surfers are attracted, retained and *buy*. Companies with busy Web sites have learned to develop a strong brand image with community feel: visitors feel at home and wanted. The site is constantly changed with up-to-date news, comment and offers.

Niche products and services work best on the Internet. With millions of sales messages being blandished, the more tightly you can focus your offering the better, otherwise you will never be found. Specialization is the key that will draw and retain a community of Web buyers.

To the new starter going online poses three main problems:

☐ cost of setting up and Web page design;
☐ time (and expertise);
☐ attracting and retaining quality visitors to the site.

Costs

To get online you need to pick an Internet Service Provider (one of the established names – BT, Demon, Virgin – or perhaps a smaller, local provider of which there are more than 200). It is difficult to choose in this frighteningly changing sphere, as league tables of performance may attract floods of new business that weaken their edge. Broadly speaking, the large providers will have more expertise, quicker servers and more facilities, but will be more expensive. Smaller, newer and cheaper ISPs may be able to offer more personal service. Ring a few and see how long it takes to get through – in office hours and in the evenings. Check out what software is provided (should be free, and maybe includes filters for pornography and junk mail) and how the charges are worked out. Ask how many email addresses are provided, the cost of a domain name (jimsmith-cars.co.uk) and which usenet newsgroups are available.

The costs of going online will be the Internet account and 10 Mb of Web space – that together may cost £500 – and for designing a Web page. Like adverts, the design is crucial for getting your message across and to build brand loyalty. While there are many cheap DIY packages around, employing a skilled designer could cost £1500 to produce ten pages of revenue-earning material.

Time

One of the main attractions of marketing online is the ability to constantly update the message, but this all takes time. Stale sites don't pull or sell and unless you have the expertise and willingness to keep your Web site attractive and topical you will not get the results. Before attempting to either design your own, or brief a professional, spend some time visiting some of the better sites and evaluate what makes them successful. Try the Electronic Telegraph (www.telegraph.co.uk), The Guardian (www.guardianunlimited.co.uk), Amazon books (www.amazon.co.uk), the BBC (www.bbc.co.uk), research (www.scoot.co.uk) and of course the grand-daddy of them all, Yahoo! (www.yahoo.com).

Design

New starters on limited budgets will probably design their own Web site using one of the many cheap packages (MS Word includes templates for free that can be easily adapted). If you DIY or use consultants you need to bear in mind that:

- [ ] complicated graphics look pretty but take time to download: 15 seconds is the average time spent visiting a site;
- [ ] the site needs to look professional and carry forward your corporate image from whatever else you produce;
- [ ] find out about your customers by asking more questions than just their address;
- [ ] make it easy to buy and give ordering and delivery timings;
- [ ] include plenty of factual topical information/problem solving, Frequently Asked Questions, industry trends and gossip, news columns and chat forums, articles and even cartoons.

To be successful, your site should always look interesting, informative, lively and responsive to the needs of your customers. All this takes time, but the effort will be repaid in repeat business.

Attracting visitors

Marketing your presence on the Web is split into offline activities (advertising and conventional PR) and online (getting on to search engines, usenet groups, links, etc). Every piece of printed literature should carry your Web site address and any newsworthy items placed on your site deserve promotion out to the printed media.

Most visitors look for Web sites via search engines (Yahoo!, HotBot, AltaVista, etc) and it is not easy to get accepted and maintain a presence. As the search is by keywords make sure the vital distinguishing words are on your home page and the site is kept up to date.

Links with other Web sites are a vital part of your strategy and you need to explore other non-competing businesses (newsletters, trade associations, etc) and areas where visitors are likely to be calling. PR online is much the same as PR offline – it needs the same flair and imagination combined with solid news to generate hits. Surveys and reports are usually worth promoting.

Never forget that online marketing is no different from offline – it is the quality of the visitors rather than quantity. Repeat visits from your niche market will only be made if the site is kept alive and friendly with the promise of more to come. Because your time is limited it is worthwhile encouraging your customers to contribute by sharing problems, starting news groups, posting classified ads, etc.

SHOWS AND EXHIBITIONS

Running a stand can be an effective way of widening your market. Apart from rural craft and agricultural shows there are some 3000 trade and other significant public exhibitions run each year at venues as expensive as the NEC at Birmingham to an off-season hotel in Torquay. There are shows to cater for everyone's interests, from _Hotelympia_ (now at Earls Court) to the Royal Show at Stoneleigh (300,000 visitors). If you have designed a new dog collar, head for _Petindex_ at Harrogate, a better tractor then go to Smithfield and so on; these shows are worth attending. To find major shows look in _Exhibition Bulletin_ (updated every month), or for smaller rural shows, _The Showman's Directory_ (copies probably in your reference library).

Whatever your budget, get hold of last year's show catalogue and gauge from the exhibitors if it is the right arena for you. General shows are usually of less use than those more specific. If you can't afford to rent an entire stand, try contacting another exhibitor to share the costs and manning by offering a commission on leads generated. Shows are also good places to visit to meet key players and keep up to date on the competition.

Multi-level marketing

Once outlawed as pyramid selling, network marketing or multi-level marketing has returned under more ethical rules. There is still the need to be wary about venturing into such a field with its promises of easy riches for little effort. It works well in the States, but is still viewed with some scepticism over here. Do your own sums and work out if the balance of profit is too heavily weighted in favour of those at the top, rewarding the humble foot sloggers with very little margin.

SALES

Your sales force is your front line and it is your salesmen's skill that ensures a healthy turnover of contracts. Although this is stating the obvious, no matter how many administrative systems or accounting procedures you have, your company could not exist without sales. Selling is a skill, it is a combination of job commitment, product knowledge and the ability to put across the point which tells the client what he wants to hear so that he buys the product or service on offer. The closing of the sale is as necessary as initiating

health, wealth and happiness

That's what we enjoy at Neways – is it what you're looking for?

- Unique products from a world-wide company.
- Build your own business – don't be tied to someone else!
- Very low start-up cost – only £10.00
- Work the hours that suit you – not the hours that suit your boss!
- Products that really make a difference to people's lives.

NETWORK MARKETING – A SELF-EMPLOYED BUSINESS WITH "BIG FIRM" HEART

In your search for the best business opportunity available, you may have come across the terms, network marketing or multi level marketing (MLM), and wondered exactly what was involved. What are the advantages over other forms of self-employment? What kind of commitment, financial or otherwise, is required? Who are the people this kind of business opportunity suits best?

Network marketing involves self-employed "distributors" buying a company's products, often exclusively, for own use and retail sale. Part of their income is derived from the profit made on their own retail sales and, by building a network of other distributors below them (their "downline") they qualify to receive bonus payments based on their own "personal" volume plus the "group volume" sales of their downlines. This is the second arm of a distributor's income, and it is these bonus payments that change network marketing from a limited, sales-based income to an exciting career with unrestricted financial potential.

One of the big advantages of network marketing is that, unlike many others in self-employed businesses, you are working for yourself, but also with the support, not only of the company whose products you are selling, but also from the distributors above you, your "upline". These experienced networkers have a vested interest in your business as, although you are independent of them financially, your sales contribute directly to their income through the bonus schemes that network marketing companies have. Therefore, they are keen to see you do well, providing you with help and information, particularly when you are just starting out.

Let's look at one company, Neways International (UK) Ltd, in more detail. Neways is an ethical multi-level marketing company that has been in the United Kingdom since 1994. It has nine superb ranges of products: personal care; dental care; body contouring; skin care; nutritional supplementation; cosmetic care; household and automotive systems and essential oils. With one of the best marketing plans in the business, and an exciting car bonus scheme that gives senior distributors the chance to obtain new cars, paid for by the company, Neways is one of the fastest growing network marketing companies in the country.

Rod Catherall, partner in Optimum Health Products Limited and with Neways for over two years, tells us more about the kind of support that new distributors receive, even when they aren't members of an established team. "Early in 1998, I was invited by Neways to advise on the feasibility of contracting out their warehousing, storage and distribution in their rapidly expanding business. In the process, I learned about Neways' background and something of their very impressive products. I bought some products thinking that my partner, Maggie, would be as taken with them as I was. She is a complementary health practitioner and I believed they would extend the services provided from her clinic. When I explained that Neways is a network marketing operation, it was the kiss of death - she simply did not want to know. Maggie had been modestly involved with networking previously and it had not been a happy experience."

"Some months later, I became decidedly under the weather, having one cold after another. Maggie decided the time had come for some drastic action. This prompted her to look closely for the first time at the Neways products, which I had bought and which had lain unopened ever since. The product selected was VMM, the powerful immune system booster. The result was truly astonishing. Within a week the cold had gone and what's more, I have not had one since."

"At about this time, an invitation came from Neways asking if we would like to attend their annual convention in London. What a day it was! We met Tom and Dee Mower, the founders, Dr Samuel Epstein the renowned cancer prevention campaigner, top distributors and many others relatively new to the business. We decided there and then that Neways was for us and signed."

"As the weeks went by, it became apparent that we were disadvantaged, as we had unwittingly signed up to a group whose leaders where in Australia and not the UK. We felt like orphans! It meant that we did not have the benefit of experienced networkers to show us how best to operate and build our business. We quickly came to terms with the situation and set about attending every Neways meeting we could find. In the process, we have made many friends, all of whom have been very supportive. As it has turned out, being orphans has almost been an advantage! Neways is truly an extended family of like-minded, friendly and helpful people ready and willing to support others without any question of personal gain. This has played a major part in enabling Maggie and I to build our business. We have also had the opportunity of repaying some of the kindness by doing all we can to help others new to the business. One of the ways we can achieve this is by running monthly meetings where we regularly get 200 attendees."

"We are delighted to say that our business is now growing at a pace and we fully expect within the next few months to achieve the top rank of Diamond Ambassador. Neways really is a first rate company and we are proud to be part of that "extended family""

Another big advantage that encourages many people to get involved with network marketing is that the amount of time and money involved can be flexible. In the early stages of their networking career, many people will start by just selling products to friends and family and the time taken will be minimal. As time goes on, and they start to develop their own downline, more and more time will be taken up with training and encouragement, but the income generated will rise proportionally.

Dick Jeeps CBE is an ex-England Rugby captain and former Chairman of the British Sports Council. His wife first joined Neways soon after the company came to this country in 1994, but Dick was not initially impressed. He himself takes up the story: "My wife, Jennifer, joined Neways about a month after they came to England in 1994 - she was attracted to them as her background is in Beauty Therapy and Cosmetics Consultancy. She joined because of the quality of the products that Neways produce and also because they are totally ethical products that have never been tested on animals."

"She had not enjoyed good health for some years and was having hormone replacement therapy (HRT) twice a year. After starting with Neways' cosmetics, she soon decided to try some of Neways' nutritional products to see if a natural approach would help her condition. Within a short time, she was feeling much better and what really impressed us both most of all was how well she felt in terms of mood i.e. very balanced."

"During this time, and after I had retired as Chairman of the British Sports Council, we were running a restaurant. In 1995, I had a colon cancer removed and was still quite ill 6 weeks after the operation.

Jennifer contacted Tom Mower, the founder of Neways International, and he sent over supplies of Revenol, a powerful anti-oxidant, which has subsequently become available in this country. I started taking Revenol and, within a few weeks, I began to feel much better; within four months, I was back working in the restaurant. I continued to take a maintenance dose and this seems to have rid me of all my aches and pains from old rugby injuries, left over from my days as England Captain. In addition, I haven't suffered from colds or sore throats since."

"In 1996, and having sold our restaurant, I joined Neways full-time, a decision I will never regret. Initially, I had severe reservations about network marketing but soon discovered that my wife had joined a company that is run by the Owner/Founder and his family, is totally debt-free and one that is innovative and constantly evolving to meet the needs of its distributors. With an exciting new product catalogue just issued and several other projects, like a new headquarters, a new starter kit and a new party-plan package in the pipeline, Neways is always keen to provide the tools its distributors need to sell the best products currently available in this field."

"With their tremendous marketing plan, we, like many other distributors, are reaping the financial rewards whilst promoting a wonderful, safe range of products. The future will see further expansion into many other countries but if I were to be asked the question "Have we reached saturation point in Great Britain?" my reply would be "We have not even scratched the surface!"

With some people, it may be the ability to work from home, at times that suit them, that attracts them to network marketing in the first place. Everyone's personal circumstances are different but full-time employment is not always flexible enough to deal with that. This particular aspect of network marketing was part of the appeal for Dr Surjit Virk, a Ph D in Biochemistry, and father of two young girls. "As a student at the University of Birmingham, I revelled in the time spent researching in my chosen field of Biochemistry. The freedom to work the hours that I wanted, whether that was at night or weekends was something that I really enjoyed and, whilst I needed to report to a project supervisor, I was left pretty much to my own devices. What a shock, therefore, when I left university and went into full-time employment, virtually tied down to a desk. I very quickly decided that I felt cramped and, although I tried different jobs to see if I could find something that suited me more, I was not happy working for others and wanted to regain the freedom I had felt before."

"In 1992, my wife, who has her own full-time career as a careers adviser, gave birth to our first daughter and I was faced with a choice; either carry on working full-time and find a child minder or find some form of self-employment that would give me the flexibility to look after my daughter as well as providing an income. It was at this time that I first became involved in network marketing. Finally, I had found something that gave me the flexibility to look after my daughter during the daytime but the opportunity of working in the evening, and at weekends, to build my networking business. When our second daughter was born a couple of years later, I knew I had made the right decision."

"I worked for a number of different network marketing businesses and learnt a lot along the way. I enjoyed the opportunity of seeing other successful people, of always having goals to aim for and making life-long friends along the way. At the back of my mind, however, was the concern that so many of the senior people in the companies I tried seemed to be totally money-oriented."

"In 1999, I found Neways and realised my search had ended. Here, finally, was the right company with the right product and the right organisation; a company whose owners were totally debt-free and whose concern was with introducing as many people as possible to their superb range of products. Of course, the money is very nice but far more fulfilling is the opportunity to introduce people to products that can really make a difference to their quality of life. In fact, at a recent training meeting I ran for twenty of my downline, we spent the whole day talking about the products and the marketing plan wasn't mentioned once! We all knew that, if we can get the products to people, that side would almost take care of itself."

the contact. This holds true for both on-the-road sales personnel and for telephone sales (the latter is more cost-effective and can be used with great benefit as a back-up or customer supply service).

Many businessmen find it difficult to sell and this comes across to the customer. If you are a sole trader or in a small partnership or company, you will have to train yourself to go out and sell your product – remembering that selling is a two-way communication. Remember that the national average for selling situations is supposed to be one successful call to seven rejections, so your hardest task is probably going to be maintaining your own morale and enthusiasm. Good salesmen enjoy meeting people and are interested in what makes them tick. Much of selling is trying to understand that simple psychology of the individual buyer.

Meet the buyer

While there will always be 'born salesmen' many can master enough of the rudiments to earn a living. You must first grasp that people buy people: in other words you have to sell yourself first, the product later. Image, personality and belief in oneself are vital, for no-one buys from bored and disinterested salesmen. Appointments should be made where possible. You need to identify the correct decision maker and get past the receptionist whose job may be to deflect all salesmen. Providing you adopt an honest, straightforward approach and avoid time wasting irrelevance, you should be able to make appointments in most cases. Be firm and authoritative, yet polite. Record all names, as it flatters people's egos to use the name next time. It sometimes helps to offer alternatives: 'I am in your area next Wednesday and Thursday. Which is more convenient?' The choice then is not whether the buyer will see you or not but which day is the more suitable.

Good salesmen are good listeners but not good talkers. Selling is a two way conversation – the trick is to show interest in the buyer's problems and provide the attractive solution. Keep the initial pleasantries to a minimum and then:

☐   always ask open questions that cannot be answered by just saying 'yes' or 'no';

☐ know your product and have correct prices and delivery dates to hand;

☐ look for buying indicators: questions that mean 'I'd like some of those.' If the buyer asks 'Do you do them in red?' it really means sell me some;

☐ take samples where possible and encourage the prospect to handle or try them on. Involve all the senses. If the product needs demonstrating make sure it works properly beforehand;

☐ ask for an order and probe the objection.

Handling objections

Inevitably there will be objections: too dear, existing supplier, budget already allocated, wrong time of the year, don't deal with new (or small) suppliers, not enough discount or margin, no brand awareness or national advertising – and doubtless many more. Don't be discouraged and don't expect to walk out with an order every time. First visits are fishing expeditions to find out if the prospect has any need for your product range, what price and quantity tend to be bought, and to learn of any seasonality in purchasing. The first sale should be in the nature of a sample order: 'try us out, compare our service with your existing supplier, keeps him on his toes.' Once a relationship and trust has developed between you, real selling is more likely to take place. Buyers, be they in industry or in the home, tend to stick with suppliers they trust and it takes time to break down those prejudices. As a race we tend not to be adventurous and risk our – or the boss's – money.

Presentations

A professional image must be presented at all times.

Here are a few further 'golden rules' to bear in mind when presenting to customers or speaking to them on the telephone:

☐ never promise what you cannot deliver;
☐ never let your customer see that you have a problem;
☐ never be too pushy or aggressive as this can lose a sale;
☐ never criticise your competitors – the attitude to take is 'they are good, but we are better', or simply do not mention them;

- ☐ never criticise your colleagues or the business or its product(s);
- ☐ never argue with the customer – turn the point around by asking questions.

The main area in which sales are lost in a presentation is in the closing of the sale. Some people are frightened to ask for a commitment and avoid the closing question. Be positive, ask the customer: 'When shall we deliver?' 'Do we agree that ...?' 'Do I have your approval on ...?' 'Do you want it if we can get it?' 'How many would you like?' It is a waste of time to make a presentation, get the customer interested and then back away from asking for a commitment at the last moment. The customer will not mind being asked.

Closing the sale

Closing the sale means obtaining an order and this is where the better salesman scores. Answers to objections can often be turned into a closing question.

- ☐ 'I need them by next week.' 'If I can rush them through how many would you like?'
- ☐ 'I've spent my budget for this year.' 'Tell me when your new year starts.'
- ☐ 'I've no room to hold stock.' 'Fine, we'll make weekly deliveries instead of monthly.'
- ☐ 'I need a bigger margin.' 'We'll meet your price if you order 10% more.'

Never be afraid of simply asking for an order. The buyer is then forced to come to a decision, and often an objection, which may lead to an opening if you listen and react. Often the buyer will have to consult with others, perhaps a committee, and further appointments will have to be made. Keep up the momentum by writing a reminder letter or phoning after a sensible period.

It sometimes helps to leave a sample behind so that the buyer's colleagues can handle the product, and this also provides a further opportunity to call back. And before you leave, ask for someone else, perhaps within his organisation, that you can see: 'By the way is there anyone else I might usefully see?'

MOTIVATING SALESPEOPLE

Salespeople need management, motivation and control; recognition of a job well done develops a sense of achievement. It is relatively easy to see when a salesman is not working well but it is more difficult to find out why. Be sympathetic and try to find out the reasons for the lack of or decrease in sales performance. It is a good idea to have a commission rate system based on performance but at the same time it should be linked to security by the provision of a basic salary. An appreciative thank you is often worth nearly as much as a bonus. Selling is a lonely, often dispiriting, and misunderstood job, so always give your sales force support and encouragement. It helps to learn what motivates them: we are all individuals.

Sales are the life-blood of a business: without the selling of your product, you would not be in business at all.

Some golden rules

☐ Identify your market segment and look for the gaps.
☐ Study trends, decide where there is growth and profit.
☐ Think about what the customer needs and talk about benefits.
☐ Always answer the question 'What's in it for me?'
☐ Make your product different and your ads distinctive.
☐ Find other goodies to sell into your growing customer base.
☐ Cosset the customer and always keep your promises.

Checklist: Marketing

- ☐ Have you a marketing plan?
- ☐ Have you costed your publicity effort?
- ☐ What should your publicity achieve?
- ☐ Will you provide transport?
- ☐ What packaging and delivery policy will you have?
- ☐ Have you prepared your pricing policy to meet the market opportunity?
- ☐ Will you avoid undercutting your experienced and established competitors' prices?
- ☐ Are your quality, service and price strategies adequate?
- ☐ Is there any unique feature about your offer?
- ☐ Are you better, cheaper, quicker, or all of these, than your experienced competitors?
- ☐ Will you do your own selling?
- ☐ Will you offer sales people commission (on profit or turnover)?
- ☐ What will your selling effort cost?
- ☐ What else should be considered in your case?

Source: _DfEE, Small Firms Section, Running your Own Business_

6 Control and Financial Management

The economic climate is difficult for anyone setting up in a new business and the risk of failure is very high. But if you do set out on your own, or seize an opportunity for growth and development of an existing business, then effective control is vital if you are to survive and succeed. Yet very often we find that it is exactly this ingredient which is missing. The businessman gets on with what he considers the real work – and neglects the controls and forward planning – and his business suffers accordingly.

PLANNING

One factor which affects small and large businesses alike is the rate of change. During the last few years we have seen an accelerating rate of change: products are on sale today, some of them by using new technology, that were not even thought of ten or even five years ago. In this climate, planning – especially financial planning – is of the utmost importance. The well-managed company needs to be constantly alert to change. The prime questions to ask yourself are:

☐ Where are we now?
☐ Where do we want to go?
☐ What resources (financial and manpower) do we have?
☐ What is our performance like?
☐ What are our objectives?
☐ How are we going to reach them?

☐   What is holding us back?
☐   What tactics do we use?
☐   What is the competition?

Then, as managers, we have to start to make it happen.

FIXING YOUR OBJECTIVES

Let us start at the beginning. Where do we want to go? Write your objectives down. If you do not know where you want to go, your chances of arriving are not good.

Identifying the constraints

The next step is to ask: 'What constraints are holding us back?' Typically the answers fall into three main areas: finance, management and markets.

Finance

The worst time to go to your bank and ask to borrow money is when you are in desperate need of it; when this happens it is often the result of poor financial control. Statistics show that a high proportion of companies go bust within the first four years. Most insolvencies can be avoided if the management directs proper attention to cash-flow problems. A major deficiency in small businesses is often a lack of 'information' about the cash requirements. But information concerning what? The answer is: cash flow and profitability.

Financial control involves dealing effectively with each of the individual steps in the cycle:

☐   having the necessary information to facilitate day-to-day management of the assets and liabilities of the business, particularly the debtors and creditors;
☐   having the right information to plan the overall cash needs of the business and to evaluate the worth of future projects and alternative proposals;

- [ ] having the information needed for measuring actual results and comparing them with the plan;
- [ ] having advance information to enable the business to do a proper job of tax planning.

Each business has different financial pressure points, ranging from effective debtor control to seasonal peaks and sudden large payments. It is the gathering of such information that is an important ingredient in solving potential financial problems.

It is vital to make sure that either you have sufficient cash reserves, or you are able to look ahead to when you may need the money. If you can make a good case for it and show that you have a profitable idea, often it is not that difficult to raise the money (in which case, it was not really a financial constraint in the first place). Alternatively, when you work the proposal out carefully, it may not look such a good idea after all and you will be unable to raise the money – but in that case it was only because the business plan was faulty in the first place.

Management

Starting off in a small business you may not be lucky enough to have any managerial assistance, in which case you have to become a 'jack of all trades'. This situation may not last, however, and once you start to expand, increasing your turnover and the size of your company or business, you need to consider the extra managerial layer needed – middle management. The first type of management expertise you need may be in the financial and sales/marketing areas. You could find that some of your employees 'in the back room' have hidden talents which could be useful to you. But in any case this is the time when you have to be very careful that your control structure and overheads are in line with your activities.

As your business grows and your middle management expertise needs to be 'bought in', make sure first of all that it cannot be found in existing employees. Consultants can be expensive and selecting those suitable to your business's needs is time-consuming. Before employing a consultant seek recommendations first. Always select a reputable firm and one which has had previous working experience in your field of business. Enquire as to the size of company the firm normally works for. Above all, consider whether you can afford their fees. To some extent these points apply to any external professionals you engage, such as your accountant or solicitor.

As each department is formed, you must be careful that guidelines are laid down so that the workload and personnel supervision are clearly defined. This is often a weak point in medium-sized companies. As your company expands further and you find that you are no longer able to oversee all the departments, the time has come to appoint a general manager.

Arthur C Clarke, the science fiction writer, sums it up very nicely: 'The company which concentrates on the present may have no future; in business as in everyday life, wisdom lies in striking a balance between the needs of today and those of tomorrow. It is true that the farmer whose house is on fire must stop the sowing to put out the fire, but he will lose much more than his house if he doesn't prepare for next year's crop.'

Markets

Financial planning is not just looking inwards – it must look outwards as well. One of the hardest things for a small business to do is to keep an eye on what is going on outside. It is very important that you do not lose sight of what is happening around you. All products go through a traditional cycle: introduction, growth, maturity, saturation, decline and obsolescence. Sometimes it takes generations, sometimes it takes two or three months. Skateboards are a good example. They were introduced in early 1980 and grew to maturity by early autumn but the fad was virtually over by December. Lots of people made a lot of money on skateboards but most of them lost it again at the end of the cycle because they did not get out quickly enough. This all boils down to 'timing'. In later years, skateboards re-emerged with more sophisticated designs that allowed greater manoeuvrability and enhanced performance, so starting a new product cycle that was to prove more lasting if not as frenetic.

It is often recommended that you keep an 'Ideas' file in which you and your employees can put down any feasible suggestions.

Look at the prevailing market influences and consider whether or not you can afford to produce (in both monetary and physical terms) a new product. It may be too late once your competitors have introduced a new product to decide whether or not you should attempt to match it. Once you have borne all these considerations in mind, however, you will be wise to plan to move with the market force.

Let us consider the case of Brut, the range of men's toiletries, which was introduced many years ago as a very high-class product. It went through the inevitable cycle, and when it began to decline the company made it available through outlets like Boots, Woolworths and so on. In this way they gave new life to the product by widening the market. When sales began to drop off again, they introduced not just aftershave but also body lotion and talc, as well as all toiletries they already sold under a different brand-name. Once more they widened the product range and the market, and Brut took off again. Then when it began to decline once more they brought in Henry Cooper with a big advertising campaign to promote their products. The big companies can afford to do that – they have the resources – but as a smaller company you will not be able to take such an aggressive market line, and so you will have to be prepared to move with the market.

This is where market research helps. If you cannot afford to hire the services of a specialist firm, compile a simple questionnaire and ask your sales force to circulate it. The information gained from it can then be analysed, and will help in making overall decisions about your product. Get to know your marketplace and which products it can take; it is no use producing a walking, talking, tail-wagging toy if there are others like it on the market, or if potential buyers will not accept it.

TYPES OF CONTROL

The structure of the business

The organisation of the business itself is a control. The fact that there is an organisation with directors and divisional managers, with even the simplest of administrative/financial/sales/production functions, demonstrates this. The business is structured in a pyramid fashion. When applied to the company's organisation this means a formal workload/personnel ratio. When a company becomes either too top heavy (with too many senior managers or middle managers) or the opposite, where there are not enough senior/middle managers, it is harmful for business and should be avoided at all costs.

Job functions

Segregation of functions is a control much loved by accountants. The fact that, in a business, people will have to do different things to the same document is a form of control. In a typical situation one person in a department will place an order, but another person in a different department will pay the invoice relating to that order. If fraud is to take place it will require collusion between at least two parties. So too in the preparation of the payroll, segregation of duty helps to prevent loss to the business.

Physical controls

Physical controls include the lock on the petty cash box, the fence round the factory, the list of who uses the company cars and how many miles they have done, who has the authority to order what, etc.

Authorisation

Authorisation means that everything has to be approved by somebody. The most common example is that cheques can only be signed if they are authorised by a senior manager in charge of that section. If there are two directors then a system should be arranged whereby two signatures are needed. Orders too have to be signed by someone in authority to be valid.

Finance

Accounting controls include such things as someone going through invoices to check that they are added up correctly and relate to goods and services actually received. Other examples are ensuring that ledgers are balanced, that bank statements are reconciled, that management accounts balance and that in annual accounts the balance sheet adds up. All outgoings and incomings should ideally be analysed and accounting controls established for prompt invoicing, stock control and credit control. The production of a budgeted profit and loss account will enable a comparison with the actual results to identify variations, as shown in Figure 6.1 (on page **XX**). It will also provide the major part of the information required to enable you to produce a cash-flow forecast which will give you and your bank manager a forewarning of any future cash problems (see Chapter 7).

PERSONNEL CONTROLS

Ensure that you employ people fit for the job, that they have had appropriate training, that they know what to do and that they are reliable.

Management

Supervision of members of staff is a form of control. If you have an invoicing section, there could be a need for a supervisor of that department, depending upon the size of your company department and your turnover. If you have a shop, there will be one person who is in charge of the other assistant(s). The staff then know that if they have a problem there is a supervisor to approach, and that they do not have to go right to the very top, which might put them off.

Management has the task of ensuring that their employees' job specifications are in line with the company's objectives, and that all jobs are carried out satisfactorily. They, along with the other employees and the owners, should have the company's best interests at heart, from making sure that the products are selling at the right price and making the right profit, through receiving the cash and seeing that it does not go astray, to making sure that

ANY COMPANY LTD
Last year

MANAGEMENT ACCOUNTS FOR THE MONTH ENDED:

	This month				Cumulative year to date					
	Actual		Budget		Actual		Budget		Variance	
	£000	% of sales	£000	% of sales	£000	% of sales	£000	% of sales	£000	% of budget
SALES		100		100		100		100		
Cost of sales										
GROSS PROFIT										
Commission payable										
Carriage and packing										
Bad debts provision										
Rent and rates										
Light, heat and power										
Insurance										
Repairs and renewals										
Directors' remuneration										
Other employment costs										
Travelling and motor expenses										
Printing, stationery and advertising										
Telephone and postage										
General expenses										
Audit and other professional fees										
Hire and leasing costs										
Depreciation										
Bank charges and interest										
Other items (service charge receivable)										
TOTAL OVERHEADS										
NET PROFIT (LOSS) BEFORE TAX										

Last year columns:

| Month | | Year to date | |
| £000 | % of sales | £000 | % of sales |

Figure 6.1 *Monthly management account report*

production is up to standard and looking after the welfare and status of the staff.

Cash management is a vital function in the overall management role, with the main aim being to generate more capital for the company, as well as to conserve the existing capital. There are a number of areas where this principle can be effectively applied, such as cost reduction, aggressive pricing, elimination of cash liquidation of excess assets, and cautious borrowing. Credit control (see Chapter 7), prompt invoicing, good banking arrangements and payments to suppliers are all areas which need attention.

The continuous monitoring of a business is an important management function. Monitoring may be broadly defined as the preparation and review of regular accounting information. It should include preparation of budgets, product costs and cash-flow forecasts, followed by the comparison of these projections with actual results on a regular basis.

The fact that your business is doing well does not mean that you can sit back; indeed, it can be said that you need to work even harder. Priorities need to be established concerning the day-to-day financial controls of the business and the regular reporting of results. Do not rely on the annual audit to determine the future of the company; by its nature, an audit deals in historical information and cannot normally be used to determine the strategy of the company.

The importance of regular financial information does not lie in its preparation; it is the intelligent review of the results and trends shown by that information which is essential to the successful running of the company. For example, the accounts may show that sales have fallen, but it is more important to understand why. There could be a simple answer, or the answer could rest with any one of a number of problems, from production problems to understaffing or defaulted deliveries. The information should be prepared on a regular basis. It is a good idea to prepare these accounts monthly, near the middle or the end of the month.

Controls prevent you getting lost. If things go wrong you can find out why, and do something about it quickly. If your business is going into loss or stops making a profit, then your controls (management accounts, cash figures and cash-flow forecast) will sound warning bells in time for you to take action. You will not be waiting until the end of the year or perhaps several months after that for your accountant to tell you that you made a loss of £10,000 last year. Your controls will have warned you that this is happening and you can do something about it.

Benchmarking

This term is applied to an ongoing control process to improve products, services and systems, by reference to the best practices in other companies. Financial and operational performance measures are compared with other organisations and working practices changed in those areas found to be weak.

The law

Controls also stop you breaking the law. If you pay people's wages without deducting tax or pay the wrong amount of VAT or are not observing the Health and Safety at Work Act – you are breaking the law. Controls in business prevent mistakes which, while they may be quite innocent, are nevertheless unlawful. Ignorance is no defence in the eyes of the law.

The essential thing for any business, large or small, is to have a strategy: to know where you are going and how you are going to get there. If you have the right controls then the organisation will follow naturally, and in turn you will be able to monitor your plans and see if they are on course and if not, why not. The following financial checklist will set you in the right direction.

FINANCIAL CHECKLIST

Cash control

Day-to-day financial management needs to be applied continuously, and in detail, to the ever changing cycle of expenditure and revenue. In the course of this cycle, cash is converted into trading assets such as stock and work-in-progress, then into debtors and finally back into cash. The cash generated by this process should exceed that which is invested in it, and control is needed to maximise the cycle, to prevent leakage and to ensure that it moves as fast as possible. There follows a series of questions to which you should already know the answers – if you don't, you should find them out.

Cash

- ☐ Have you reviewed security arrangements and insurance?
- ☐ How long is each element of the trading cycle?
- ☐ What changes can be made to improve the cycle?
- ☐ Are budgets expressed both as cash-flow and profit forecasts?
- ☐ Can performance in cash flow be compared with expectations?
- ☐ What is the regular difference between bank statement and cash book?
- ☐ Are bankings sufficiently frequent?
- ☐ Are bank accounts grouped for interest and bank charges purposes?
- ☐ What is the ratio of cash and liquid assets to current liabilities?

Stock and work-in-progress

- ☐ Is stock kept securely and is it adequately insured?
- ☐ Have you taken your accountant's advice on recording and valuation?
- ☐ How much stock is surplus to expected requirements?
- ☐ How many stockouts occur?
- ☐ What is the cost of stockholding?
- ☐ Are reorder quantities established and safety stocks reviewed?
- ☐ How often can you determine stock levels?

☐ How much production is for stock or for specific orders?
☐ Can stock lines be rationalised?
☐ Are bulk orders cost-effective?
☐ Do checking procedures prevent under-deliveries or damaged goods being accepted?
☐ Can you identify and reduce slow-moving stock?
☐ What is the ratio of: stock to purchases?
                              stock to sales?
                              work-in-progress to production?
☐ What is the importance/proportion of seasonality and sales trends?

Accounts receivable – debtors

☐ What time lag occurs between sales and invoices?
☐ Can payment on account or in advance be obtained?
☐ Are invoices clear and correct?
☐ Can direct debiting or banker's orders be introduced?
☐ What is the effect of discounts for prompt payments?
☐ Is special clearing of large cheques worthwhile?
☐ What about credit insurance?
☐ What about debt factoring or invoice discounting?
☐ Are customers' credit ratings checked before accepting orders?
☐ Is the use of a credit agency justified?
☐ Have you considered a debt collection agency?
☐ Do you ensure prompt and regular chasing of overdue accounts?
☐ What is the ratio of debtors to sales (expressed in days)?

Accounts payable – creditors

☐ How many suppliers do you deal with?
☐ Are there single source suppliers of key materials?
☐ Can payments be delayed?
☐ Are buying costs known?
☐ Are payment discounts worth taking?

☐ Are all purchases properly authorised?
☐ Could you pay twice for the same goods?
☐ What are the price indices for main supplies?
☐ What are the lead times for main suppliers?
☐ What is the ratio of: orders overdue to orders placed?
                          creditors to purchases (days)?
                          goods returns to purchases?

Assets employed

☐ Can you measure the use of assets in output, value, units?
☐ Can you measure contribution from the output?
☐ What is maximum capacity?
☐ Are there any bottlenecks?
☐ What are the fixed costs of the capacity?
☐ What is the realisable value of assets employed?
☐ Are assets properly insured?
☐ Can you time investment or defer taxes?
☐ Should you use discounted cash-flow techniques?
☐ What are the advantages of buying, hiring or leasing?
☐ What is the ratio of: operating profit to operating assets?
                          operating profit to sales?
                          sales to operating assets?
                          actual output to maximum output?
                          unproductive time to total time?

Capital structure

☐ What proportion of funds are borrowed and on what terms?
☐ Are loans due for early repayment?
☐ Are corporate plans prepared?
☐ Are cash-flow forecasts and plans available?
☐ Is liquidity adequate?
☐ Are there special tax considerations?
☐ Have capital markets been explored?
☐ What about the Alternative Investment Market?

☐ What about industrial co-operatives and management buy-outs?

☐ What is the ratio of: profit before interest to total assets employed?
borrowed money to equity?
interest payable to borrowed money?

7 Bookkeeping and Administrative Systems

This chapter explains an essential aspect of your business: book-keeping and administration. Whether a manual- or PC-based method is used, the chapter describes a simple and easily kept system of administration and accounting that can be tailored to the needs of most small businesses.

A word of warning – do not try to run before you can walk. Start with simple systems and let them grow with you – your time is extremely valuable and you do not want to find yourself working at an over-complicated system far into the night. You may ask: Why have a system at all? Why keep the books? At the end of the day, the success or failure of your business is not measured primarily in the quality of your product, but in financial terms – in other words, profit. If, for instance, you forget a delivery date or miss invoicing, you will not get cash coming in. A permanent record of your business affairs is therefore required. The Inland Revenue will require its share of your profits, and they will demand – whether or not you have made a profit – evidence to support your self-assessment tax returns of the income and expenses of your business. When the turnover of your business exceeds £52,000 based on a rolling year's turnover, you will have to register with HM Customs and Excise and charge the relevant rate of VAT on your sales. You will be able to set off any VAT charged on incoming invoices against VAT on sales. You will be required to keep adequate records and declare all VAT charged on a regular basis. The VAT inspector may come to check your records. To ensure that your business runs smoothly, you will need to set up systems for ordering and its control, a system for keeping your records in easily accessible files, and personnel records when you take on an employee, etc. All these aspects of your business require systems.

BOOKKEEPING

For your own benefit it is necessary to monitor the well-being of your company, and you will wish to keep a close control of your cash flow and results. One of the major factors that contributes to the failure of many small businesses is a simple lack of financial control. Hard evidence of your trading record will always be required should you find it necessary to raise further capital or even to continue your bank overdraft.

So what does bookkeeping entail and how do you go about it? It is a procedure for recording your business transactions, both receipts and payments, in a way which is easy to understand and makes sure that the information is readily available when you need to refer to it.

The method of recording is designed to take up a minimum amount of time but still provide a level of control to ensure that you have recorded the information correctly. Always complete the 'books' regularly, not allowing the volume to build up to unmanageable heights or left to a later time after you have forgotten the transactions.

Whether you trade as a limited company, sole trader or partnership, you are required by law to be able to provide accounts for the Inland Revenue. A further requirement when trading as a limited company is to provide accounts, in a format required by law, to Companies House with, if necessary, a Registered Auditor's report showing his opinion of the accounts and compliance with the law.

At the end of the year you will probably need to engage an accountant to prepare the final accounts for completion of your self-assessment tax return.

The more time he has to spend on your records the more he will charge you. Any work you can do during the year to write up your own books will save him time and you money.

Of course, each business is different and has its own accounting requirements. The most important thing is to set up a bookkeeping system that can develop with your business. To start off you will require books to record:

- [ ] an analysis of receipts and payments in your bank account;
- [ ] your daily take, split, if necessary, into categories;
- [ ] analysis of miscellaneous cash expenditure, e.g. petty cash;
- [ ] adequate VAT records;
- [ ] adequate wages records;
- [ ] a means of filing invoices, receipts, correspondence, etc.

The first essential task is to record the receipts and payments of money – in cash, cheques and credit-card transactions – in a cash book. For this purpose, if records are kept manually, it is best to use an analysis book which can be purchased from most high street stationers. It has several cash columns, making it easy to analyse types of receipts and payments to individual columns. Take care, however, to choose the right one – compare the suggested rulings shown in the subsequent pages with what is available, and remember it is better to get one with too many columns rather than too few. Ensure that you keep an adequate filing system.

Finally, remember that your accountant, like your bank manager, will prove an invaluable friend to your business. Do not hesitate to consult him and act on his advice when you start. He will have a wealth of experience in dealing with new businesses and five minutes spent with you, even on the telephone, may well save him hours at the end of the year as well as giving him, one hopes, a more successful client.

PC (computer) accounting will show details in a different form, with the analysis in numbered registers. These may be required to be set up first with titles or you may find most of the titles are given already. This operates in much the same way as a manual system without the work of adding up the registers. The more advanced systems may produce invoices, remittance advices and reports for you and your accountant. Again, remember to discuss the type of system and applications with your accountant before purchasing or using a system. Always back up your work and make paper copies so that you, your accountant and the taxman can see them. Understanding of a manual book system will help you to use PC systems and add meaning to your final accounts.

THE CASH BOOK

The cash book is used to record and analyse all receipts and payments in your bank account. If it is written up regularly it will tell you instantly how much, or how little, money you have in the bank. This is something your bank statement will only tell you when you actually receive it, once a month.

The cash book is divided into two sections. Receipts are entered on the left-hand side and payments on the right. A suggested ruling is shown in Figure 7.1. You will note that there are only five columns of analysis for receipts; this is because your major income will usually be from sales, which can be sub-analysed through the sales day book (Figure 7.2). The sales day book is a record of people who owe you money – your debtors. When you receive payment for the invoices which have been entered, the whole amount of the invoices must be analysed to the 'Debtors' column. Do not separate the VAT in the cash book because this has already been done in the sales day book. Think about the type of receipts you will expect to have in your business and if necessary choose an analysis book with more columns.

When you first start in business you may not require a purchases day book (Figure 7.2) for the analysis of your expenditure; it is often easier to do this analysis in your cash book (Figure 7.1). Hopefully, suppliers will soon grant you credit terms. They will then give you an invoice for your purchases and allow you time, perhaps 30 days, before payment has to be made. You will need to record these invoices in a purchases day book because they represent your creditors. Then you will need a column for 'Creditors' on the payments side of the cash book. When you make your payment remember to enter the whole amount in this column. Do not separate VAT because this will already have been done in the purchases day book. Figure 7.2 shows a typical analysis but you must tailor the headings to suit your own business; your accountant will be able to advise you on this. It cannot be over-emphasised that a detailed breakdown of your expenditure is of great importance to you and your business as well as to your accountant in producing your accounts at the end of the year.

You will note from the headings that sales receipts are itemised by individual invoice; this is by far the best method for small

RECEIPTS

Date	Detail	Ref	Bank	VAT	Sales	Debtors	Sundry	
2000 Feb 3	Brought fwd		110.20					
6		112	53.85			53.85		
8		113	845.47			845.47		
11		114	126.02			126.02		
12			63.45	9.45	54.00			
			62.00				62.00	Sale of cabinet
28	B. White	126	147.78			147.78		
	T. Green	127	1127.70			1127.70		
			2536.47	9.45	54.00	2300.32	62.00	
Mar 1	Balance b/d		205.82					

PAYMENTS

Date	Detail	Cheq No.	Ref
2000 Feb 5	Spencer Ltd	012	47
	Brit. Telecom	013	48
16	Alf's Garage	014	49
	Brookharts	015	50
	Browns	016	51
	Printus Ltd	017	52
17	Ins. Brokers Ltd	018	53
28	A. White	037	
	Inland Revenue	038	
28	Balance c/d		

PAYMENTS (continued)
Assuming that a purchases day book is not being used

Bank	VAT	Creditor	Material	Power	Stationery Post	Tele-phone	Travel exps	Repairs	Rent & Ins	Wages PAYE	HM Customs	Sundry
63·84	9·50		*	*	*	*	*	*	*			
167·21	17·17		54·34									
85·79	12·78					150·04	73·01					
176·25	26·25											
1107·53	164·95		942·58									150·00 Accountant
55·42	8·33				47·59							
117·15									117·15			
450·82										450·82		
106·14										106·44		
205·82												
2536·47	**239·98**		**996·92**		**47·59**	**150·04**	**73·01**		**117·15**	**556·96**		**150·00**

* These columns will not be needed if you are doing this analysis in a purchase day book.

Figure 7.1 *Cash book*

businesses. (When you come to file these invoices away number them in sequence, noting the number in your ledger book. This will make for a quick and easy referral.)

Receipts

As you receive money, either by cheque or in cash, you will want to pay it into your bank account. This you will do by entering such item's details into your paying-in book and presenting it and the cheque, or cash, at the bank. Enter the details from the paying-in book into the receipts side of the cash book, recording sales in the sales column, sundry receipts in the sundries column, etc, making sure that all items add across to the total amount entered in the bank column. Remember to separate the VAT from all receipts except for entries in the 'Debtors' column. This should be the amount shown subsequently on your bank statement. If items are credited directly to your bank account you will also have to enter these in your cash book.

Payments

You will draw cheques on your bank account and in the same way you will enter these on the payments side, making sure that the total of the individual cheques and the relevant details are clearly entered. The analysis of the expenditure is then entered into the relevant column. When you are using a purchases day book several of the analysis columns will not be needed in the cash book. If you are registered for VAT you will have to enter the VAT amount in the VAT column leaving only the net amount to be entered in the analysis column except for entries in the 'Creditors' column. Similarly, items appearing directly in your bank statements, such as standing order payments, bank charges, etc, will also have to be entered in your cash book.

Keep a running total of the two bank columns; the difference between the two will give you your bank balance. At the end of each month, total up all the columns and enter the totals. All the subsidiary columns should add back to the two bank columns. If they do not, check your additions and the analysis of your items – five minutes spent now will be amply rewarded in the future. When both sides agree enter the balance to equal up the receipts and payments, and carry this balance forward to the next month.

The bank reconciliation

When you receive your bank statement covering your transactions up to the end of the month, tick off the items, both receipts and payments, in your cash book. In so doing you will find the following items, apart from those which appear in both the statement and your cash book:

☐ Receipts and payments not entered in your cash book. Enter these (see example on page 106).

☐ Items in your cash book but not in the statements. If these are receipts, check to see whether they have been credited by the bank in the first few days of the next month and list these. If they are cheques they are probably 'outstanding', meaning that it may be some time before the payee of the cheque pays it into his bank and it is presented, through the clearing bank, to your bank. Again, list these.

You can then prepare a reconciliation as shown below.

Bank reconciliation as at 29 February 2000

Balance from bank statement (overdrawn)		(455.95)
Add receipts credit 2 March 2000		1,157.00
		701.05
Less outstanding cheques	450.82	
	106.14	
	40.45	597.41
Balance as per cash book		£103.64

If it reconciles, pat yourself on the back. You have probably written your cash book up correctly. It it does not then you will have to look for the difference. Again, do not begrudge the time.

SALES DAY BOOK

Date	Detail	Inv No.	Total	VAT	Net Sales		Amount Paid	Discount	Date Paid	Cheq or Cash
2000 Jan 1	F. Ingram	112	55.23	8.23	47.00		53.85	1.38	3.2.00	Ch
	B. Jones	113	867.15	129.15	738.00		845.47	21.68	6.2.00	Ch
	I. Smith	114	129.25	19.25	110.00		126.02	3.23	8.2.00	Ch
	T. Andrews	115	130.13	19.38	110.75					
2	J. Press	116	448.85	66.85	382.00					
28	B. White	126	151.57	22.57	129.00		147.78	3.79	28.2.00	Ch
	T. Green	127	1207.90	179.90	1028.00		1127.70	30.20	28.2.00	Ch
			7261.20	1081.45	6179.75		2300.82	60.28		

PURCHASES DAY BOOK

This is similar to the sales day book but records all invoices from suppliers for goods or services bought on credit terms. Analyse each invoice according to the type of expense and remember that, when payment of the invoice is recorded in the cash book, the total amount must be entered in the 'Creditors' column.

Date	Detail	Ref	Total	VAT	Material	Power	Stationery & post	Tele-phone	Travel exps	Motor exps	Date paid

Figure 7.2 *Salesday book and purchase day book*

The evidence

As you enter up your cash book, make sure you have some evidence for every entry. On the receipts side it will be your daily takings record, your sales day book (see Figure 7.2) or a note about a sundry receipt. On the payment side it will be the electricity bill, the purchase invoice, the garage bill, etc. Cross reference all these to your cash book and file them in date and number order.

The result

The monthly totals for each column will show your expenditure for the month in each category. The monthly figures will make up the annual figures that will appear in your accounts.

SALES DAY BOOK

If your business is in retail, or you only take cash, or if you issue your invoices and collect payment at the same time, it would be simple for you to record your sales directly in the cash book. In this case, you will need a book with a few more columns on the receipts side, according to the detail you need, and, of course, a column for VAT analysis if you are registered. You will not need to keep a separate sales book.

If you do issue invoices in advance (see Figure 7.3) of receiving payment, your cash receipts will not reflect your sales on a daily basis; you therefore need to keep a separate record of the sales invoices that you issue. Use a sales day book for this purpose.

You should keep a record of each invoice you issue. It helps to have printed invoices in sets so that, for instance, the top white copy goes to your customer, the second copy (green) is your accounting copy and is filed in numerical order, and the third copy (blue) goes in the individual customer file. The VAT regulation lays down what information should be shown on an invoice and an example is shown in Figure 7.3.

As you issue your invoice, enter it in your sales day book as shown in Figure 7.2. Again, you will note the individual details

SUPPLIERS 54 High Street Newtown NA2 3QZ Telephone: 0803 96481			**SALES INVOICE NO**		
INVOICE ADDRESS		**DELIVERY ADDRESS (If different)**			
Your Order No	**Contract No**		**Date and Tax Point**		
Description	**Quantity**	**Price**	**Tax Exclusive Value**	**VAT Rate**	**VAT Payable**
			£	%	£
		Tax Exclusive Value	£	%	£
		Plus VAT	£		
		Invoice Value	£		

TERMS OF PAYMENT: 30 days net   VAT No 300 3000 03

Figure 7.3 *Sales invoice*

shown for each invoice. You have the choice with two or more columns to split your sales between types. Note that the VAT is shown separately and that only the *net* amount is analysed. Make sure you file the copy of the invoice in the same order.

All being well, your customers will pay your invoices, and when they do, enter the amount and date in the columns provided. If you allow them a discount for prompt payment, enter the discount given in the appropriate column so that the amount received plus the discount clears the invoice amount. If your customer settles more than one invoice at a time, cross-reference the receipt to the respective invoices. If you issue credit notes make sure these are entered, placing the details in brackets to show that they should be deducted, in the sales day book.

The receipts entered will form the amounts that are paid into your bank and will be shown in the cash book.

At any time the invoices with no 'paid' entry against them will be those that are unpaid. You will then be in a position to remind the client via a letter, phone call or statement. Similarly after the end of the year, your accountant will be able to pick out those unpaid by the year end by checking the dates of subsequent payment.

Each month, total up the columns and enter the totals, checking that subsidiary columns including VAT balance by adding across to the total. This total will be your monthly sales, including VAT, while your cash book figure will be the cash received from your customers. Any difference will be cash received during the month from invoices issued in the previous month or, conversely, invoices issued but still unpaid.

PETTY CASH BOOK

The petty cash book is used to record small items of expenditure which you pay for in cash. Figure 7.4 illustrates a typical layout for a petty cash book although, again, you must tailor the headings of analysis to suit your business.

Receipts of cash from the bank are shown on the left-hand side and payments on the right-hand side. The easiest method of dealing with petty cash is to draw an initial 'float' of cash for you to hold, preferably in the petty cash box. When any expenditure is

Receipts   Payments

Receipts

Date	Detail	Cash		
2000 Feb 1	Balance B/f	270.00		
17	Cash book	107.14		
26	Cash book	114.08		
			491.22	
March 1	Balance	165.12		

Payments

Date	Detail	Voucher No.	TOTAL	VAT	Post	Stat.	Travel	Motor expen.	Clean	Sundries
2000 Feb 1	Postage	41	18.00		18.00					
2	Cleaner	42	8.40						8.40	
	Mr. White	43	116.71	8.38		16.03	90.30			1.00 Telephone
3	Petrol/van	44	11.50	1.50				10.00		
4	Grocers Ltd	45	.63							.63 Coffee
10	Mr. Smith	46	171.86	22.43		141.43				
Feb 28	Total		326.10	32.31	18.00	165.46	90.30	10.00	8.40	1.63
	Balance		165.12							
			491.22							

Figure 7.4 Petty cash book

made, a petty cash numbered voucher is marked and usually at the end of every week the vouchers are entered in numerical order in the petty cash book. The book is totalled regularly and you then draw a cheque for the total spent in order to 'top up' your float to the original level. Vouchers should always be kept for your accountant at the end of the year and are probably easiest kept in marked envelopes.

The petty cash book should be reconciled monthly so that the balance in the book – the difference between the two sides – should equal the money in the box. If it does not you have probably forgotten to enter some item of expenditure. Note that there is a VAT column and that the analysis is net of VAT.

At the end of each month the subsidiary columns are totalled and agreed by adding across to the total column. As with the cash book, the balance is carried forward to the next month.

WAGES BOOK

You will have to keep a wages book and employee records as soon as you start employing others to help you run your business. It is necessary to follow the rules of the Inspector of Taxes and your accountant will assist you in this. It is advisable to arrange all this before you take on any employees so that you will be able to start paying them correctly as soon as they start work.

A new Small Business Service (SBS) to coordinate advice and support for SMEs was announced in the 1999 Budget. The SBS will have a new role helping businesses to comply with regulation and will offer an automated payroll service to new small employers.

The Inspector of Taxes will send you the relevant booklets explaining how income tax and National Insurance contributions are deducted from the wages you pay to your staff and remitted to the Collector of Taxes. The Inspector will also send you stationery on which to record the individual employees' deductions.

In addition to this, you will need a wages book to summarise weekly or monthly payments made. There are several available on the market and Figure 7.5 illustrates a typical layout. It is also necessary to keep personal records of each of your employees, giving:

Full name
Address
Date of birth
National Insurance number
Date of starting work with you
Salary
Position held
Date of leaving (if relevant)

You will need to give your employees payslips which detail how their wages are made up. You will also need to keep records of your employees' absences due to illness and you are required to compute and pay to them sickness pay, which may then be reclaimed from your payment to the Collector of Taxes. This is called Statutory Sick Pay and the Inspector of Taxes will furnish you with all relevant forms and documents regarding this; since April 1994 the refund is only available for employers whose National Insurance bill for the year is less than £20,000. (Chapter 10 discusses the details of recruitment and employment law.)

Irrespective of whether you pay your staff weekly or monthly, you will need to draw a cheque or cash to pay them. This will be entered in the cash book or petty cash book as will the cheque drawn to remit to the Inland Revenue for the PAYE and National Insurance deductions. Note that the employer also contributes to National Insurance.

Summarise your wages book and check that the figures agree with the wages column of your cash book. The figure that will appear in your accounts will be the gross cost of the wages, that is, the net amount paid to employees plus the PAYE and National Insurance deducted, plus the employer's contribution. The wages book should give you the breakdown of this figure.

Individual entries should agree with the tax deduction cards supplied by the Inland Revenue. Wages envelopes with a printed summary on the outside are readily available. If you have more than a few employees it is probably a good idea to look at one of the proprietary systems which allow you to deal with the payslips, wages book and deduction card all at the same time.

Month Ending **FEB 2000** Week No. _____

NAME	National Insurance No	Contribution Table Letter	Gross Amount Due	EMPLOYER'S DEDUCTIONS				Net Amount Due	EMPLOYER'S CONTRIBUTIONS	
				Tax	Class 1				Class 1	
A. White (Code 220L)	YK90 21 19 B	A	636.07	135.82	57.42			443.05	66.67	

Figure 7.5 *Wages book*

Remember that if your business is a limited company and you are a director, even if you are the sole director or jointly with your wife, any money taken from the firm will be your wages and should be taxed through the PAYE (Pay As You Earn) system. The Inland Revenue is now quite strict about this and will penalise directors for drawing untaxed lump sum amounts.

If you are a sole trader or partnership, your tax is assessed on your real results and the amounts you take are your drawings. These do not have to be taxed at the time, but remember that you are still liable to pay National Insurance and will have to pay, depending on your results, tax on your profits in the future.

VALUE ADDED TAX (VAT)

For most small businesses, the VAT return is relatively easy to complete, always given that your books are kept up to date and totalled on a regular basis. If you have followed the advice of the earlier parts of this chapter then you will have already recorded all the details necessary for completing the VAT return.

It is advisable to keep a separate book for your VAT workings. Figure 7.6 gives an example of this. The information in the official VAT return is in the VAT column of the book and in the 'totals excluding VAT' columns. Do be especially careful not to claim in the input column any VAT paid over to HM Customs and Excise. This is a very common mistake; unfortunately they do not take kindly to you boosting your income by claiming back the VAT already paid over. VAT is discussed in detail in the following chapter.

CREDIT CONTROL

This area is very important to the continued success of your business. It relies on information found in the sales book and cash book previously covered.

What are your terms of credit? And how long do your clients take to pay? Are you currently overdrawn at the bank and still owed outstanding monies?

It is a fallacy to believe that applied credit control will upset your customers. What is the point of selling your product if you are not going to get paid? If done in a proper and efficient way, credit control is not only effective but will not offend your clients. They will respect you for it as they in turn have to do the very same thing.

Do not be heavy handed. Your first action should be a statement of account sent out between 14 days and 21 days after the invoice (or with an existing credit chasing system) or at the end of every month. After a reasonable period of time, a pleasant telephone call to your customer's 'bought ledger' department should gain some response. Again allow a few weeks to elapse and then if nothing happens send a polite letter as a reminder that the account is now overdue by 'XX' days and that you would appreciate prompt settlement of the outstanding amount. A rapport often builds up between yourself and the 'bought ledger' and if this is kept on a pleasant business footing then you can succeed in calling in outstanding money where a hard-handed approach will often fail to win prompt action. You should not, unless it is absolutely necessary, resort to solicitors' letters. Should recovery, after completing the credit-chasing procedure, become difficult you can try to reclaim the debt by issuing a summons in the small claims section of the County Court. However, the recent introduction of legislation does now allow for interest to be added to unpaid invoices of over 30 days.

After some time a pattern will emerge showing you the clients who pay promptly and those who take longer to settle their account. Large firms will often take 60 to 90 days to settle, sometimes longer than that, so do ensure that this is taken into account or, if not acceptable, that the matter is discussed in advance with your client and credit terms agreed.

If a client is consistently overdue in paying your invoices, to the extent of using between 60 and 90 days over and above the credit term agreed, then you should consider whether or not to withdraw credit terms or to cease trading with them. This decision, of course, rests entirely with you and should not be taken lightly. If either eventuality occurs, make clear to your client the reason why the step has had to be taken.

If you allow a discount for prompt payment ensure that, should the client not pay within the time, the discount is not deducted from the paid invoiced amount.

ADMINISTRATIVE SYSTEMS

This section is based on administrative principles vital to the success of an existing or proposed small business. It also assumes that you know in detail the product or service of your business.

Paperwork and legislative controls hold little attraction for many people – indeed, most would tell you that they hate paperwork – but they are essential to the success of a business. These controls do not have to be either time-consuming or sophisticated.

Earlier in the book you will have read about how to obtain additional finance, whether or not it is best to operate in a partnership or as a sole trader, and rules on sales and marketing. Basically, in operating your business you will have three main factors to consider:

- ☐ the knowledge of your product/service;
- ☐ money;
- ☐ people.

Each of these areas requires records and administrative procedures of one sort or another to comply with statutory or just sound business requirements.

Simple systems

Financial

The first area to examine when implementing systems is the financial one. If you go to a bank for additional funds the first thing you will be asked is, 'How soon can you pay it back?' and/or 'Can you let me have a cash-flow statement?' This cash-flow statement is a vital part of your administrative records. It must project for at least a year ahead, preferably three years, and it must show what bills you expect to receive month by month for rent, rates, light and heating purchases, wages, even VAT. You must then estimate the volume of your sales receipts over the same period – remember to be realistic when working on future projections. Then and only then can you estimate what your cash balance or overdraft figure is likely to be at the end of each

For VAT RETURN – quarter ended ....   For quarter ended ....

	Month Feb 2000 £	Month £	Month £	TOTAL £	Month £	Month £	Month £	TOTAL £

OUTPUT TAX

	Month Feb 2000 £	Month £	Month £	TOTAL £	Month £	Month £	Month £	TOTAL £
Sales	1081·45							
Cash	-							
Bank	9·45							
	1090·90							

INPUT TAX

Purchases	-							
Cash	32·31							
Bank	238·98							
	271·29							

NET Payable
TAX Receivable

NET Payable
TAX Receivable

122

OUTPUT (excluding VAT)

Sales	6179.75						
Cash	–						
Bank	2527.02						
	8706.77						

INPUT (excluding VAT)

Purchases	–						
Cash	293.79						
Bank	2297.49						
	2591.28						

Figure 7.6 *VAT summary*

month. Naturally, any hire purchase, leasing or loan repayments must be similarly noted.

Accounts records should be kept and an explanation of what books to keep and how to keep them has already been given. You must remember to set aside time to keep these accounts up to date and accurate, otherwise the entire accounts system will grind to a halt.

Stock levels

An area often forgotten is your existing stock level. This stock represents money tied up and not available for use. Whether it is for your own use or for resale, what is the level of your stock? Stock records, kept up to date, can tell you what the present level of stock is, with the added bonus that they can also tell you the length of time the stock has been held and the quantities, and you can then do something about it where necessary. If you review stock records regularly, you can see at a glance what is moving and what is not, and this can be a great help in controlling the capital outlay necessary when keeping stock up to the right level. Again you need a simple card index showing commodity, pack, supplier, minimum and maximum stock, incomings and outgoings, and balance with a value column.

Personnel

Another area of administration to look at is personnel. All details relating to your employees must be assigned a file – one file for each individual. All appropriate records must be kept in this file, such as job application forms, references, your copy of the contract of employment, letter of appointment, etc. These files must be kept private and confidential and noted as such. Notes from discussions should also be filed away and any letters of complaint too. Wages cards (and your account files and books) can also be kept in the private and confidential filing drawer as this will save on space initially.

Keep copies to hand of the different leaflets given out by the Department for Education and Employment and the Department of Social Security.

The key to good administration is to keep it simple, creating a file only if you really need it. A correspondence filing system is the most basic and the easiest to start; all you need to do is put one client's correspondence in one file, that of another client in the next file, and so on. You then build up these files and put them away alphabetically. Your business administration files should be divided into six parts – office, personnel, legal, accounting, equipment (purchases) and sales (customers). Keep the files separate at all times, preferably in a safe, fireproof location. Do consider keeping duplicate records. Should any unforeseen accident occur, such as a fire, it would take some time to compile replacement documentation. Consider purchasing a safe in which to place your valuables. Your office insurance payments could be reduced should you acquire a safe.

A first-aid kit will have to be purchased and a first-aid system set up. It is extremely important that your office and/or factory complies with the Health and Safety at Work Act. The Department for Education and Employment will send you all the necessary details; you may already have had a visit from your local factory inspector to ensure that you are complying with the Act. A book will need to be kept to record any accidents.

What about office equipment – should you buy or lease it? If you are a new company starting up you could find leasing difficult to obtain. On the other hand, if you purchase, you are allowed to write off part of the value of the machine each year. As there are so many different machines, at varying prices, it is often best to look at the situation carefully in the light of your own requirements and business. If you are thinking about buying a computer, shop around and decide what sort of work you want the machine to do. However, unless you have a manual system up and working it is pointless trying to match an existing computer program to take over the existing workload. You must know what you need and want from a system before you buy it. Many companies have run into serious administrative difficulties (and financial ones too) over the purchase of a computer. Telegraph Publications have produced a comprehensive book on the subject entitled _How to Choose and Use Business Microcomputers and Software_ which will be most helpful.

Part of successful administration is making sure that your business is covered by insurance. Obtain quotations and compare the price and content of different policies as they vary, and do read the small print. You are required by law to have a policy called 'Employer's Liability' and the policy must be displayed in a prominent position. Your machinery, premises, vehicles, etc, will all need to be covered by insurance.

Administration is just as important an ingredient in the success of a business as the rest of the business disciplines. To run a business you have to amalgamate the various skills involved, and you will find that at any one time one particular skill will be needed more than the others. But remember that clear and simple administrative systems will ensure that you will not run foul either of the law, the various government departments or your customers.

The list of further reading in Appendix II is a useful reference should you wish to locate a book that goes into more detail on a specific business or financial topic.

Checklist: Preparing finance and administration

- ☐ Have you set up your bookkeeping system?
- ☐ Have you considered and set up a credit control system?
- ☐ What other business controls have you set up?
- ☐ Are you aware of tax, including VAT, and National Insurance requirements?
- ☐ Are you aware of welfare and health & safety regulations?
- ☐ What special paperwork is necessary?
- ☐ What records and filing must be arranged?
- ☐ Will you require telephone, telex or fax services?
- ☐ What else should be considered in your case?

Checklist: Purchasing

- ☐ Do you know how much stock to buy, when to buy it and at what cost?
- ☐ What will unsold stock cost you?
- ☐ Can you store your purchases securely?
- ☐ Have you prepared a stock control system?
- ☐ Have you sought several quotations for supply (in writing)?
- ☐ Have you planned to keep all expenditure to a sensible minimum?

Source: *DfEE, Running your own Business*

---

8 National Insurance, Income Tax, Corporation Tax and VAT

'No man in this country is under the smallest obligation, moral or otherwise, so to arrange his legal relations to his business or to his property as to enable the Inland Revenue to put the largest possible shovel into his stores.'

This was Lord President Clyde's view, adding that the taxpayer is 'entitled to be astute to prevent, so far as he honestly can, the depletion of his means by the Revenue'.

When you start your business, you have to decide the form it is going to take: sole trader, partnership, unlimited liability or limited liability company. The tax position can decide which form you start off with, although no good tax adviser will ignore the commercial requirements. But just a slight adjustment here and there can make a material difference to the amount of tax that you pay – and not only to the amount but also to when it is paid. At the end of this chapter you will find an invaluable checklist of the key points which you need to know about tax and your business. (While every effort has been made to ensure that the figures given in this chapter are correct, please refer to the latest DSS and Inland Revenue leaflets for the most up-to-date figures.)

NATIONAL INSURANCE

Although we talk of National Insurance (NI) as 'contributions', it is, of course, just another form of taxation. NI is easy for the government to levy as it is an efficient system of collecting tax; it does not cause too much aggravation or need many staff to administer it.

National Insurance is often the forgotten element in tax planning. The amount involved these days can be quite considerable and it can tip the balance when you are trying to decide whether or not to set up as a sole trader, partnership, or whether to start off straight away as a limited liability company. One practical point to remember when employing additional staff is that the employer, in addition to deducting NI from that person, also has to pay to the government its own NI contribution for that employee.

NI: AN OUTLINE

The employed

Class 1 contributions are in general payable by employees over the age of 16. Contributions are normally paid by the employee and the employer. However, if the employee has reached pensionable age (65 for men, and 60 for women) only the employer has to pay the contributions. Employers are required to deduct contributions from the employee's pay and to pay over the total to the Inland Revenue along with income tax deducted under the PAYE scheme.

☐   Rates of contribution are expressed as a percentage of earnings where these are at present between the 'earnings limits', which are in turn expressed in weekly, monthly or yearly terms to be used according to the normal pay intervals of the employee. Earnings limits and the new NI Class 1 rates are as shown in Tables 8.1 and 8.2.

☐   No contributions are payable if earnings are below the lower earnings limit subject to rules for persons with more than one employment.

☐ Where the employer has an occupational pension scheme which satisfies certain requirements, he can 'contract out' of the state scheme. The full rates apply to the part of the earnings up to the lower earnings limit but there is a reduced rate for the part of the earnings in excess of that figure.

☐ Earnings for contribution purposes are gross earnings before PAYE or pension fund deductions, but do not include redundancy payments, payments in lieu of notice, termination payments, pensions, benefits in kind, meal vouchers, expenses or tips not paid by the employer.

☐ Primary contributions due from an employee with more than one employment in one year are limited to a maximum of the full rate applied to 53 weeks times the weekly upper earnings limit. There is normally no limit on the employer's contributions.

☐ There are special rules for persons entering or leaving the country. These may be modified if the movement is between EU countries or between Great Britain and a country with whom it has a reciprocal agreement.

The self-employed

☐ Self-employed persons over 16 and under 65 (men) or 60 (women) can be liable to pay flat-rate Class 2 contributions and earnings-related Class 4 contributions. There are exemptions from Class 2 contributions, the most important being if profits (as shown by the accounts) are expected to be below £3,825 (for 2000/2001).

☐ The rate of the Class 2 contribution is £2 per week. Contributions may be paid by direct debit through a bank account or Giro. The option of payment by purchasing stamps is no longer available.

☐ Earnings-related Class 4 contributions for any year are based on the profit assessable under Schedule D Class I or II for that year, after taking account of capital allowances, balancing charges, loss relief, and annual payments incurred for trading purposes. For 2000/2001 the rate of contribution is 6 per cent on assessable profits between £4,385 and £27,820 per annum.

Table 8.1 *Contracted in on all earnings. NI Class 1 contributions from 6 April 2000*

Earnings per week	Employees		Employers
	On first £76	Remainder	
up to £76.00	0	0	0
£76.00 to £84.00	0	10%	0
£84.00 to £535.00	0	10%	9.2%
£535.00	no additional liability		12.2%

Table 8.2 *Contracted out on all earnings. NI Class 1 contributions from 6 April 2000*

Earnings per week	Employees		Employers	
			Remainder	
	On first £76	Remainder	Salary-related	Money-purchased
up to £76.00	0	0	0	0
£76.00 to £84.00	0	8.4%	0	0
£84.00 to £535.00	0	8.4%	9.2%	11.6%
over £535.00	no additional liability		12.2%	12.2%

The businessman can no longer obtain 50 per cent relief for income tax purposes on his graduated Class 4 contributions.

☐ Class 4 contributions are collected along with income tax on the Schedule D Class I or II assessment.

☐ Where a person is both employed and self-employed, his total maximum contribution under NI Classes 1, 2 and 4 is equal to 53 weekly Class 1 contributions on the upper earnings limit at the standard rate.

The unemployed

☐ Class 3 contributions are entirely voluntary and are payable by those who wish to secure a measure of entitlement to benefits and whose contribution record is not otherwise good enough. Class 3 contributions can only be paid by a person who has not paid, in Class 1 or 2, contributions equal to 52 Class 1 contributions at the standard rate on the lower weekly earnings limit.

☐ The rate is £6.55 per week. Contributions are paid by direct debit through a bank Giro or account.

CONTRIBUTIONS

The rates of Class 1 NI contributions effective from 6 April 2000 are as shown in Table 8.1.

If you or your employees are contracted out of the state pension scheme, you pay at reduced rates on the amount of salary over the lower earnings limit. The applicable rates effective since 6 April 2000 are shown in Table 8.2.

The benefits available to the self-employed through their Class 2 and 4 contributions are a great deal less than those to which employees and directors are entitled through their Class 1 contributions.

BUSINESS TAX

Calculation of trading profits

You calculate your trading income on normal accounting principles. In other words, not on a cash basis but on an invoicing basis, so you count the income when you become entitled to it rather than when you actually receive the cash. Similarly with expenditure, you bring in the liability when it arises, not when you pay out the money. Trading income is the only type of income dealt with on that basis; most other income is dealt with on a receipts basis.

For the individual

If you go into business as an individual or in partnership, your profits will be assessed for income tax.

If you are a sole trader or partnership setting up business, you are entitled to count as part of your trading expenses any revenue expenditure incurred by you in connection with the business for up to seven years before you actually started trading (or five years if you started trading before 5 April 1995). For example, you may own a workshop for some three to six months before starting any work in it. But you are going to be paying rent, and you may have other outgoings such as gas and electricity. You can offset those against the income that you eventually generate when you do start trading. Those expenses, plus, for example, capital allowances, can normally be used to reduce your profit or generate an income tax loss if you are setting up on your own. If you make a trading loss then there are all sorts of things that you can do with the loss: you can carry it forward against the future income from your trade; if you have other income in the same year in which you make the loss, then you can set that loss off immediately against the other income.

Furthermore, if you make a trading loss in the first four years of trading, it can be carried back and set off against your other income in the three years prior to the loss. If you have a capital loss on a chargeable asset, you can set that off against capital gains in the same period or you can carry that capital loss forward. But you *cannot* set a capital loss against income – that is a basic rule of revenue law.

Table 8.3 *NI contributions Classes 2 and 4 self-employed 2000/2001*

Class 2 fixed per week	
no liability if earning below £3,825	£2
Class 4 earnings related	
on profits between £4,385 and £27,820 a year	7.0%

If you are an established self-employed person, whether working as a sole trader or as a partner, the system running until 1995/96 was that you paid tax on what was known as the preceding year basis. However, new income tax rules came into play in the tax year 1997/98. From 9 April 1997, the existing 'preceding year' basis was replaced by the 'current year' basis. This means that tax is charged on the profit of the accounting year that ends in the tax year itself (current year), rather than the profit of the accounting year that ends in the previous tax year. Tax is payable in two instalments on 31 January in the tax year and 31 July of the next tax year.

Once you have calculated your total profits, there are certain things you can deduct. The main element is non-bank interest paid for business purposes. If you pay interest to someone other than a bank, it is allowed not against your trading income but against your total profits. So, if you knock off the non-banking interest, you arrive at the profit chargeable for corporation tax (CT).

For your company

If you choose to operate through a UK limited company, the company will be liable to pay corporation tax (CT) on its profits. Companies pay tax on a current year basis, on whatever they earn in the particular accounting period. Companies pay corporation tax (CT) on both income and capital gains (Table 8.4).

For most companies the date of payment for corporation tax will generally be nine months after the end of the accounting period. If the companies receive income from which income tax has been deducted they are given credit for that income tax, and it is set off against the corporation tax due. If they have no profits liable for CT, they get the income tax back.

Marginal small companies' relief

Below £300,000 profits you pay 20 per cent and over £1,500,000 you pay 30 per cent in 2000/2001. In between these two amounts is the 'marginal small companies' relief'. This is an effective tax rate of 32.5 per cent for year ending 31 March 2001.

Table 8.4 *Corporation tax*

| | Accounting period commencing 1 April | | | |
	2000	**1999**	**1998**	**1997**
Full rate	30%	30%	31%	31%
Small companies rate	20%	20%	21%	24%
Charged up to	£300,000	£300,000	£300,000	£300,000
Marginal relief up to	£1,500,000	£1,500,000	£1,500,000	£1,500,000
Marginal rate	32.5%	32.5%	33.5%	33.5%
Marginal relief fraction	1/40	1/40	1/40	1/40
Starting rate	10%	N/A	N/A	N/A
Charged up to	£10,000			
Marginal relief up to	£50,000			
Marginal rate	22.5%			
Marginal relief fraction	1/40			
Advance CT rate	N/A	N/A*	1/4	1/4

* after 5 April 1999 (1/4 from 1 April to 5 April).

For a family company, making profits slightly over £300,000, it may be worth paying out extra cash to, say, directors' bonuses. In addition, it is worth taking on a little more plant and equipment and paying in a little more to the company's pension scheme in order to stay out of this £300,000 plus band, which results in you paying CT at 32.5 per cent on the difference between £300,000 and £1,500,000.

The limits of £1,500,000 and £300,000 are reduced if you have more than one company under your control, or more than one company in a group of companies. It would be very nice, of course, if you were making £500,000, just to set up four companies, with £125,000 profits at 20 per cent tax on each. However, it does not work that way.

For the year to 31 March 2001 and subsequent years, there is a starting rate of 10 per cent up to £10,000 with marginal relief for profits between £10,000 and £50,000. It works in the same way as the small-companies rate.

What are dividends?

In small companies the shareholders and directors are usually the same. If you have any surplus profits they can be allocated as directors' bonuses, in which case they will count as earned income. If, however, you take out the cash as a dividend, the company will not get a deduction from the profits in respect of the amounts that you pay out. On the other hand, dividends do not attract NI contributions and carry a tax credit which discharges the shareholders basic-rate liability.

It is important to note that a company is a separate legal entity from its directors. This is true even if one director controls all or most of the share capital. The controlling director himself may regard the company and himself as essentially one business entity. This can cause practical difficulties. For example, all his expenses, both business and private, may be paid by the company. Where this happens, any private expenses must be charged to his current account. If this causes the account to become overdrawn, there can be a tax charge both under the fringe benefits rules relating to beneficial loans and under the close company 'loans to participators' rules (as to which, see below under close companies). Overdrawn balances can be dealt with by way of a dividend or remuneration or a combination of both.

Generally, a director who holds shares can take his reward in the form of dividends, remuneration, or a combination of both. This requires careful consideration.

What about salaries?

One important aspect, as mentioned above, is that dividend payments do *not* attract NI contributions whereas salary and bonuses do and these can be quite costly. Where the shareholders and directors of a company are one and the same, it may be worth paying out a part of their 'reward' by way of dividend instead of remuneration. Where the company is paying corporation tax at the 20 per cent rate, this change makes no effective difference to its tax position, but could lead to a useful saving of NI contributions.

There are a number of other factors, however; the timing of tax payments, effect on pension scheme contributions and social security benefits, valuation of the company's shares – all these factors need to be taken into consideration. Each situation needs to be looked at on its own merits and professional advice is strongly recommended before any decision is taken.

What is a close company?

Most small companies will be what are known as 'close companies', defined as being controlled by five or fewer shareholders or by any number of directors who are also shareholders. The vast majority of companies in this country are close companies. Bearing in mind that you can still pay 40 per cent tax on your own income, it would be very handy to put some money into a company and leave it to grow, knowing that the bulk of it will never pay more than 20 per cent tax.

The Inland Revenue was aware of this dodge of using companies as money boxes to hold cash that would have been paying tax at fairly high rates as individuals' income, and there is a 30 per cent CT charge on close investment companies which retain most of their profit.

Furthermore, if your company pays tax at 20 per cent, you do not want to take the money out of the company and pay tax on it. You just borrow it from the company and carry on borrowing larger and larger amounts and never pay back the sums borrowed. But the Revenue have spotted this loophole too. Now, when a shareholder receives such a loan, the company has to put on deposit with the Collector of Taxes the equivalent of the recently abolished Advance Corporation Tax (ACT) so the loan is treated virtually as a dividend. In addition, the recipient could be assessed to income tax on the benefit of the loan. The annual benefit would be equal to the amount of deemed interest on the loan at the 'official rate' (6.25 per cent since 6 March 1999).

There are stringent rules under the Directors and Insolvency Act 1985 which have particular relevance for close companies and their director-shareholders. Under this Act anyone who acts as a director is considered to be a director and is personally liable for any debts arising should the company continue to trade while insolvent. (The definition of director includes shadow directors, non-executive directors, etc.) The Act does not allow for the excuse of incompetence or lack of knowledge, and assumes that directors must be responsible for their actions and those of their companies. In certain circumstances directors can be jointly liable for the actions of fellow directors. Financial implications aside, should a director fail to fulfil the administrative obligations as laid out in the Companies Act and the Insolvency Act 1986, fines as well as imprisonment can be enforced. Directors can also be disqualified from acting as a director for up to 15 years. Careful study of this Act is therefore advised.

Running costs

Now that the corporation tax rate for very small companies has been reduced to 10 per cent, and the rate for small companies has been reduced to 20 per cent, tax alone should not be a reason to stop you from incorporating the business. However, the running costs of a limited liability company are higher than those of a trading business, and this should be borne in mind. And although it is called a limited liability company, you may not get the full benefit of limited liability because the company's bankers may require the director-shareholders to put up personal guarantees to cover the company's borrowings.

WHAT ARE CAPITAL ALLOWANCES?

Capital allowances can also be deducted from trading income provided they have been incurred before the end of the accounting period. While you are not allowed to deduct depreciation in arriving at your taxable income, you are allowed instead to deduct capital allowances. These are given on a wide range of capital expenditure, for example, plant and machinery, industrial and agricultural buildings, with special treatment available for 'short-life' assets. In some cases, it does not matter whether the asset is in use or not; provided that the expenditure has been incurred, the business will qualify for relief.

Allowances on plant and machinery

There has never been a definition of plant and machinery but the term encompasses not only machines, but also many fixtures and fittings, office equipment and motor vehicles.

The allowance generally available is a 25 per cent 'writing down' allowance. This is given on the 'pool' of expenditure calculated on a reducing balance basis. Expenditure on new assets is added to the pool and the proceeds of plant disposed of are deducted from the pool so as to arrive at the amount on which the 25 per cent allowance is given. If the accounting period is less than 12 months, the allowance is reduced accordingly.

For expenditure on or after 2 July 1999 by small and medium-sized businesses, an initial allowance of 40 per cent of the cost can be claimed on certain expenditure.

Special treatment is given to motor-cars costing more than £12,000: the writing down allowance on each such car is limited to a maximum of £3,000 a year.

Allowances on industrial buildings

If you buy an industrial building or have it built for use in your own trade or to lease to someone else in their trade, you may be entitled to capital allowances on the building. That amount of allowance will depend on whether the building is new or second-hand when you acquired it. If the building is new you may claim an annual 'writing down' allowance of 4 per cent on the cost of the building, but not the land. If you buy a second-hand building, you may be entitled to 'writing down' allowances but the level of these will depend upon the allowances claimed by the vendor of the building. If you buy a new commercial building in an Enterprise Zone, you are entitled to an initial allowance of 100 per cent. You need not claim this allowance in full; instead, should you wish, you can claim a 25 per cent 'straight line' allowance on the balance in subsequent years.

If you sell an industrial building, part or even all of the allowances you have claimed may be clawed back, ie added to your income, depending upon the price you receive for the building and when the expenditure in respect of which the allowances were claimed was originally incurred.

RELIEF FOR TRADING LOSSES

☐ These can be set against other income or chargeable gains of the same or the preceding accounting year.
☐ Relief can be carried forward against future trading profits on the same trade.
☐ On cessation of trade the losses of the last 12 months can be carried back against trading profits of the three previous years.

CAPITAL GAINS

☐ The gains on the disposal of business assets can be deferred if another business asset is acquired with the proceeds, though normally not more than one year earlier or three years later. This is known as 'rollover relief'.
☐ Capital losses can be set off against capital gains in the same accounting period, and net losses can be carried forward to future periods.
☐ Capital losses cannot be set against income.

You should also remember that as the company and its shareholders are separate legal entities, a double charge to capital gains tax can arise if the shareholders wish to realise the assets in the company. First, there may be a charge within the company to corporation tax on the gain arising on the disposal of the assets concerned by the company. Second, there may be a further charge to capital gains tax on the gain arising to the shareholders when they realise their shares, for example, on liquidating the company.

On the other hand, where an individual disposes of his business or sells his shares in his family trading company when he is over 50 or is obliged to retire under that age through ill health, he may be able to claim substantial relief against the chargeable gains arising on him in this way.

VALUE ADDED TAX (VAT)

VAT is charged by most businesses on all sales and the tax collected is paid over to HM Customs and Excise quarterly. A business can usually claim a set-off for VAT which it has paid. Small businesses may not be liable to register, but this means that they cannot recover it either.

Where a business is exempt – the major ones are property investment, banking and insurance services – VAT is not charged but the business cannot recover VAT which it pays.

You should be aware that VAT on certain expenses is not recoverable: the most notable example is entertaining customers or suppliers and the cost of buying (but not running) motor cars.

Registration

You do not charge VAT unless your annual turnover exceeds £52,000. It is important to register if:

☐   at the end of any month the value of your taxable supplies in the previous 12 months has exceeded £52,000; or

☐   at any time there are reasonable grounds for believing that the value of taxable supplies you will make in the next 30 days will exceed £52,000.

The VAT inspector will want tax on your sales from the date of your registration. If you do not register in time, he will still want to collect tax from the date you should have registered, and will not allow you to set off the VAT on expenses incurred during the intervening period.

Where the turnover limits are not likely to be exceeded, a business can, in certain circumstances, still register. This may be advantageous, particularly if supplies are being made to other taxable businesses which can recover VAT charged. It is only by registering that the VAT paid can be recovered. Also, where a business intends to make sales subject to VAT at some time in the future, it may be allowed to register as an 'intending trader' (subject to certain conditions imposed by Customs and Excise) so as to be able to recover VAT on its expenses in the meantime. It is also possible for a newly registered business to reclaim VAT on goods bought prior to registration where these are still held at that time and on services supplied to it for up to six months prior to registration.

Voluntary registration is also useful if you make mainly zero-rated supplies because it enables you to get back the VAT you have paid out. Most supplies attract VAT at the standard rate of 17.5 per cent but certain categories are zero-rated, i.e. there is no VAT payable, and these include most foods, books and newspapers, transport, and children's clothing. Export of goods and many supplies of services to foreigners are also 'zero-rated' or 'exempt' categories. Domestic fuel attracts VAT at 5 per cent. The only person who suffers VAT, and this is the usual peculiar approach of most tax legislation, is someone who is exempt from it. It might be the ordinary citizen, or someone in the property business, or bankers, but whoever is exempt cannot reclaim VAT despite having paid it out.

Companies register separately, but if they are part of a group or commonly controlled they can register together. For unincorporated businesses it is the proprietor of the business who has to register and all his business activities are looked at together. So if he has a turnover of £20,000 a year on a fruit stall in the local market and another £33,000 as a consultant, he must charge VAT on the lot as it is over the £52,000 limit. This does mean keeping records and in recognition of this there are special schemes available to small traders.

Registration for VAT requires extra record-keeping, but this should not be significant unless the business is using one of the special schemes for antiques and certain second-hand goods under which VAT is only charged on the margin between cost and selling price, and not on the whole selling price. There is also a variety of schemes for calculating the VAT liability of a retail business.

As the payment of VAT can handicap the entrepreneur starting off in business, when compiling sales forecasts it is advisable, should they show that the VAT limit is going to be exceeded, to allow for the relevant amounts of VAT in the overall forecast. Forewarned is forearmed. Leaflets on VAT can be obtained from your local Customs and Excise office.

Cash accounting and annual accounting

The payment of VAT due on a cash accounting system is widely publicised by HM Customs and Excise. This optional system benefits businesses which have a turnover of up to £350,000 per year. Late payment of invoices in the past has left small businesses with an extremely vulnerable cash-flow situation. Now these businesses do not have to pay VAT until the related invoices have been paid.

In addition, there is also an option of annual accounting for VAT, up to an annual turnover limit of £300,000. Under this scheme, businesses have to complete only one VAT return per year; however, there will be nine *advance* payments on account to be made.

Bad debt relief

Bad debt relief of VAT can be claimed after six months if the debt has been written off in the business's accounts.

WHAT TAX CHOICES DO YOU HAVE?

For the sole trader

Let us suppose that you are in a fortunate position in that your pretax profits after capital allowances and all the other things (but not remuneration for yourself, as you are not incorporated) are £70,000. Let us take the example of a small businessman who is married. In 2000/2001 he pays income tax of £20,951.60, Class 2 contributions of £104 and Class 4 contributions of £1649.45. His total contribution to the Exchequer is £22,703.05.

For the partnership

If he formed or was part of a partnership, our businessman could take his wife into equal partnership and her share of the income would be taxed separately. If this is done each would earn £35,000. Each would get the personal allowance. Each would pay tax of £6951.60, Class 2 contributions of £104 and Class 4 contributions of £1647.45. The total for both is £17,406.10 which shows a reduction of £5,296.95 when compared with the sole trader example. However, the wife must genuinely work in the business in a capacity likely to earn the sum of money being paid.

If you are starting a business, never set up as a husband and wife; make sure that one or other is an employee for the first year, as your first year's accounts usually form the basis of assessment for the first three tax years. The earnings of an employee are only taxed in one year so if one of you is an employee for that first year you pay tax on those earnings once, but the employer gets the deduction two and a half to three times over. Often it is the husband who sets up on his own and takes the wife as the employee and then the wife is introduced as a partner at the end of the first year.

For the company

Let us suppose our married couple choose to incorporate and form a limited company. The company has £70,000 of taxable profits before they draw anything out of their business to live on. Let us assume they each take a salary of £20,000. Income tax on that for 2000/2001 works out at £3252.90 each. Class 1 NI is £1604.80 from each employee plus the company's contribution of £1907.10 per employee.

The company's position is as follows:

	£	£
Profits before directors' remuneration		70,000
Remuneration 2 x £20,000	40,000	
Secondary Class 1 NICs: 2 x £1907.10	3,814	43,814
Corporation tax profits		26,186
Tax at 10% on	10,000	1,000
Tax at 22.5% on	16,186	*3,642
Corporation tax payable		*4,642

* to nearest £1

The taxes are therefore:
2 x (£3252.90 + £1604.80 + £1907.10) = £13,529
    plus   £4,642
                           £18,171

to the nearest £1. This compares with £17,406 for a partnership.

Table 8.5 *Income tax*

	Tax rate %	2000/2001 band £
Basic rate band	22	28,400
Higher rate band	40	28,400+
Personal allowance (under 65)		4325

Benefits in kind ('perks')

One of the advantages of the company structure is that it is possible to provide employees (in particular the directors) with various benefits in kind. These are likely to give rise to some additional tax on the individual, based on the cost incurred in providing the benefit that he receives. However, the cost of this is likely to be significantly less to him than if he had to provide this benefit entirely at his own expense.

A particularly popular form of 'perk' is the company car. Here the benefit is measured by reference to scales laid down by the Inland Revenue depending on the list price and age of the car. The benefit is calculated as 35 per cent of the list price of the car when new plus accessories, but less any capital contributions made by the employee. The value of the benefit is reduced by one quarter for cars more than four years old. When the employee uses the car for between 2,500 and 18,000 miles during the tax year the benefit is reduced to 25 per cent of the price and to 15 per cent if the business mileage is over 18,000 in the tax year. An additional charge scale applies where the company petrol is supplied for private use.

Remember that the actual cost to the employee is the tax on these scale charges.

Pensions

Pensions can make all the difference to you, whether you are self-employed or not.

Personal pension schemes came into force on 1 July 1988. These schemes are available to both employees and the self-employed. The employer is able to contribute to personal pensions. Our couple could normally pay only up to 17.5 per cent of their relevant earnings into a pension scheme, though this limit is higher for people more than 35 years old. Alternatively, the company could set up an occupational pension scheme for the directors. It might be able to pay much higher contributions (subject to Inland Revenue approval) and so reduce the CT charge correspondingly. However, if you are going to start a pension scheme you have got to be sure you want it in addition to finding the cash to pay for it.

Let us look at the finances. Take a man aged 53 with a salary of £15,000 out of his company. He wants to retire at 60 with a tax-free lump sum of one and a half times his final salary and a pension thereafter of two-thirds of his final salary or a reduced pension in view of the lump sum. The annual contribution for the next seven or eight years would be determined by actuarial contributions. It might be as high as £54,000 simply because of the applicant's age. The older you are, the higher the premiums become for the same amount of money.

There are a number of special schemes now and it is advisable to contact your independent insurance consultant to find out the most suitable one for you. Your decision, however, should rest on commercial principles rather than on purely tax considerations.

Stakeholder pensions will be available soon. Telegraph Publications have published a pensions guide which is available through bookshops or directly from the *Daily Telegraph*.

IMPLICATIONS

The different types of taxation dealt with in this chapter must be considered separately and, unless the businessman has a financial background, it would be advisable for him to discuss the implications with his accountant *before* he starts trading. The *Daily Telegraph* publishes a series of tax guides specifically aimed at small businesses, whether or not they are trading as limited companies or are self-employed.

Before the reduction in the level of corporation tax, many companies considered their accounts in the light of how much tax they would have to pay rather than from sound business principles. This has changed and will in all likelihood continue to change. None of us likes paying tax; the small businessman finds it unrewarding to work all hours only to have his hard-earned money taken away by the taxman. If it makes it easier, consider that if you were not earning money you would not be liable for tax.

Further changes were announced for the tax year 2001/2002 in the Budget of March 2000. These changes will be addressed in the next edition of this book.

Checklist: Preparing tax

☐ Check with your accountant that the form of your business (ie: sole trader, partnership, unlimited liability or limited liability) is the most tax efficient.

☐ Have you included National Insurance within your tax planning and recruitment costs?

☐ Consider ways to stay below £10,000 or £300,000 profit if you are close to these figures, such as increasing the company pension scheme or taking on additional plant and equipment.

☐ Examine the advantages of registering for VAT, if your annual turnover is under £52,000, such as recovering VAT on expenses.

☐ Identify additional record-keeping required for VAT registration.

---

9 Planning for Tax and Using the Incentives

The small business entrepreneur is currently fashionable in government circles, and a number of schemes have been introduced to make life easier for him. A summary at the end of this chapter lists the more recent changes and incentives. This chapter also looks at planning for tax and lists a number of relevant points which need to be taken into consideration. It cannot be stressed too strongly that for sole traders and partnerships consultation with your tax consultant is essential, as no two personal situations are ever the same. The other section in this chapter looks at the effectiveness of some of the government schemes and introduces you to some key questions you ought to be asking yourself, whether as a new business or as an investor. Chapter 8 has already explained the possible benefits and drawbacks of the graduated tax rates, and the dangers of getting caught in the marginal relief band. It has also pointed out the pitfalls for the small company which has not as yet registered for VAT or the dangers of forgetting to do so.

INITIAL COSTS

If you are going to start a new business you will spend money on printing, advertising, legal fees and perhaps rental of an office or factory. The incentive for the small business is that your expenses for up to seven years before you trade will be allowable against tax on commencement, provided that those expenses would have been allowable had you started to trade.

Table 9.1 *Which form of business should I choose?*

	Sole trader/partnership	Company
General	unlimited liability	limited liability (but note possibility of personal guarantees by directors). Also note the stipulations laid out in the Insolvency Act 1986 with regard to directors' liabilities and responsibilities
	statutory audit not required	statutory audit may be required
	annual returns need not be submitted or statutory books kept	annual returns must be submitted and statutory books kept
	no legal continuity on death	legal continuity
	no restrictions on drawings from business	company law in general prohibits loans to directors. Share capital may only be withdrawn:
		☐ in the winding up of the company, or ☐ where there is a reduction in the company's share capital sanctioned by the courts, or ☐ where the company buys back its own shares under the arrangements allowed under the Companies Act 1981 and the Finance Act 1982

Table 9.1 *Continued*

	Sole trader/partnership	Company
Taxation	income tax charged at rates from 10 per cent to 40 per cent depending on profits	corporation tax for small companies 20 per cent. This tax increases as a company grows and depends on profits. At present the top rate is 30 per cent
	'current year' basis from April 1997 (except in opening and closing years of trading)	'actual' basis of assessment
	lower total NI contributions (but fewer benefits)	higher total NI contributions by company as well as directors if employees, but better benefits
	relief for personal pension premiums	relief for contributions to personal pension schemes or occupational pension scheme
	single charge to capital gains tax on disposal of assets and subsequent withdrawal of funds	possible double charge to capital gains tax on disposal of company assets and withdrawal of capital, e.g. on liquidation
	no capital duty on formation	no capital duty payable on formation
	interest relief on money borrowed to invest in business, as capital or as a loan	interest relief to individuals only on money borrowed to invest in company as share capital or by way of a loan

WHICH STRUCTURE IS BEST?

There is no golden rule about which particular form of business structure is best. They all have to be individually examined and applied to your personal circumstances; Table 9.1 summarises the main differences.

The difference between a sole trader and a partnership from a tax point of view is small; whether you are a sole trader or partnership depends on whether you are going into business on your own or with somebody else. The costs of running this sort of operation are considerably less than those incurred when running a company.

The main additional expense of running a company is probably the audit fee. However, limited companies with an annual turnover of less than £350,000 can choose not to have a statutory audit. For all companies, a shareholder can request an audit, regardless of turnover, providing that he holds at least 10 per cent of the shares.

Despite these audit exemptions, the 'true and fair' annual accounts must still be prepared in the existing prescribed format and sent to Companies House nine months after the year end. Many banks are likely to request audited rather than unaudited accounts when they consider overdraft and loan positions, and the audit exemption may not therefore be entirely at the discretion of the shareholders.

On the other hand, as a sole trader or partnership you will certainly need to have accounts prepared to send to the tax inspector and these may well also be required by the bank in the case of a loan or large overdraft; in any case properly prepared accounts must be an important ingredient in the management of your business. The other costs which you can incur in a company that you do not have in a partnership or as a sole trader are those arising out of certain statutory obligations imposed in the running of the company: having meetings, keeping statutory books, sending in the annual return to be registered at Companies House, and so on.

It is also generally easier to withdraw money from a sole trader's business or from a partnership. Let us say you are a director of a company. Now it is generally contrary to company law for a director to take money out of a company as a loan, so if you want to draw money out it has got to be by way of salary or bonus. If you take it out in this way you have got to deduct income tax under PAYE (Pay As You Earn). With an established sole trader or partnership you can have drawings throughout the year and pay the tax on the profits in two instalments.

As an example, take somebody who is starting in business after being made redundant and who has received a redundancy payment of, say, £20,000. To start a business, he will have to spend, say, £10,000 on capital equipment – plant and machinery, fixtures and fittings. After the first 12 months most businesses might make a loss. However, let us say that he does quite well and comes out even; therefore there is no profit or loss. But he needs to take some money out of the business to live on; let us say he takes £6,000 out.

If it was a company, it would have made a loss of £6,000 because he paid himself a salary of that amount and all he can do is carry it forward and set it off against future profits. He has actually paid some tax – PAYE on the salary of £6,000.

As a sole trader, his drawings of £6,000 do not count as salary; he is just drawing in advance of profits, although he has not made any. (He might, however, be deemed to have repaid £6,000 of any qualifying loan that he raised as business capital, thus restricting his interest relief.) All he has done is break even. If, however, he has made a loss in this first period, apart from his drawings, he can carry that loss back for three years into all his previous earnings. In fact, this relief is available for trading losses in the first four years of business. If he paid tax during those years he may therefore be able to recover it up to the level of the losses incurred, provided he is operating as a sole trader or in a partnership. In a company, it would cost him the PAYE and NI on £6,000 which might amount to, say, £950.

An employer has to pay higher NI contributions in respect of his employees, including the directors of his company. It costs a bit more, but the employee receives better benefits out of those contributions. If you are operating as a company you can generally set up better personal pension arrangements than a sole trader or partnership.

The tax rules about converting a sole trader or partnership into a company can be quite complex but there are special tax reliefs covering the assets transferred to the company and covering unrelieved trading losses.

In practice you may find that large suppliers prefer to do business with a limited company rather than with a sole trader or partnership; therefore some commercial pressure may be brought to bear on the need to incorporate. All these aspects should be kept under constant review in consultation with your accountant.

TAX PLANNING

This subject has never been more important. The progressive reduction of the rates of corporation tax has meant that the deferment of corporation tax liabilities will be a certain means of saving tax. This section does no more than indicate areas which may be worth examining more closely. The operation of the tax system, company law and practice in all these areas is complex and once again it is essential that professional advice is taken when looking at particular situations.

Year-end planning

The planning for the review of a company's tax position should take place well before the year end as part of an ongoing programme involving directors and advisers. Areas for consideration include:

☐ Hire purchase of machinery or plant; claim capital allowances on full cash price.

☐ Lease or buy? Can the business absorb the full capital allowances? How do interest rates compare on a lease contract and bank borrowing?

☐ Rent or buy premises? Again, can the business absorb full capital allowances? Consider the impact of industrial building allowances and the 'machinery' element in buildings.

☐ Are your investments tax efficient? What is the best use of surplus funds?

Salaries and dividends

The extent to which the director–shareholders should take their reward in the form of remuneration and dividends requires careful consideration, as does the timing of payment. The following points are relevant:

☐ Salaries in excess of the justifiable commercial level may be challenged by the Inland Revenue. Not generally a problem except where directors' wives are employed with no real duties.

☐ The aim should be to raise directors' remuneration up to a level where the individual's marginal rate of income tax at least equates to the company's marginal rate of corporation tax. This can be achieved by fixing bonus payments after the year end.

☐ PAYE on remuneration may be due for payment to the Inland Revenue earlier than the company's corporation tax liability. A cash-flow problem may be avoided or reduced by providing for payment of the bonus (as noted in the above point) some time after the balance sheet date. However, remember that PAYE is due when the individual is able to draw down against his bonus entitlement, *not* when he actually does; it is generally accepted practice that if PAYE on a bonus is paid within nine months after a year end, the bonus can be treated as part of that year's expenditure in the accounts.

☐ Remuneration is subject to secondary (and possibly primary) Class 1 NICs, but dividends are not.

☐ Remuneration is 'relevant earnings' for pension purposes, dividends are not.

Fringe benefits

Although legislation is much tighter now, scope still exists for providing directors and higher paid employees with various forms of non-cash benefits. There are a number of points to remember, not least of which is the wide definition of the word 'director'.

Earnings for directors and for employees earning over £8,500 per annum include:

- [ ] all salaries as generally understood;
- [ ] value of all benefits received;
- [ ] all expenses reimbursed before any allowable deductions.

Benefits include living accommodation and the use of company cars.

Pension schemes

Although at present pension schemes offer the best opportunity for tax planning which will benefit both the company and its employees in all categories, currently the main advantages of an approved occupational pension scheme are the substantial tax reliefs and exemptions that are allowed, particularly in the payment of tax-free lump sums on retirement or on death in service.

Purchase of own shares

Subject to certain constraints, companies may purchase their own shares. Where this happens, the company may apply to the Inland Revenue for clearance so that the shareholder who is selling his shares can treat the sale as a normal capital gains tax disposal. Where clearance is not obtained, cash passing from company to shareholder must be treated as an income distribution, to the extent that it exceeds the amount subscribed for shares, with possibly a higher rate liability on the shareholder.

There are a number of stringent requirements that have to be satisfied, but this is a route that may well be worth examining when an investor in the company wishes to realise some or all of his investment and there is no market readily available.

What type of capital is best?

The question of how much money you should put into the business by way of share capital (in the case of a company) and by way of a loan – in other words, your own money, not outside finance – should be decided on commercial factors. It is something which you will need to go into with your advisers at the time. In general, interest payable on business borrowings attracts tax relief, but interest on private borrowings does not. Therefore, unless you have plenty of capital, it is better to borrow business and use private capital to fund new-business acquisitions and activities. Table 9.2 sets out the options for acquiring a business.

BENEFITS FOR THE INVESTOR

Benefits for the investor:

☐ Tax relief can be claimed on the money borrowed to put into a company or partnership, provided the borrower is active in the management of the business.

☐ If unquoted companies in which you have invested lose money, you can set your loss off against your other income.

☐ Where a tax loss arises in either the tax year of commencement or any of the following three years, the loss can be set against the taxpayer's total income for the three previous years (relief is given for the earliest available year first). In certain circumstances, therefore, relief for a trading loss will be given in a tax year before the trade commenced.

Legislation designed to ease the tax burden

☐ Corporation tax for small companies is 20 per cent if taxable profits do not exceed £300,000. Marginal relief at 32.5 per cent applies if taxable profits are between £300,000 and £1,500,000. Profits exceeding £1,500,000 are taxed at 30 per cent. The starting rate is 10 per cent if taxable profits do not exceed £10,000. Marginal relief at 22.5 per cent applies if taxable profits are between £10,000 and £50,000.

☐ VAT registration is only required if taxable supplies exceed £52,000 or if there are grounds for believing that the value of taxable supplies made in the next 30 days will exceed £52,000.

☐ A business raising self-billed invoices will be responsible for establishing the precise VAT liability.

Relief for certain pre-trading expenses

Expenditure of a revenue nature which is incurred before trading begins is eligible for relief:

☐ if it is incurred within seven years if trading starts after 5 April 1995 (five years if trading begins before 5 April 1995); and if

☐ it would have been allowed as a deduction for tax purposes if it had been incurred after trading had begun.

Examples of pre-trading expenses which are eligible for relief include rent, rates and employees' wages.

Relief for interest paid on money borrowed for investment

1. Interest relief on borrowing to invest in close companies: an individual has to satisfy one of two conditions before he may be able to obtain any tax relief for interest on funds borrowed in order to invest in or lend to a close company. These are:

    ☐ he must have a material interest in the company (i.e. greater than 5 per cent of the ordinary share capital); or

    ☐ he must work for the greater part of his time for the company or an associated company and hold some shares in the company.

2. Interest relief on borrowing to invest in employee-controlled companies: where shares in a company are acquired by its employees so that they obtain control of the company (e.g. an employee buy-out), an individual who borrows money to fund his purchase of shares may be able to obtain tax relief on the interest paid, subject to various conditions being satisfied.

3. Interest relief on borrowing to invest in partnerships: provided that he is a member of the partnership, an individual who borrows money to invest in a partnership, either as capital or as loan, or to buy an interest in the partnership from another partner, e.g. one who is retiring, may be able to obtain tax relief on the interest paid.

Table 9.2 *Share capital or loan capital?*

	Share capital	Loan capital
Tax relief on payment of dividends/interest	No, but dividends carry a tax credit which discharges the shareholders' basic-rate liability	Yes
Voting rights and a say in the running of the company	Yes	No
Right to participate in profits	Yes	No
Receipts of dividends/ interest taxable	Yes	Yes
Can be issued at a discount	No	Yes
Dividend/interest payable if the company is making a loss	No	Yes

Income tax relief for capital losses on shares in unquoted trading companies

An individual, subject to certain conditions, may set against his taxable income a capital loss arising on the disposal of shares in an unquoted trading company. This relief does *not* normally apply to the loss of money *lent to the company*.

A claim for the relief may be made for the year immediately following and must be made within two years of the end of the year for which the relief is claimed. Any unused balance of the loss will be available to set against earned income and then against unearned income.

The Enterprise Investment Scheme

The Enterprise Investment Scheme is discussed in Chapter 22. However, it is worth mentioning that for investments that qualify, an investor is able to claim tax relief at the lower rate (currently 20 per cent) of income tax. The amount invested in the tax year, up to a maximum of £150,000 each tax year, can be set against income for that year, with a potential tax saving of £30,000 for the investor. Capital gains tax relief also applies. If sold at a profit, the capital gain is exempt from tax. If sold at a loss, or if the company ceases trading for genuine commercial reasons, the capital loss less the income tax relief already received on the investment can be set against income for the year or set against any capital gain in the usual way. The shares must be held for five years to qualify for all the reliefs.

Relief for costs of raising business loan finance

Expenditure which has been incurred on the incidental costs of either obtaining or repaying qualifying loan finance is allowed as a deduction in computing the trading profits of a business for tax purposes, or, if appropriate, as a management expense for investment companies. For this purpose incidental costs include, among others, fees, commissions, advertising and printing.

In this connection a qualifying loan is defined as being any borrowing which meets either of the following conditions:

- ☐ the interest on the loan is deductible in computing the trading profits of the business (e.g. bank loan); or
- ☐ the interest on the loan is treated as a charge on income (e.g. loans from institutions to finance trading).

The relief is extended to the incidental costs of raising convertible loans, provided that the conversion date of such loans is not earlier than three years from the issue of the loan. Any abortive costs of obtaining finance are also deductible if the finance would have been a qualifying loan. There is no corresponding relief for the costs of raising equity capital.

Checklist: Planning for tax incentives

☐ Discuss the relative merits of the different forms of business for your personal circumstances with your accountant.

☐ Schedule in the review of your tax position well before the year-end to consider all areas that affect tax liability.

☐ Examine the pros and cons of paying dividends or salaries from companies.

☐ Identify non-cash benefits for directors and higher paid employees.

☐ Discuss with your adviser how much personal capital should be put into your business.

☐ Consider whether a local Enterprise Zone can offer benefits and contact the Department of Environment, Transport and the Regions for details.

☐ Consider whether you qualify for interest relief on investment borrowing.

☐ Examine the details of the Enterprise Investment Scheme if you want to encourage investors.

10 | Employing People – Your Legal Obligations

If you employ only one person in your business, the employment laws that you have to obey are virtually the same laws as those that apply to a major company or public body with thousands of employees.

You need to be aware of these laws when you are recruiting, during the whole of the time in which you employ anyone and also when you are considering whether to dismiss an employee. The right which employees have not to be unfairly dismissed is particularly important, because if you act unreasonably in dismissing an employee you could now face a compensation claim of more than £50,000.

We shall look at unfair dismissal later in this chapter, but the first laws that you need to consider are those against racial, sex and disability discrimination. You need to obey these laws from the time when you take the first steps to recruit employees. Rights are given to job applicants as well as to employees. Compliance with the discrimination laws is of the utmost importance to your business, because there is no limit on the compensation that can be awarded. There have been cases of six figure awards, usually where a decision to dismiss an employee has been influenced by that employee's colour, sex or disability.

RACIAL AND SEX DISCRIMINATION

The laws on sex discrimination cover discrimination against men as well as against women and also discrimination against married employees or job applicants. The laws against racial discrimination cover discrimination in relation to ethnic or national origin and nationality as well as colour.

The law forbids indirect as well as direct discrimination. Job requirements, selection criteria and other employment rules and practices must not be indirectly discriminatory, unless they are job related and can be objectively justified. For example, it could be indirect sex discrimination to overlook part-time workers for promotion, or to be inflexible on working hours and shift arrangements, because it still tends to be women rather than men who have child-care commitments.

You must not discriminate either personally or through your managers and other employees or through an agent, such as a recruitment agency.

The following are some of the key rules that you must obey:

☐ Never be influenced by a job applicant's or employee's gender or marital status or any racial factor.

☐ Never act on assumptions, for example that a physically demanding job would be unsuitable for a woman.

☐ Be objective in your recruitment and other employment decisions and focus on the needs of the business.

☐ Never discriminate against a woman because she is pregnant, whether by rejecting her job application or overlooking her for promotion or dismissing her.

☐ Take effective steps to protect your employees against racial or sexual harassment.

☐ Apply the same standards to all your employees, whatever their gender, marital status or ethnic background.

☐ Keep records relating to job applicants and employees, so that you can explain your decisions in the future if you are faced with a discrimination claim. Keep recruitment records, such as job applications and interview notes, for at least six months. You will need to keep records about employees for much longer.

☐ You must make sure that no employee is victimised for having made or supported a discrimination or equal-pay claim.

☐ If your business is a small one, you may be able to make sure through your direct management and supervision that no harassment or other unlawful discrimination takes place. If your business is, or becomes, larger, you will need to ensure that your managers and supervisors receive adequate training on the legal requirements and their own responsibilities.

Leaflets and further information can be obtained from the Equal Opportunities Commission (0161 833 9244) or the Commission for Racial Equality (020 7932 5286). The two Commissions, in conjunction with the National Disability Council, have produced a free booklet entitled *Equal Opportunities is Your Business Too*.

DISABILITY DISCRIMINATION

For the time being, the employment provisions of the Disability Discrimination Act 1995 only apply to you if you have 15 or more employees. You also need to include in the total any employees in an associated business (for example if you employ staff directly and also run a business through a company). This is one of the very few cases where employment law grants an exemption to a small business.

The definition of disability is a very broad one. It takes in not only workers with obvious physical handicaps but also, for example, many workers who have learning difficulties or who are suffering from long-term clinical depression or who have serious progressive conditions such as cancer and HIV.

One of the key legal requirements, if you have 15 or more employees, is that you make reasonable adjustments for job applicants or employees whose disability puts them at a substantial disadvantage. This obligation can include obvious physical adjustments, such as wheelchair access, special desks or chairs and modifications to equipment. It can also include changes to working hours or job duties or even offering a transfer to a different job.

The second key requirement is that you must not treat a disabled job applicant or employee unfavourably (eg by not appointing an applicant or by dismissing an employee), unless you have a good and substantial reason. An obvious example is dismissing an employee because of a poor attendance record, if absences have been caused by a disability and are not causing any significant problems for your business.

There are two very useful publications, which you can obtain from the Stationery Office. One of them is *Guidance on the Definition of Disability*. The other is the *Code of Practice on Disability*.

RECRUITING STAFF – OTHER OBLIGATIONS

The law does not permit you to turn down a job applicant because the person does not belong to a union or will not join some particular union. Equally, you must not discriminate against a job applicant because he *does* belong to a union or is a union activist.

You are legally required to check that new employees are entitled to work and remain in Great Britain. If the worker does not have a National Insurance number, you will need to see some other documentary evidence of work status, such as a work permit, UK birth certificate or European Union passport. You should take and keep a copy of the document that is produced to you. You must not act in a discriminatory way, for example by assuming from the colour of the worker's skin that he is or is not entitled to work in Great Britain.

Every new employee must be given a written statement of the main terms of his employment, unless these terms are contained in an employment contract. This must be done within two months after the commencement of the employment. You will be able to obtain a leaflet from an Employment Office with full details of the matters that must be covered.

Any change to these particulars must be notified in writing to the employee within one month after the change takes place.

CONTRACTS OF EMPLOYMENT

A binding contract of employment can be a formal contract, often a very lengthy document, or it can be an offer letter combined with the acceptance of the offer by the prospective employee. A binding contract can also be made by word of mouth, but it is better for contract terms to be clearly stated in writing, because otherwise there could be a dispute about what has been agreed.

There are three particularly important matters that you should consider when preparing a written offer of employment. First of all, you may want to make the job offer conditional on satisfactory references, passing a medical or some other requirement. You must make this clear in the offer letter. If you take up references that you find to be unsatisfactory, you will be in breach of contract if you then go back on an unconditional job offer that has been made and accepted.

Secondly, the offer letter should state how much notice you will have to give in order to terminate the employment and how much notice the employee will have to give you. If the offer letter states a fixed or minimum period for which the employment will continue, you will not be entitled to terminate the contract earlier if the employee proves to be incompetent or otherwise unsatisfactory. Once you have committed yourself to a fixed-term contract, only gross misconduct by the employee would entitle you to dismiss him before the fixed period expires.

Thirdly, it is good practice for the offer letter, and also the formal contract if one is prepared, to specify a probationary or trial period (for example three or six months) during which you will be entitled to dismiss the employee with the minimum of notice or formality if he proves to be unsatisfactory. If you have a contractual disciplinary procedure, under which warnings would normally be given for unsatisfactory conduct, performance or attendance, you should expressly state that this procedure will not apply during the probationary or trial period. You should also include the right for you to extend the period. When we look at unfair dismissal, later in this chapter, we shall see that the general rule is that employees have unfair dismissal rights only after one year. It is important, therefore, that any contractual documents should also give you the flexibility to dismiss unsatisfactory employees within that first year.

An employment contract can give you rights as well as obligations. A prospective employee who will have access to confidential or technical information, or who will be dealing with your customers, may be in a position to damage your business by leaving you to set up on his own account or joining a competitor. You should have the contract drawn up by a solicitor if you wish to impose restrictions on what the employee can do after the employment ends. The restrictions need to be carefully worded, to make sure that there is no ambiguity. They must also be reasonable in all respects. A restriction will not be enforceable if it goes further than is reasonably necessary to protect your business or if the period of the restriction is unreasonably long or if it covers an unreasonably wide geographical area.

If you have a growing business, you may well wish to keep paperwork to a minimum. There are, however, some records that the law requires you to keep. Examples are given later in this chapter. There are other documents that you do not have to produce, but which may help to avoid disputes in the future. These include:

- [ ] Carefully prepared and clearly worded employment contracts. You will, for example, find it easier in the future to change working hours or shift patterns, in the light of the needs of the business, if the change is clearly provided for in the contract.
- [ ] A job description (including some degree of flexibility) for all employees. It is much easier to assess and monitor an employee's performance if the duties that need to be performed have been clearly identified.
- [ ] Disciplinary rules. If you need to take disciplinary action against an employee, you will be on much stronger ground if you have clearly identified both the offences that you would treat as misconduct and the more serious offences that would be regarded as gross misconduct (so as to justify dismissal for a first offence). You should make it clear in each case that the list of offences is by way of example and not exhaustive.
- [ ] Policies on equal opportunities and on sexual and racial harassment. These policies can serve several purposes. They should make employees aware of the conduct that will not be tolerated. They should give guidance to potential victims of harassment or of other discrimination on the steps that they can take to raise the matter formally or informally. They should also remind you of the steps that you need to take in order to prevent unlawful discrimination.

HEALTH AND SAFETY

It is a mistake to think of health and safety only in terms of preventing factory accidents. Accidents and damage to health also occur in shops and offices. They can be caused, for example, by faulty wiring, unsafe equipment or badly designed office furniture. Workers have also brought successful claims against their employers, and obtained substantial damages, in cases where the employer has failed to take reasonable steps to prevent damage to health caused by stress at work.

You could also face claims if one of your employees, acting in the course of his employment, causes injury or damage to a fellow employee or to a third party. You must take out employer and public liability insurance cover in respect of your premises and all your business activities. You must also ensure that the appropriate cover for business use is in force whenever cars or other vehicles are being used for the purposes of your business.

As an employer, you have a responsibility to provide a safe and healthy working environment. If you have at least five employees you must also have a written statement of your general health and safety policy and the arrangements for carrying out the policy. Many guidance notes, leaflets and codes of practice are available from the Health and Safety Executive (HSE) and some of them are free of charge. You can obtain information and advice from the HSE Information Centre, Broad Lane, Sheffield S3 7HQ or by telephoning a different office on 0541 545500.

You must also carry out all necessary precautions against fire. Guidance on fire precautions is contained in several official publications, which you can buy from the Stationery Office. You will need a Fire Certificate if more than 20 persons are employed in total on your premises (or more than 10 persons elsewhere than on the ground floor).

You must never dismiss an employee, or victimise an employee in any other way, for taking any legitimate action in relation to health and safety. For example, if an employee refuses to work in unsafe conditions, and you sack the employee because of this refusal, you will have no defence to an unfair dismissal claim. The employee will be able to bring the claim even if he does not have one year's service.

The Working Time Regulations

The Working Time Regulations contain restrictions, on health and safety grounds, on working hours. The Regulations also give several rights to employees and other workers.

Working time (including overtime) must be recorded. Weekly working time has to be averaged over a set period, which is usually 17 weeks. The average must not exceed 48 hours per week, unless the worker has signed a written agreement opting out of this restriction.

There are further provisions restricting the hours of night workers. These workers also have the right to free health assessments. The Regulations also give workers rights to rest breaks and daily and weekly rest periods.

The Regulations also give employees and other workers a right to paid leave. A person has this right once he has worked for you continuously for 13 weeks. The minimum annual paid leave is four weeks. You cannot require your workers to take pay in lieu.

MATERNITY RIGHTS

Pregnant employees have the following rights:

- □ time off for ante-natal care;
- □ protection against dismissal;
- □ statutory maternity pay (SMP);
- □ maternity leave.

You must not dismiss an employee because she is pregnant or because she has been off work with a pregnancy-related illness. If it is unsafe for a pregnant employee to continue to do her job (for example because it involves heavy lifting) you must find her suitable alternative work or, if none is available, suspend her on full pay.

Every expectant mother has the right to take maternity leave of up to 14 weeks and to return to work at the end of that period. During this maternity leave period of up to 14 weeks, the employee is entitled to retain all her contractual benefits other than pay (e.g. use of a company car if you provide one under the terms of her contract).

For employees whose expected week of childbirth begins on or after 30 April 2000, the 14-week period for maternity leave is to be increased to 18 weeks. The maternity leave period will then match the period for which SMP is payable.

There is a right to a much longer period of leave (but without SMP beyond the 18 weeks and without a continued right to contractual benefits unless you have agreed to provide them) if the employee has worked for you for two years up to the beginning of the eleventh week before that in which the baby is due. An employee taking this additional leave must comply with various notice provisions and must generally return to work within 29 weeks from the start of the week in which the actual confinement falls. For employees whose expected week of childbirth begins on or after 30 April 2000, the qualifying period of two years is reduced to one year.

If an employee is unable through illness to present herself for work after her maternity leave (whether the standard leave or the extended leave), you cannot treat her employment as automatically terminated.

This is a bare summary of the employee's rights. For the detailed rules you should obtain a leaflet from your local Employment Office.

Parental leave

Both male and female employees now also have a right to parental leave. This is a right to take unpaid leave to care for children who are born or adopted on or after 15 December 1999.

The maximum leave is 13 weeks for each child, to be taken (except in adoption cases) before the child reaches the age of 5. Unless you agree otherwise (or the child is disabled), the leave must be taken in instalments of one or more weeks, not a day or two at a time, with a maximum of four weeks in any one year.

The employee must give you at least 21 days' notice before the start of any period of parental leave. You will then have the right to give written notice within seven days to postpone the leave, for up to six months, to a time which would be more convenient for the business. The only exception is where the employee wishes to take the leave to coincide with the birth or adoption of the child. You have no right of postponement in those circumstances.

Time off

In addition to maternity leave and parental leave, there are several other grounds on which your employees could have a right to paid or unpaid time off. For example, an employee who is under notice on grounds of redundancy is entitled to a reasonable amount of paid time off to look for a new job.

Since 15 December 1999, all employees have also had the right to take a reasonable amount of unpaid leave in order to deal with a variety of family emergencies, for example to provide assistance when a child or other dependant falls ill or to take any necessary action when arrangements for the care of a child or other dependant are unexpectedly disrupted or terminated.

There is also a right for certain employees aged 16, 17 or 18 to take a reasonable amount of paid leave in order to study for a relevant qualification.

WAGES

You must pay your workers the minimum wage that is required by law. The current minimum is £3.60 per hour. The reduced rates for young workers are £3 from 18–21 and £3.20 for certain workers aged 22–25 who are still in the first six months of their employment and have entered into an appropriate training agreement with you. There are special rules for certain categories, including apprentices. There are also special rules for workers who are paid by results, for example commission on sales or payments based on output. You must keep the necessary records to show that you are complying with the minimum wage laws.

You are also of course required by law to deduct tax, under PAYE, and National Insurance from wages, pay the money to the authorities and keep the necessary records.

Apart from these deductions, and also cases where you have overpaid wages or expenses, you cannot deduct money from wages without the employee's prior agreement. For example, if there is any suggestion that you should lend money to an employee and take it back by instalments out of his wages, you will need to have the employee's written agreement to the deductions before the loan is made.

You must also comply with the laws on equal pay. An employee could make a claim if an employee of the opposite sex is being paid more, so long as they are doing broadly similar work or work of equal value. Claims can be made not only about differences in pay but also about differences in other contract terms and conditions (such as a right to a car or other fringe benefits). You will, however, have a defence to a claim if the difference in pay or other contract terms is genuinely due to a material factor other than the difference in sex (such as longer service or better qualifications).

Sick Pay

Your employees will generally be entitled to statutory sick pay (SSP) for the first 28 weeks of any sickness absence (except the first three days). There are special provisions where there are two or more absences with short gaps between them.

You will be able to set the SSP paid in any month against your National Insurance contributions, to the extent that the amount of the SSP paid in the month exceeds 13 per cent of your contributions for the month. You are required to keep detailed records. You should obtain a leaflet from an Employment Office for full details of the scheme.

Some employers operate more generous arrangements than the SSP scheme (eg full pay for a month and half pay for a further month in any calendar year). You cannot, however, impose a scheme that is less favourable to your employees than the SSP scheme. If you do pay more than under the SSP scheme, you should clearly state in writing (for example in the contracts of employment or in the staff handbook if you have one) whether the arrangements are contractual or discretionary.

WORKING WITH TRADE UNIONS

A new law will come into force during the year 2000 under which you could be required to recognise a trade union, if you do not already do so. This law will not apply to you, however, if (taking into account any associated employers) you have 20 or fewer employees.

This law on union recognition is very complicated. The basic principle is that recognition will be compulsory in either of two cases. The first is where a majority of your employees have joined the union that is seeking recognition. The other is where, on a ballot of your employees, a majority vote in favour of recognition and that majority amounts to at least 40 per cent of the employees.

Whether you recognise a union or not, you cannot lawfully prevent your employees from joining a union. The law prohibits you from penalising an employee or job applicant in any way for belonging to a union, for trade union activities or for not being a union member.

Whether you recognise a union or not, employees have the right to be accompanied by a union official at disciplinary and grievance meetings. The employee may instead choose to be accompanied by a colleague.

If you do recognise a union, members of the union are entitled to unpaid time off for certain union activities and officials or representatives can take paid leave for certain union duties.

There are special rules on collective consultation if you are proposing to transfer your business or to declare redundancies affecting 20 or more employees at one establishment. There are detailed requirements on the advance written notice which you must give to an official of any recognised union and on the consultations which must then take place. If you do not recognise a union in respect of any of the affected employees, then you must arrange for them to elect representatives for consultation purposes. Failure to comply with the consultation requirements can result in awards of substantial compensation against you.

ENDING EMPLOYMENT

There are four main kinds of claim that you could face if you dismiss an employee. First, a person has the right not to be unfairly dismissed once he has been continuously employed by you for a year or more. It does not matter whether the person is employed full-time or part-time. If you wait until the last week of the year before dismissing the employee, you will be too late to deprive him of his unfair dismissal rights. If the person had become your employee because of the transfer of a business or another undertaking to you, it will be necessary to take into account the length of service with the previous employer as well as the time for which the person has been employed by you.

You should note that the one-year qualifying period does not apply if you dismiss an employee for:

☐ being pregnant, a pregnancy-related absence or returning from maternity leave;
☐ trade union membership, non-membership or activities;
☐ asserting certain statutory rights or rights under the Working Time Regulations;
☐ claiming the minimum wage;
☐ certain action taken in relation to health and safety;
☐ 'whistle blowing' under the Public Interest Disclosure Act.

In all these cases, an employee can bring an unfair dismissal claim no matter how short his service is.

Secondly, you could face a discrimination claim as well as or instead of an unfair dismissal claim, if the employee alleges disability discrimination or direct or indirect racial or sex discrimination in relation to the decision to dismiss him. As already mentioned, there is no qualifying period in discrimination cases and there is no limit on the compensation that can be awarded.

Thirdly, there could be a breach of contract claim, if you fail to give the full notice required under the contract or if you fail to follow a contractual procedure. Whatever the contractual notice period is, the law requires that you should give at least one week's notice to employees who have been with you for four weeks, rising to one week for each year of continuous employment (up to a maximum of 12 weeks' notice).

Finally, an employee is entitled to a redundancy payment if he is made redundant after at least two years' continuous service. The rules for calculating redundancy payments are quite complicated. The relevant factors are length of service, the age of the employee and gross weekly pay. For example, an employee aged under 41, with 10 years' continuous service, would be entitled to one week's gross pay (up to a maximum of £230.00) multiplied by 10 (the number of full years of continuous service).

Unfair dismissal

Dismissing an employee could have very serious consequences for you if you act unreasonably, either in making the decision or in the way you go about the matter. The maximum amount of compensation that you could be ordered to pay for an unfair dismissal is more than £50,000. If the dismissal amounts to racial, sex or disability discrimination then there is no limit on the compensation that could be awarded against you.

You must always have a substantial reason for dismissing an employee. The most common reasons are misconduct, incapacity or redundancy. Incapacity can include long-term or regular sickness absences as well as poor performance.

It is not enough to have a substantial reason for dismissing the employee. You must also follow a fair procedure and arrive at a decision that is reasonable in all the circumstances.

You should not dismiss an employee for poor performance, an unsatisfactory attendance or timekeeping record or unsatisfactory conduct (other than gross misconduct) unless the employee has received previous warnings, culminating in a final written warning which is still current. Preferably you should have a written disciplinary procedure spelling out the various warning stages, such as oral, first written and final written. You should remember that warnings are not simply stages that you have to go through in order to reach the point where you can lawfully dismiss the employee. The purpose of warnings is to give the employee a genuine opportunity to meet the required standard. If you operate a warning system fairly this can mean that you have to put up with an unsatisfactory employee for a lengthy period of time. This is why it is important to weed out unsatisfactory employees during the first year of the employment, before they have unfair dismissal rights.

You should not take any disciplinary action, whether a warning or dismissal, without thoroughly investigating the matter and giving the employee a fair hearing. These requirements are particularly important in gross-misconduct cases. Even an employee with a clean disciplinary record can be dismissed for gross misconduct, but you must give the employee a fair hearing and you must have reasonable grounds for deciding that the offence is being made out. You must then be sure that the offence is so serious that dismissal is reasonable in all circumstances. You need to consider whether the offence is one that you have specified as a gross misconduct offence in your disciplinary rules or at least one which is as serious as those that you have specified. The fact that an offence is described as gross misconduct in your disciplinary rules is not, however, conclusive. You must consider carefully what the employee has done and be satisfied that the matter is so serious that immediate dismissal is appropriate. You must take any mitigating circumstances into account and also consider how you have dealt with any similar cases in the past.

Long-term absence cases are particularly difficult, not least because there are frequently disability discrimination implications. Before making a decision to dismiss the employee, you will need to obtain up-to-date medical evidence, identify any specific problems that the absence is causing for your business and consult with the employee on his state of health, the effect of the absence on your business and the matter generally.

Consultation is also a key requirement before you dismiss any employee on the grounds of redundancy. A redundancy dismissal without prior consultation will always be unfair. The fact that you are having consultation meetings with union or other representatives does not excuse a failure to consult individually with all the employees who are facing redundancy. The consultations must be genuine consultations and they must take place when there is still time for the employee to influence the outcome by putting forward objections and alternatives to your redundancy proposals. You must also, in redundancy cases, consider whether there is any alternative employment which can be offered to the employee and discuss this matter as part of the consultation process.

It is always prudent to take advice before dismissing an employee. Some possible sources of advice are mentioned below.

Constructive dismissal

Sometimes you may stumble into a dismissal without intending to do so. If you break an express or implied term of the employment contract, your employee may be entitled to walk out and claim to have been dismissed.

A common example of a constructive dismissal is where the employer imposes a pay cut or some other change in the employee's terms and conditions. If you have a business need to vary an employee's terms of employment, then you should take advice on how to achieve this variation.

It could also lead to a constructive dismissal if you take an action that, without breaking any of the express terms of the employment contract, undermines the employment relationship. Examples are bullying, publicly insulting or humiliating an employee, refusing to discuss a grievance or failing to deal with a complaint of racial or sexual harassment.

GETTING HELP

The matters on which you are most likely to need expert advice include preparing an employment contract, varying contract terms, responding to complaints of discrimination, complying with the Working Time Regulations, handling redundancies and other dismissals and dealing with Employment Tribunal claims against you.

You may be able to obtain legal advice through an employers' or trade association to which you belong. Otherwise you should go to a solicitor who is experienced in dealing with employment law. You may be able to obtain recommendations from other employers or from your other professional advisers.

The Advisory, Conciliation and Arbitration Service (ACAS) is an important source of free advice for employers who are considering a dismissal or who have some other employment problem. ACAS has public enquiry points at its regional offices throughout the country. There are also important ACAS publications, such as the code of practice on disciplinary practice and procedures.

There are currently public enquiry points in the following towns and cities:

Birmingham	0121 622 5050	Liverpool	0151 427 8881
Bristol	0117 974 4066	London	020 7396 5100
Cardiff	029 2076 2636	Manchester	0161 228 3222
Fleet	01252 811868	Newcastle	0191 261 2191
Glasgow	0141 204 2677	Nottingham	0115 969 3355
Leeds	0113 243 1371		

ACAS also plays an important role in achieving settlements in unfair dismissal and other Employment Tribunal cases and disputes. The general rule is that you can achieve a binding settlement only through ACAS or by means of a compromise agreement, on which the employee must receive independent advice, for example from a solicitor or a union official.

Sensible decision making

Much of employment law is technical and complicated. The laws relating to equal pay, maternity rights, the transfer of undertakings and union recognition are particularly difficult. You cannot hope to comply fully with the legal requirements without studying some areas in more detail, or taking advice. There are also unavoidable record-keeping requirements, for example in relation to working hours and the minimum wage.

You will, however, vastly improve your prospects of complying with the law, and avoiding expensive compensation claims, if you adopt the following approach:

☐ make recruitment and other employment decisions objectively, having regard to the needs of your business;
☐ make or confirm agreements in writing;
☐ talk to your employees before you make decisions affecting them;
☐ tackle problems, such as unsatisfactory work, promptly and constructively;
☐ record important decisions and the reasons for them.

Checklist: Employing people

- ☐ Have you obtained public and employers' liability insurance?
- ☐ Have you issued contracts of employment or statements of terms?
- ☐ Have you adopted and issued disciplinary rules?
- ☐ Are you alert to discrimination and equal-pay issues?
- ☐ Do you have written policies on equal opportunities and harassment?
- ☐ Are you paying the minimum wage?
- ☐ Are you honouring all your employees' entitlements to paid or unpaid leave?
- ☐ Do you regularly review your health and safety measures?
- ☐ Do you keep all the records that the law requires you to keep on wages, PAYE, National Insurance, SSP, SMP and working time?
- ☐ Do you keep proper records on other important matters, such as selection and promotion decisions, disciplinary warnings and grievance meetings?
- ☐ Are you aware of the potential consequences if you dismiss an employee without careful consideration and without full consultation or a fair hearing?

11 | **Starting Off in Export**

BEFORE YOU START

The need to take export seriously is today more important than ever because we live in a Single European Market, which now has a single currency for the conduct of trade with 11 of its 15 member countries. Even as a small business you cannot escape the implications of living in a single market, because competitors from other European Union (EU) countries are able to compete for your customers here in Britain. Your best defence is probably to compete with them in their own nations. You may, if you prefer, think of this as extending your domestic business and not as exporting. Indeed this would be more forward-thinking than considering other EU countries as export markets. Even so, dealing with customers elsewhere in Europe will inevitably involve you to a considerable degree in export procedures.

While you may be more or less forced to 'export', you need take this no further than Western Europe. However, you may well feel that if you can handle business from other countries in Europe, you could equally well handle it from countries outside Europe. But whatever you do, your aim should be to do profitable business, otherwise it will not be worth having, and, moreover, will almost certainly fail. But bear in mind you must not try to go too fast, or take on too much, while you must certainly limit the amount of any money you may need to borrow.

Look at your company

Before beginning to export it is best to take a good look at your own company and its business. If you have any doubts have a word with your nearest government export assistance office, and see if specialist consultancy help would be beneficial in areas such as marketing, design, manufacturing systems, business planning and financial and information systems. This will ensure that your business is soundly based before you go ahead and expand into export. In England you should ring your local Business Link office, in Scotland, the Scottish Trade International Service, in Wales, the export section of the Welsh Office and in Northern Ireland, the Industrial Development Board for Northern Ireland.

Next, have a word with your accountant, and discuss what you are thinking of doing; in particular, talk about the costs of the project you have in mind, and the facilities you may need. Then talk to your bank, and discuss the figures you showed to your accountant. Make sure the facilities you may require will be available, and for how long.

The DTI publishes a range of useful booklets on exporting and export markets through its 'Business in Europe' service, which gives information and advice on documentation, trade fairs, credit insurance, choosing representatives, and many other aspects of export. The first thing to do is ring the Business in Europe Hotline on 01272 444 888, which is open 24 hours a day, seven days a week, and ask for details of government services in the areas in which you have an interest.

Gather information

Another source of information about exporting is the Association of British Chambers of Commerce, which operates an export marketing research scheme. Moreover, your own Chamber of Commerce may well have an Export Development Adviser (EDA), whose job it is to help a small company devise a coherent and practical plan for export. Your initial consultation is free, and at this stage you will only need that initial guidance, but any further help has to be paid for.

If you still need some reassurance, remember that more and more buyers in the world are demanding specialised goods and services, instead of mass-produced goods and services from enormous multinational companies. As a small business you can take quick action to exploit unexpected opportunities because you do not have the cumbersome procedures which seem obligatory in larger companies. You may be able to avoid the effects of a slump in your domestic trade if you have export business since not all countries experience slumps at the same time. Exporting is exciting, and a welcome change from the rather more prosaic round of domestic business which you will have probably been engaged in for some time.

At this stage, however, you need only decide whether you will or will not start off in export. How and where you do this cannot yet be decided, nor can the extent to which selling overseas will affect your business. There is a good deal more to examine before you have to come to those decisions.

EXPORT MARKET RESEARCH

You may well be advised to start your strategic planning for export by carrying out export market research. This suggestion should be treated with caution because not only does research cost time and money, but it fails to generate business immediately. Moreover, it will not tell you what to do, but merely help you to make up your mind.

What you need to know

Even so, some research will be necessary, but it should be kept to an absolute minimum, and you should obtain as much information as you can for free. Most of what you will need for starting up in export is known as secondary information, i.e. information that has been published. Primary information, which you must obtain yourself, is unlikely to be needed in the initial stages.

The areas you will have to check by research are:

1. The local conditions of any area to which you propose to export. For example, you cannot hope to sell to people in Hong Kong unless you know something about the Chinese people there, their methods of buying, their needs and wants, etc.

2. You will need to make sure that what you sell, whether goods, services or know-how, is suitable for your prospective customers. For example, it is difficult to sell a milk jug to French women who drink their tea with lemon or their coffee black. Nor can you expect to sell food labelled in English to Dubai.
3. You must understand how goods can be made available to their final users. For instance, you must appreciate the part played by street vendors of household goods in places like Nigeria and Turkey.
4. You should be familiar with the various aspects of physical distribution, i.e. getting your goods delivered overseas. If you sell to Cyprus do you send the goods by sea or air? What documents will be needed, and how do you obtain them? And just as important, how do you get paid by your customers, and how long does this take?
5. If you are going to trade profitably, you must establish your costs and then arrive at prices that are acceptable to your customers, in order to obtain a reasonable contribution to your revenue and a worthwhile return on the capital employed. If you are selling in, say, Saudi Arabia how do you negotiate with the Arab traders, who know only too well how to drive a hard bargain?

Some sources of information

A range of government services are on offer, which are aimed specifically at helping small companies to obtain the essential information they need to start off in export. Details of these can be obtained from the previously mentioned government offices (the telephone number will be in your local directory).

Chambers of Commerce have a great deal of information readily available. Moreover, they have introduced an export marketing research scheme, whereby if a company wants specialised information they will contribute towards the cost of having this obtained locally. Because you will wish to visit places where you are trying to start selling, aim to do this travelling cheaply. One option is to join an Outward Trade Mission, sponsored by a Chamber of Commerce. You cannot take advantage of their help for countries in Europe, but elsewhere you can save most of the travelling costs since these will be paid for you. Moreover, you will meet many people on these missions who can be invaluable to you, and this is particularly important when you are visiting an unfamiliar place.

The problem with information is that there is almost too much of it. So do not become bogged down by market research; only try to find out what you really need to know. A useful publication is *Croner's Reference Book for Exporters*, because it provides a mass of useful facts about countries in addition to the documents needed, transport facilities, etc. Also obtain for any country in which you are interested a copy of the *Hints for Exporters Visiting* ... booklet, published by the Overseas Trades Services (OTS). The books are written by the commercial officers of the British Embassies and High Commissions overseas and are excellent small summaries of local conditions. There are also numerous Web sites of interest to exporters, many of which are listed at the back of the book. A good starting point is the Department of Trade and Industry at www.dti.gov.uk.

Finally, you should start some simple system in your office for collecting any interesting information you come across in your daily life about people and places overseas. It is amazing how quickly this becomes an invaluable source of information, and at little or no cost to the company.

WHERE TO EXPORT

There are, of course, several criteria for choosing where to start trying to sell, the main one being that you should find an area containing customers who are as much like your domestic customers as possible. After all, if you can sell to these people at home then you should also be able to sell to them overseas. In practice it will probably be very difficult to find an identical market, but the closer you can get the better.

Which countries to exclude

You could start by eliminating all those parts of the world where import restrictions or a lack of foreign currency more or less prevent importers buying from you. These are the areas you can best deal with by licensing, and may well include some Eastern European countries and places like Burma, as well as most countries in Central and South America.

Exporting to Europe

Alternatively, you could start in the European Union, because not only does it take over 70 per cent of all British exports, but there are no customs duties payable on EU-originated goods. So, for example, British goods sent to Italy pay no duty, although VAT or its equivalent is payable in all European countries, albeit at different rates. Outside Europe, many regulations affect what you may sell in particular countries, and these regulations may require you to choose some areas in preference to others.

Research your market

Before finally choosing where to start examine the exports of British goods in your field as set out in the _Statistics of Exports_ published by the Government Statistical Office. You can see these figures in the DTI's Export Intelligence Library or any Chamber of Commerce; they will show you where there is business, since if others can trade there you can probably do so too.

Dismiss any parts of the world where you feel there are severe transport problems and decide on where you would feel happiest doing business. Have you perhaps received some approaches in the past which you have not followed up? Or have you relations and friends who could help?

Areas of Western Europe

If you are going to tackle Western Europe, try to think in terms of areas rather than countries. For example, you will find that customers in the north-western part of Germany have much in common with those in Holland and the north of Belgium, where Flemish is spoken, but both German and Dutch are understood.

Another area in northern Europe which is easy enough to reach from the UK is north-eastern France, the south of Belgium, where French is spoken, and the western half of Switzerland. But if you prefer a more Latin market, why not look at the east of Spain, the south of France, the north of Italy and the south of Switzerland – where Italian is spoken.

What you are looking for are groups of compatible customers to whom you can sell. For example, one small company concentrated on Embassy and High Commission staff all over the world, because they have virtually no foreign exchange problems, or customs duties to pay, and found their exports grew rapidly in several countries; another small company began in Portugal because the Chairman had a Portuguese wife. So there are endless reasons why small companies start in different parts of the world; you should choose carefully where to start but be prepared to change if sales do not materialise.

WHAT TO EXPORT

There are three main choices: goods, services and know-how. Taking the last one first, as a small company you may well have valuable assets in the way of a patented process or a good trade mark and name which you can sell overseas by means of some licensing arrangement.

Licensing

The great advantage of licensing for a small company is that you do not have to extend your factory to produce more goods to earn foreign exchange. Moreover, you do not have to be concerned with shipping the goods overseas, arranging their documentation and then worrying about how you will be paid for them. And there are a great many parts of the world where licences to manufacture and sell are eagerly sought, such as Eastern Europe and Central and South America. Hence you export with the minimum of effort, and cash an asset you probably did not realise you possessed.

Export of services

If you sell services remember that a great deal of our foreign currency comes from what are called invisible earnings, i.e. services of various kinds, like banking, insurance, education, design, engineering, etc. If you are a professional selling personal services you can earn commissions from other countries. For example, UK companies specialising in the disposal of waste have secured contracts in the Middle East because local people do not like to be associated with that kind of work.

Where major projects are concerned, such as the building of a hospital or school, or new roads or an airport, these days the originator will demand a package deal so that he can deal with one person and not a whole host of suppliers. Such deals are handled by what are called consortia, and you can as a professional person or company join such consortia, and benefit from the major contracts they handle; for example, an architect may be involved with the building of several hotels in the Caribbean on this basis. Hence a road haulage contractor, for example, is able to seek business wherever he likes, and no longer be restricted in the return loads he carries from outside Britain. Services can be offered under the competition policy of the EU wherever you choose. We have seen the growth of estate agency services on a joint basis between UK companies and those in northern and southern Europe, as people buy a second home or go to live and work in other parts of Europe.

Goods needing modification

When you export goods you may well have to modify or alter them according to local regulations or local customer preferences. Many countries do impose regulations on the exact specifications of goods sold, and these regulations have to be met by the exporter. For example, there are strict fire regulations imposed on all children's toys in Germany. As all countries have regulations to some degree, check before you export your goods that there are no regulations or if so, what they are by contacting the Technical Help to Exporters section of the British Standards Institution. They will provide you with details of what countries control individual products and the points you must check. You will have to pay for detailed answers to how your produce may be affected in any one country, but the service is invaluable.

Customers abroad may demand changes in many goods to suit their tastes. If you produce clothing you may have to vary the weights of cloths to suit local climatic conditions. You may also have to alter sizes and cuts because the average size and shape may vary from country to country. Moreover, in many countries quantity is important in that not everyone can afford to buy much at a time. Cigarettes, for example, are often sold singly, as are razor blades, which need individual packaging. Packaging, especially of foodstuffs, may also have to conform with local regulations. The goods may have to be renamed or trade marks altered should they be unsuitable when rewritten in the local language.

Your aim, however, must be to sell where you have to make the fewest number of changes to what you produce, because such changes increase your production costs, often out of all proportion to the size of the changes made. Hence the suggestion that you find customers as close in all ways to your domestic customers as possible.

Export merchants

There are two other possibilities for exporters, the first being for those whose skills are in selling rather than in manufacturing. In this case you can set up as an export merchant, buying in from suppliers in the UK, or indeed from any part of the world, and reselling to customers overseas. Merchants do carry out a great deal of export work, and if you wish to develop a merchanting export business get in touch with the British Exporters Association.

Exporting unlabelled goods

The second possibility is for those whose skills are mainly in manufacturing and who might wish to concentrate on this aspect of exporting. In this case exporters can offer to make goods for sale by customers under their own labels or names. You may supply in bulk and leave the local buyer to package as he wishes. Or you may supply goods which only need labelling, such as clothes.

In both these cases you are concentrating on either selling or manufacturing and many companies would agree that it is better to do what you can do best, rather than try to do it all. Many Japanese successes have been built on one company making goods and another selling them.

WHO TO EXPORT TO

Having decided what and where to export you must then pin-point the customer to whom you wish to sell.

This person will not necessarily be the same as the user because with consumer goods and durables the goods may pass through several hands before they reach the actual user. Sweets, for example, will go from an importer to a wholesaler, and on to a retailer before reaching the hands of the child who eats them. But with many capital goods and raw materials the customer may well be the user, because he buys, for example, some machinery to manufacture things he proposes to sell.

As a small business you will be concerned primarily with your actual customers, and here you have a choice depending on what you sell and where you sell.

Selling to manufacturers or export agents

In the first place you need not go outside your own domestic territory to export, because you can sell components to other manufacturers who incorporate them into the finished article, which is then exported. Having started this way you can expand to selling those components to manufacturers overseas. Second, you may supply export merchants with goods and leave them to sell them to their customers overseas. Merchants buy and resell for their own account. There are also 'confirming' houses who buy on behalf of principals overseas. In both cases you are relieved of all shipping and documentation problems, and are paid promptly in the UK. If this kind of exporting appeals to you contact the British Exporters Association. They will put you in touch with their members who specialise in your type of goods. Moreover, they can provide services like finding you an export manager to work for you on a purely part-time basis (often only being paid a commission). Department stores overseas also have representatives and merchants buying for them, so here you can start exporting by dealing with people and companies in the UK – an ideal way to start for a small company with limited money and manpower.

Commission agents and distributors

When a small company starts to develop business more extensively in one or two parts of the world, it can consider appointing an agent of some kind to represent it there, and get more business. For capital goods usually a commission agent is appointed, i.e. one who obtains orders for his principals, has them executed by the exporter direct to the customer, but who is paid a commission for every order he obtains. Commissions vary from 2.5 per cent to 15 per cent depending on the goods, the territory and problems of selling. For consumer goods a distributor is more common, i.e. one who buys goods from the exporter and resells them for his own account, making his money on the difference between the cost of the goods and their resale price locally. Both commission agents and distributors are widely used by small companies in export, the main problem being that there are so few good ones available. The DTI will help you to find them through its Export Representative Service, for which there is a charge if they find someone suitable. You must give these overseas agents every assistance; you must visit them regularly to keep them up to scratch; and you should really only consider them in your best overseas markets.

Using your own salespeople

As an alternative, and this might well apply within other EU countries, why not use your own salespeople? True, you may have a language problem, but there are always interpreters if your customer does not speak English or your people cannot manage the local language. But increasingly people are learning each other's languages in the EU. And as no one sells better than a company trained and employed person, every effort should be made to use the same sales force in the EU as at home. That is a proper integration of effort.

There are two instances where direct selling is most important. One is where services are concerned, because most exported services are one-offs, i.e. tailored to the exact requirements of the buyer. The other is where technical goods are concerned, and as many small companies deal with these, it is important that whoever deals with the customer overseas is technically competent. This is a weakness with many commission agents and distributors, and it really takes an engineer, for instance, to sell to an engineer. So if you wish to export highly technical goods or services you should consider using your own personnel to do the selling.

Information on opportunities

Of course, there are many opportunities occurring all the time overseas for business and you can, instead of concentrating on any particular part of the world, deal with opportunities as they arise. To be aware of them you have two good sources of information. The first is the OTS's Export Intelligence Service, which brings you (via computers) details of all published requests for goods all over the world.

Joint ventures

Another option of finding and dealing with customers overseas is to set up a small joint venture with a local small company. This is not as daunting as it may appear, and it may well be the answer for small businesses in specialised fields in the EU. One of the advantages here is that the UK exporter will then have the chance of expanding his domestic business by selling his partners' goods in Britain, while they sell his in their countries.

Your options

Do not think that you have to choose from these options. Most companies use some or all of them depending on where the customers are. For example, start by getting all you can out of export merchants and confirming houses. Start selling to the representatives of overseas department stores in Britain before tackling the stores in their own countries for greater business. Only select and appoint commission agents or distributors where you can find good ones and where you have gained some business. Use your own sales staff where you can see a need for them, preferably not too far away, and especially in highly technical fields. Perhaps develop joint ventures where you can find willing partners with similar interests to your own.

THE INTERNET

One of the most important developments in business over the last few years has, of course, been the proliferation of the Internet (covered in more detail in Chapters 5 and 12). More and more small firms now have a Web site which provides information about themselves and their products.

In a sense, having a Web site is akin to having a permanent stand at a trade fair or exhibition. You can explain and demonstrate your products and make direct sales (via interactive dialogue with customers). Internationally a site on the World Wide Web can give your business a vast potential reach, while the same messages can penetrate the narrowest of niche markets among information seekers.

There can be no doubt that the Internet greatly eases the marketing tasks of firms wishing to export. It removes all geographical constraints and permits the establishment of virtual branches instantly throughout the world and allows direct and immediate foreign market entry to the smallest of businesses. An Internet connection substantially improves communications with foreign customers, suppliers, agents and distributors, helps identify new customers and distributors, and can be used to generate a wealth of information on market trends. Arguably the availability of the Internet removes 'at a stroke' a number of the organisational and resource constraints supposedly associated with exporting.

PRICES AND TERMS

As you most certainly know, if you can estimate your costs of producing goods accurately, can fix a price to suit your customers and allow for a reasonable margin for yourself, then your sales are extremely worthwhile. This is easier said than done, but must be your aim in starting to export.

Allocating costs and deciding prices

You must first allocate some proportion of your fixed costs, or overheads, to export. As your exports grow you must increase this amount so that exports bear their full share of these costs. Next, you must calculate the variable costs of producing the goods for export, allowing for any extra costs due to changes to the goods being made to suit conditions locally. Hence you will take into account the raw material costs and labour costs plus any additional selling costs. Then allow for some reasonable margin as a contribution to the company's revenue, and altogether you should have a price at which to export. You must decide whether you will go for a small margin on a large volume of goods or a large margin on a small volume, but you will have most likely already decided that for your domestic trade. And if you are going to concentrate on EU business you must try to have your export prices much the same as those for the UK because in a Single Market customers will expect to pay the same prices for goods wherever they may buy them in Europe. This will become a vital consideration as the single European currency comes into circulation.

For most parts of the world you should calculate minimum and maximum prices, because many overseas buyers like to bargain, as in some countries that is how they customarily do business. You must take into account what buyers are prepared to pay, and this may well vary from country to country outside Europe. And you must take account of three additional factors when agreeing a final price. The first is when the order is to be placed, because in these days of ever-increasing prices most quotations should be limited to three or six months. The sooner a customer orders the lower the price. Second, how a customer is going to pay is important because export customers do take longer to pay, and if you can arrange payment when you ship the goods this is better than after the goods arrive. Third, you may well have to offer credit, and this is fine provided that the cost of such credit is reflected in the price.

Giving overseas customers quotes

Having arrived at a series of prices you must then decide how to quote your customers overseas. You will need to use one of the internationally accepted terms of delivery, known as Incoterms (these have been codified under that name by the International Chamber of Commerce). You should obtain a copy of the latest edition of Incoterms from the International Chamber of Commerce (ICC) in London. Normally you quote as your customer requests but, if he leaves it to you, most exporters quote FOB (free on board) except for Europe where it is becoming usual to quote DDP (delivered duty paid) because no duties are payable on goods in Europe, although you must remember that VAT or its equivalent is added everywhere.

For Europe your customers will prefer a quotation in their own currency or in Euros and this you may safely give provided you use what is called the forward rate of exchange. That will be explained later, under payment and finance. Customers in other parts of the world may also wish for a quotation in their own currency but you can only do this safely if there is a forward rate of exchange, and this applies only to the major currencies used in international trade. You can always use US dollars if no forward rate exists. You normally use a pro forma invoice when quoting, and you add to the cost estimated freight and insurance charges if you are quoting FOB although these are included if you quote DDP.

You should also include your conditions of sale as at home, and your lawyer should be able to suggest these, in order to protect you from unscrupulous customers overseas.

Pricing services

If you sell services you will also have to arrive at a price based on your costs and a reasonable margin of return for yourself. But the basic rules remain, especially allowing for maximum and minimum prices to leave room for manoeuvring, since all services depend very much on who is selling them, and how far the buyers appreciate the variations in prices that so often occur. Hence you must try to get the best possible price, and no one can do this better than the person who actually provides those services.

Pricing licences

When you sell a licensing agreement you must put a price on the licence which will be a down payment in cash for the actual licence. This may be difficult to establish but will depend on the value of the process, trade mark, trade name, etc. Having arranged this you must negotiate an annual royalty on sales, at so much a unit. You must also insist on a minimum annual sales royalty, because licensees have been known to buy the licence merely to keep the goods off the market because they have a competitor. In addition you must agree the terms on which you will supply any raw materials, assuming the licensee is prepared to buy these from you. Your costs will be minimal, since you are merely supplying what you already possess, so that whatever you get from selling the licence to manufacture and sell overseas is more or less profit to you. But, of course, any licence agreement will be for a long time so that you will not be able to take back the licence at a later date.

Pricing and selling in export is no different from domestic business. You will find, however, that a greater degree of flexibility in pricing may be required with overseas buyers who are more used to trading (that is, bargaining) than buyers in the UK. But this is for many companies part of the pleasure of exporting.

PHYSICAL DISTRIBUTION

If you make and export goods overseas, or act as a merchant by buying in your goods to be exported, you will need to arrange to have them transported to your customers in other parts of the world. You will also be concerned with the documents required in international trade, and you will need to ensure that the goods are insured against loss or damage while in transit. While you may sub-contract some of this work, you must know how to brief the people doing it for you, and there are certain things you will have to do yourself because the service cannot be provided.

Use of freight forwarders

In arranging transport, a company new to export should not engage special staff to do this, but should use the services of an expert. Such people are known as freight forwarders. You should, therefore, contact the British International Freight Association and ask them to recommend several of their members to you, after you have given some idea of the extent of the services you will be requiring, and the likely volume of your shipments. You then visit each and after discussing your problems with them and evaluating the services they can offer, and the charges they will make, you choose one to act for you. You must make this choice carefully because it makes no sense to obtain business from customers overseas, only to lose it because the physical transportation and documentation required are unsatisfactory.

What a freight forwarder can do for an exporter:

☐ suggest the best means of transport;
☐ book transport for you and pay advances on your behalf;
☐ documentation and ensuring that goods are put on the ship or aircraft;
☐ advise on suitable means of packing for insurance purposes;
☐ provide the necessary transport documentation after shipment;
☐ insure goods on your behalf;
☐ deal with customer clearance.

You, on the other hand, must brief your forwarder fully about the services you need for each shipment you wish him to handle, and this means having someone on your staff who can do this. Moreover, you must remember that there are certain things a forwarder cannot do: one is obtain payment for you; another is prepare the original commercial invoices, although he can handle specialised invoices such as those requiring signature by a Chamber of Commerce.

For these services he will charge and this will usually be a percentage of the freight costs involved, plus any extra costs where specialised documents have to be obtained. Is this cost-effective? For small companies the answer is almost certainly yes, especially as you will have more than enough to do to obtain payment and new orders, which you do not wish to lose because you failed to deliver promptly and efficiently.

If you are thinking in terms mainly of selling in the EU, the value of a good freight forwarder may well increase because many of them have organised their own road and rail services into Europe, as well as having special arrangements for shipments by air. To give quick and efficient service to customers in Europe you must examine all these new services offered by forwarders and make the best possible use of them. Many have extended these services to other parts of the world, and with the proliferation of transport services owing to an increased amount of international trade, the use of experts such as freight forwarders seems essential for most exporters.

Many small companies have been discouraged from starting off in export by the thought of additional paperwork, numerous complicated documents and horrific tales of shipments going wrong and customers demanding damages, etc. It need not be like this if you spend a little time learning what is involved in using a forwarder, whom you trust and pay well, to do it all for you.

If as a result of starting in export you also become involved in importing, for instance buying raw materials from overseas, you will almost certainly need someone to clear goods through Customs when they reach this country. Here the services of a freight forwarder are essential for any company.

PAYMENT AND FINANCE

For a small company tackling export for the first time being paid is a vital part of the business, because small companies cannot afford to incur bad debts or wait long for payment from customers. Most banks have a mass of helpful literature on methods of payment for exports, and you should ask your own bank for their booklet. You will in any case need to use your bank to obtain payment for your exports so talk to them at some length. Moreover, you may need their help to finance your new export trade.

Use of factors to handle payment

As with physical distribution you can, of course, opt out of handling payment from overseas by using a factor to do this work for you. A factor quite simply takes over all accounts receivable as the invoices are issued and is then responsible for collecting the money from the respective customers. But he will pay the exporter as soon as the invoices are ready, so there is neither any risk of non-payment nor any delay in the exporter getting his money. Factors deal with all problems of foreign currencies or lack of funds being transferred from overseas so you have no worries on this score. You may borrow from the factor and all you have to do is to pay the factor for the service, which can, however, be quite costly. You should bear in mind that customers may not like having a factor or his local representative chase them for the money. Moreover, you may not be allowed to deal with a particular customer if the factor feels he may be a bad risk. There are an increasing number of factors and you should obtain competitive quotations before deciding on one, if this is the way you wish to handle your payments for export.

Handling payment yourself

If you wish, on the other hand, to look after the payment yourself, and many companies new to export do, then you have several ways in which to do this. First, you can demand payment in advance. If you sell by mail order you may do this, using internationally accepted credit cards as the means of payment. But normally customers will not pay in advance. Do not accept a deposit and a promise of the remainder unless this is secured with a bank guarantee.

Second, do not offer open account terms to any customer unless you know him and are certain that he will pay. Ultimately, of course, you will have to treat customers in the EU this way as you do customers in the UK, but initially treat all customers, including those in Europe, with some caution. After all, they may well be late in paying and six months' delay in payment means, as you may know, that most of your profit has gone.

There are two generally accepted means of getting paid from overseas. The first of these is a documentary letter of credit, explained in the booklet *Uniform Customs and Practice for Documentary Credits*, published by the International Chamber of Commerce (ICC). Briefly, your customer opens a credit in your favour, which should be irrevocable and confirmed by a bank in the UK. This means that, provided you carry out the instructions contained in that credit, i.e. sending the goods as ordered, and provided the bank confirms the credit with the documents requested, you are sure to be paid. And this is usually soon after the goods have been shipped. But you must remember that all the shipping documents will have to go to the bank which has confirmed or advised you of the credit in the UK. And all the other instructions must be carried out, such as shipping by a certain date, etc. So make sure that everyone concerned with the shipment knows all the requirements of the credit.

Instead of a letter of credit you may obtain payment by means of a draft or bill of exchange. This is a document the exporter makes out, in effect asking the buyer to pay a certain sum of money for goods or services supplied, either at sight or at so many days after sight. The normal system is that the exporter collects together all the documents to enable the buyer to take delivery of the goods, and sends them to his own bank which passes them to a bank in the buyer's country. That bank in turn offers them to the buyer, handing over the documents if the buyer either pays or agrees to pay the amount of the draft. Hence the exporter can give a customer credit yet be more or less sure he will be paid. All this is fully explained in the ICC's booklet *Uniform Rules for Collections*.

Credit insurance

These are the most common ways by which buyers pay exporters and, while with a confirmed irrevocable letter of credit there is no risk of non-payment, if the credit is unconfirmed and if payment is being made by means of a bill of exchange, there is the risk that the money may not be transferred to the exporter's country because of some action by the government to prevent this (as, for example, with the Argentine at the time of the Falklands war). In both these cases the exporter should take out some form of credit insurance. The main body doing this is NCM Credit Insurance Ltd, a company that took over the short-term insurance business of the government-owned Export Credits Guarantee Department in 1991. NCM will pay 85 per cent of the value of the goods if the buyer cannot or will not pay or the money cannot be transferred to the seller. It also offers its customers domestic as well as foreign credit insurance. ECGD itself today concentrates on the insurance of payments for long-term capital projects, especially to non-Organisation for Economic Cooperation and Development (OECD) markets.

Apart from NCM, several other bodies offer export credit insurance, notably Trade Indemnity plc. Your normal broker should be able to provide you with information or alternative export credit insurers. You will need credit insurance when selling outside Europe, especially where there is a currency risk, but it is less essential when trading in the EU. The question of quoting in a customer's currency (or in Euros) has already been mentioned, and the system is that you ask your bank for a forward exchange rate which you use in your quotation. At the same time as you get the order you make a contract with your bank to sell that amount of foreign currency around the date you expect to receive it. The bank will then exchange the currency at the forward rate, irrespective of what the rate is on that day. But you must sell when you agree to or you are breaking the contract.

When you obtain an accepted bill of exchange, stating that your customer has agreed to pay you at so many days after seeing it, remember this is a valuable document because you can take it to the money market and exchange it for cash – not the full amount but at a discount. This means that you can give credit and get your money quickly, and you should allow for this in your prices.

PROMOTING YOUR EXPORTS

You clearly cannot expect your goods or services to sell themselves overseas however well known they may be at home. So you will have to go out and persuade people to buy them. First, you should try to do a good deal of selling yourself. This may not be as difficult as it sounds because, while language may be a barrier in some cases, interpreters are usually available and technical people nearly always understand each other. Learn to say a few words in any language where you have customers, but then revert to English for the negotiations. Do not be overawed by the immense amount you feel you should know.

You are unlikely to be able to allocate much money to spend on other forms of promotion, but you should try to make available as much money for export promotion as you allow, relatively speaking, for domestic business. Hence if you advertise, for instance, in some technical publications in Britain, you should also do so in countries where you hope to export. You can do this through your domestic advertising agency, who should know how to cope.

You may wish to book some space at a trade fair or exhibition overseas, both to meet customers and to publicise your goods. Check with the OTS first because they have a number of schemes whereby you can take part in these exhibitions at a reduced cost, and where a British exhibition is being organised you can become part of that for a minimal cost. If you wish to make contacts to sell in Eastern Europe taking a stand at the Leipzig Trade Fair is an excellent way of doing it.

You should take every advantage of free publicity for your company and the goods or services it exports by contacting the Central Office of Information. They are experts in obtaining free publicity in magazines and newspapers, on radio and television all over the world. All they ask is that you send them details and photographs, etc of what you offer and they will send this information out to the world media free of charge.

You will certainly require some literature in other languages and you must make sure that the words and pictures you use are suitable for any particular part of the world. While there are many translation bureaux in Britain it is generally better to have someone rewrite what you wish to say locally, and then check that what has been said is exactly what you intend. It is probably also better to have the literature printed locally, both to avoid printing errors and to save customs duties, which are often high on imported sales literature.

BUDGETS AND PLANS

No one in a small company has much time to prepare elaborate plans and budgets, but if you propose to start off in export seriously you will need to work out a simple budget, together with a strategy to show how you propose to achieve your targets. This also helps to keep you on target and equally to show you if anything is going badly wrong.

Start by preparing a simple quantified objective for the year ahead. This need show no more than what you hope to export, and what you propose to contribute to the company's revenues.

Then work out a budget which should consist of, first, the revenue you estimate you will receive from export. This gross revenue should be all the money which will be coming in. From it deduct the cost involved in producing this revenue, i.e. the production costs, both fixed and variable, and any additional selling costs. Then deduct any money needed for promotion, and you will arrive at a net contribution to revenue. This should be more than the costs or starting off in export will not have been worthwhile.

Having set out your objective and your budget, jot down the strategy by which you propose to achieve these results. This list should include:

☐ where you propose to try to export;
☐ what you propose to export;
☐ to whom you are going to sell;
☐ at what prices and terms;
☐ how you will arrange transport if goods are involved;
☐ how you will get paid;
☐ how you will promote your sales.

Try to set down some form of monitoring for the results so that you can see at a glance how you are progressing, and then, if necessary, you can halt what is in progress to see where the fault lies should things begin to go badly wrong.

As time goes by and you begin to integrate your exports in Europe more closely with domestic sales, you will have achieved a significant step forward, and you can begin to integrate all export sales with those in Britain, because a customer is a customer, irrespective of nationality or country of origin.

_____

MANAGEMENT AND STAFF

Do not immediately engage more staff if you start to export. Explain what you are doing to your existing staff and find out if any member of staff has any particular interest or abilities in export. For instance, how many can speak another language? Would any of them be interested in handling any special aspect of export? In this way export will become part of your business rather than an extraneous area which you have tacked on to it.

Where you need help, buy it in from outside – for example, using the services of a freight forwarder to handle the physical distribution side. Buy in research but make the fullest possible use of all the help that is available to small businesses, both to tackle Europe and to expand elsewhere in the world.

When you have visitors from overseas, introduce them to your staff, since buyers like meeting people with whom they deal in correspondence but rarely meet. Moreover, it keeps the staff interested in the export side of the business and encourages them to put care and effort into serving your overseas customers.

Take advantage of the many courses in export practice and procedures run by Chambers of Commerce. If you wish to learn a little more about exporting, obtain the book *Getting Started in Export*, published by Kogan Page, which is written specifically to help small companies start off in export.

Appendix III lists under Export all the organisations mentioned in this chapter and gives their addresses and telephone numbers.

Checklist: Preparing for export

☐ Talk to your accountant about the costs of the project and the facilities you may need.

☐ Contact your Chamber of Commerce to see if it has an Export Development Adviser.

☐ Research your market. Check on local conditions, find out if your goods are suitable, and how they will be sold and what prices will be acceptable to customers.

☐ Examine the exports of British goods in your field to identify potential markets.

☐ Identify relevant local regulations or customer preferences and modify your goods accordingly.

☐ Investigate the potential of setting up a Web page on the Internet.

☐ Identify a freight forwarder through the British International Freight Association.

☐ Consider which method of payment you will want to use and whether or not you will want to employ a factor to handle your payments for export.

☐ Research overseas trade fairs and exhibitions and contact the Central Office of Information to take advantage of free publicity.

☐ Draw up a budget and strategy for the year ahead and identify objectives.

☐ Discuss your plans with your staff and identify how many can speak another language and if any would be interested in handling special aspects of export.

12 Managing Communications and Information Technologies

As we advance towards the paperless economy, office systems are relying more heavily on information and communication technologies (ICTs). Playing an increasingly vital role in standard working practices, ICTs are contributing directly to business success and are likely to be a major factor determining competitive advantage as we move into the 21st century.

In particular, small to medium-sized enterprises stand to benefit from new technologies, such as computer networking and the Internet, which can improve efficiency, increase productivity and create an opportunity to gain real competitive advantage. The key is the potential of ICT's offer to share information.

Business use of technology is growing rapidly among small and medium-sized enterprises (SMEs). 'Moving into the Information Age', a 1999 DTI annual International Benchmarking Study, revealed a continued increase in the uptake and usage of information and communication technologies (ICTs). The number of SMEs using ICTs has doubled since 1987. There is a whole range of ways in which IT is helping businesses to increase the speed and efficiency of their working practices. E-mail and fax, the Internet, video conferencing, networking and e-commerce (i.e. buying and selling goods and services online) are just some of those that are becoming commonly used. These applications lead to savings in time – and therefore costs – and make doing business quicker, easier and more competitive. Failure to exploit these opportunities could lead to the erosion of UK competitiveness. If other countries take greater advantage of the benefits of new ICTs UK companies will get left behind.

The 1999 DTI International Benchmarking Study revealed that the UK's big businesses had almost closed the gap with the US in ownership of key ICT applications. However, this trend was not as strong in small and medium-sized businesses (SMEs) as in big business. The UK's position as ICT leader amongst European countries is now under challenge from other countries experiencing rapid growth, such as Germany.

SCHEMES FOR SMES

A helping hand for UK businesses exists in the Government-led Information Society Initiative (ISI) – a public-private partnership run by the Department of Trade and Industry. The aim of ISI is to promote the progress of UK businesses, particularly SMEs, towards the Information Age. Nationally, ISI seeks to raise awareness in a number of ways: a business Infoline (0345 15 2000) gives information on programme activities, and an ISI Web site (www.isi.gov.uk) is also a useful gateway to information. A wide range of materials giving basic, jargon-free information to companies is also available.

The Information Society Initiative is supporting Business Links (and equivalents elsewhere in the UK) to set up dedicated ISI Local Support Centres (LSCs). At these centres local firms can obtain experience of, and advice on, networked technologies.

The nation-wide network of nearly 100 centres offers impartial advice to companies on how technology can best be incorporated within a business strategy. Advising on everything from Internet access and Web page design through to help with video conferencing and e-commerce, they provide jargon-free consultancy and practical solutions tailored to the specific needs and aspirations of individual businesses. The ISI centres are aimed at all businesses ranging from those which do not use any IT, through to specialist multimedia hardware and software developers.

BASE-LINE EQUIPMENT

Getting started on the Internet is easier than you think. The requirements to get up-and-running are basic. As a small or medium-sized company you need only invest in the following:

- ☐ *A computer.* Either a PC with at least a 486 processor or a Mac with at least 16Mb of internal memory (RAM). To enjoy the more visual aspects of the World Wide Web you will need a machine with sufficient memory to be able to make full use of a graphical interface like Windows.
- ☐ *A modem.* The device which links the computer to the telephone network and can be either internal to the PC or external (connected by a cable). Speeds vary and while low speeds can be sufficient for simple e-mail, if you intend to download large files or use the Web you should usually go for the fastest modem you can afford.
- ☐ *A standard phone line.* Where the speed of access is important an ISDN line (Integrated Services Digital Network) should be considered.
- ☐ *An account with an Internet Service Provider (ISP) or on-line information provider.* There are over 100 ISPs in the UK. Typical subscription rates are between £10 and £12 per month. However, it is essential to compare what you are getting for your money to ensure you are achieving best value. Many free services have also recently sprung up but it is worth examining charges made for helpdesk advice, as these might well add up to as much as the ISP subscription rates.
- ☐ *Appropriate software.* This would include a minimum connection software to manage the modem and to organise the dialling, an e-mail program and a Web browser. These are usually provided free by your ISP, included within subscription rates.

MARKETING AND EXPORTS

The Internet is a global network of computers with millions of users. It consists of many thousands of permanently linked powerful computers, called hosts. Anyone with a computer and

Guide to Lump Sum Investment

Twelfth edition
Liz Walkington

Whether you have won the lottery, received a redundancy payment or inherited a lump sum, you will want to know how to invest the money to make it grow.

This new edition of this comprehensive guide describes the various short- and long-term investment possibilities, whether they are best for capital growth or income, how easy it is to withdraw money, the costs, the most efficient investments for different situations, how safe the money is, likely rates of return and so on. Topics covered in detail include:

- Fixed capital investments
- Gilts
- Equities
- Unit trusts and offshore funds ·
- Investment trusts
- ISAs

- Life insurance-linked investments
- Pension planning
- Tangible investments
- Charitable giving
- Where to go for advice.

£12.99 • Paperback • ISBN 07494 3311 6 • 320 pages • 2000

KOGAN PAGE
120 Pentonville Road, London N1 9JN
Tel: 020 7278 0433 • Fax: 020 7837 6348 • w w w . k o g a n - p a g e . c o . u k

NET◯bjects™ – putting the 'e' into e-business

With small and medium-sized enterprises (SMEs) making up 80% of UK businesses, Martin Powell, northern Europe sales manager at NetObjects, looks at two simple and viable solutions that enable SMEs to get online.

Creating a Web site with NetObjects Fusion 5.0

If you've ever wanted to create your own Website, but your experience is minimal or non-existent, then NetObjects Fusion 5.0 could be the simple answer. Fusion is the award-winning software that enables you to build and develop professional Web sites quickly and easily. It is great for individuals and small businesses that want to establish an online presence or build onto an existing Web site.

Fusion 5.0 is one of the most popular web design products available today. It is a WYSIWYG (What You See Is What You Get) html editor which allows you to design your site visually by dragging and dropping elements like images and text directly onto your page.

Focus on businesses

NetObjects Fusion 5.0 is designed to help business owners create full-featured sites that promote, inform, and sell. Many small businesses want more flexibility, individuality, and advanced features than other site-building templates deliver. At the other end of the spectrum there are the complex and time-consuming applications that cater to full-time Web designers. NetObjects Fusion 5.0 offers the combination of productivity, flexibility, and ease-of-use that SME businesses need.

e-business

Today's businesses need more than just an online presence, they need an 'e-business site', or a place where customers, employees, suppliers and distributors can reach, interact and transact with the business. E-business sites represent a convergence of publishing electronic commerce and application functionality and enable businesses to leverage the potential of the Internet.

With Fusion, a Web site can become an e-commerce site in minutes, offering several unique features, such as the ability to sell multiple items, full on-line

Martin Powell

207

ordering capabilities, shopping cart functionality with several payment options, automatic tax and shipping charge calculations, and extensive reporting.

Virtual encyclopedia for online success

NetObjects Fusion 5.0 includes an Online View, a link to everything a business needs to build a successful site. With an ever-evolving collection of valuable information and special offers, the Online View helps customers every step of the way – from finding an ISP and getting a domain name, to posting and promoting their sites. It's an integrated resource that users can turn to as their business grows to discover how to gather information from site visitors, set up an online store, and much more.

Multimedia

Fusion gives you the tools to make your Web site look simple or very sophisticated, it is up to you. It offers a full set of powerful components, allowing insertion of text, graphic images, multimedia files (such as Shockwave or Quicktime), connections with ODBC-compliant databases, Java applets, and online forms. Using DHTML, actions can be associated with any image. This allows site builders to increase Web site interactivity as well as create sophisticated animations to stimulate visitor interest.

NetObjects Fusion software includes tools that will help you to structure your site efficiently and update it automatically. The product has sold over six million copies since its initial release in 1996, and more than four million e-business Web sites and pages have already been built using NetObjects Fusion.

Gobizgo

In addition to the Fusion offering for SMEs, NetObjects recently launched GoBizGo.com, an online service that enables small companies to build successful e-businesses. Using GoBizGo.com, these small businesses can do everything from build a Web site and online store, to integrate offline and online marketing efforts, all with the advantage of online personalised assistance from experts and other business owners. The site gives small businesses an all in one solution and marketing tools, and it also encourages members to participate in communities that bring together like-minded small business owners to share resources, ideas and knowledge.

Simply put, GoBizGo.com makes creating a professional and effective Web site of up to 25 pages and 100 products as easy as a few mouse clicks. In addition to fast and effortless Web site development, membership provides a variety of other benefits, including: instant updating and maintenance, automatic search engine submission, domain name registration, e-mail services, contact management, eBay auction upload, and remote site management via any browser connected to the internet.

Finally, GoBizGo.com is a completely scalable solution. If a company finds that it has outgrown the ASP platform, they can simply transfer their current site into NetObjects Fusion to leverage its additional functionality.

It doesn't matter whether your company employs one person or one hundred, NetObjects Fusion 5.0 and GoBizGo.com can turn your business into an e-business in the click of a mouse, quickly and easily. For more information on what NetObjects can do for you, visit www.netobjects.com, or call NetObjects on 0800 0289851.

www.netobjects.com
www.gobizgo.com

THE IMPORTANCE OF COMMUNICATION

The importance of effective communications to a businesses' future are widely recognised, whether that be communicating internally with other members of the organisation or externally with customers and suppliers. In recent years, the forms in which this communication can take place have expanded from the traditional telephone and fax to include digital based communication such as the web and internet email.

Advantages of Digital Communications for Small Businesses

These new developments in digital communications are especially important to small businesses as they give them the ability to level the playing field somewhat and compete with larger organisations. Internet email enables a small business to provide better customer service through faster response times and the ability to circulate information regularly, quickly and cheaply.

Web sites can be used to create a 'virtual company' and give small businesses a marketing presence 24 hours a day, 7 days a week. Even a basic site can provide an invaluable and low cost way to interface with customers, disseminate information and take orders or enquiries. It gives a small business the marketing exposure and reach it would be difficult to achieve by conventional means such as advertising or direct mail which would become prohibitively expensive.

This all sounds great, but how does a home user or small business take advantage of the opportunities offered by this new technology? The main obstacle most will perceive would be resource, both financial and technological. As a rule, small enterprises do not have significant sums of money to invest in IT infrastructure and lack the in-house technological expertise to install complex systems and maintain them.

The ISDN Answer

The good news however, is that it is probably not be as difficult or expensive as many think. A simple, flexible and inexpensive communications infrastructure covering both traditional analogue and the new digital communications can be built around ISDN services from a local telecommunications provider such as BT and ISDN modems and terminal adapters like Eicon's DIVA family.

What are the Advantages of ISDN?

Traditional analogue telephone lines are intended to carry voice traffic and are not very well suited to transmitting digital data. This results in slow connection and low transmission speeds which translates to more time on-line and increased call charges as well as the frustration this bandwidth bottleneck causes.

ISDN (Integrated Services Digital Network) is a digital communication service which supersedes ordinary analogue telephone lines giving far greater transmission and connection speeds combined with digital security.

An ISDN line will connect within 1-2 seconds compared to 30-45 with analogue. Once connected, ISDN guarantees a transmission speed of up to 128 kbps compared with 56 kbps with the fastest analogue modem. Even this is misleading as a 56 kbps modem will rarely reach speeds of more than 36 kbps for uploading and 40 - 44 kbps for downloading making ISDN three to four times faster.

Apart from greater speed, another major advantage of ISDN over analogue is that it allows multiple simultaneous communications over a single physical line. This is because within an ISDN line there are several 'virtual' channels called bearer or 'B' channels. There are several different levels of ISDN service available from telecommunications providers with Basic Rate (BRI) having two 'B' channels and Primary Rate (PRI) having up to 30. This means that in a small office one physical ISDN line connected to an ISDN modem or card can be shared by many users giving everyone high speed digital access to the internet for surfing and email. The alternative is to have one analogue line per user with the resulting expense of having to pay line rental and installation costs on each line.

Consolidated Communications

Lastly, with ISDN, a whole office's communications can be sent over the ISDN line. This means that data files from a PC, analogue voice calls, fax calls and even GSM mobile calls can all be sent or received over an ISDN line eliminating the need for separate analogue telephone lines.

Application Scenarios

Home User

For the worker who has set up on their own and is possibly working from home, an ideal communications solution is a Basic Rate ISDN line and the DIVA T/A ISDN Modem from Eicon.

Once the ISDN line has been ordered from the telecommunications provider, simply plug the ISDN line and the PC (via the serial port) into the back of the DIVA T/A Modem. There are also two analogue ports for plugging in a telephone and fax machine. Configuration of the DIVA T/A is simple via plug and play and built in set up wizards so no great technical skill is required.

Once set up, all data, voice and fax communications can be managed through the DIVA T/A and ISDN line. The two 'B' channels allow the user to surf the internet whilst simultaneously talking on the telephone or sending a fax. Advanced features allow different numbers to be allocated to the telephone and fax which the DIVA T/A will use to route calls to the appropriate device. Other features such as call forwarding and call waiting are also supported.

Small Office

In a small office where a group of PC users need email and internet access, the DIVA LAN Modem and a Basic Rate (BRI) ISDN line will provide for all the office's communications needs.

The DIVA LAN Modem is a similar device to the DIVA T/A but also includes an Ethernet hub. With the PCs connected to it via the Ethernet ports a network is created where all the PCs can share peripherals such as printers. By adding an ISDN line into the DIVA LAN, these same PCs can share the line for high speed internet access and email. As with the DIVA T/A, analogue devices such as fax machines can be added for incoming and outgoing faxes.

A Solution to Fit Every Need

In this brief overview, we have tried to give a flavour of what is possible. ISDN is an established, standards based technology available world-wide. It is inexpensive, fast, easy to use and manage, flexible and scalable from the single user, to a large office with hundreds of users.

Together with ISDN products from companies such as Eicon, a small business can implement a communication solution to take full advantage of the opportunities offered by new digital age.

Making the Internet part of your business

Set your business free on the Internet with Oneview.net

The message is simple. To survive and prosper in today's global market place, your business can no longer afford to be without a web site on the Internet.

And with Oneview.net there's no cheaper, faster or more cost effective way to get your business there.

Our Web range packages.

We'll register your domain name, provide all programming, design and hosting of 3-15 page web sites, e-mail and e-marketing. All for a monthly subscription that starts at just £20+ VAT.

Giving your customers access to your business 24 hours a day, 365 days a year - not only locally but also globally. *Compare that to the cost of a small classified advertisement in your local newspaper!*

As your business and Internet requirements grow, we can grow your web site too. We've a complete range of Internet packages for you to choose from including the very latest e-commerce solutions.

Open your business to a whole new world of customers.

The world is turning to the Internet. Turn to Oneview.net and get your business on the Internet, hassle free, jargon free, for a minimal fee. *Before your competitors do.*

- Web site design

- Domain name registration

- E-mail

- Completely upgradeable to include e-commerce

- Expand your web site as your business grows

- No hassle, jargon or hidden costs

- No set up fee, just a monthly subscription

Don't get left behind. Call Oneview.net
01384 251111

 **oneview.net** Email: sales@oneview.net Internet: www.oneview.net

The simplest, quickest and most cost effective way to get your business on the Internet.

LEVELLING THE PLAYING FIELD:
Small business and the future of eCommerce

"What SMEs really want is a no risk, low cost entry point to eCommerce"
Michael Williams, CEO freecom.net

With all the hype and uncertainty surrounding the future of eCommerce it's hard to figure out just how your business should position itself in a digital age. Are your customers really going to be click-happy consumers or will the Internet simply fade into the ether?

At freecom.net we don't trade .in extremes. Change and innovation have always been the hallmark of good business. In our view eCommerce is part of this trend and with it comes profound consequences for all of us.

freecom.net predicts that the next five years will provide unprecedented opportunity for small and medium-sized enterprises (SMEs) to compete alongside the UK's biggest names - in whatever sector they trade in.

This is because technology and supporting software are developing at break neck speed. The cycle of research, development and implementation is getting shorter all the time. Those businesses that recognise change and innovation as a permanent feature of doing business are likely winners in the digital age.

freecom.net believes that change favours the small over the FTSE100 giants with their cumbersome bureaucracies headed by chief executives who've never even surfed the world wide web.

Since 1996 we've helped thousands of UK middle market and SME customers broaden their digital horizons. We hope you'll find that reassuring in an age of uncertainty. Our customers may not have the clout or the budget of corporate clientele but this does not mean their needs are any less bespoke or complex.

And unlike others in our industry we're not in the habit of dazzling you with research reports designed to scare you into going online. We think our unique approach to working with SMEs has met with considerable success.

To date freecom.net has developed eCommerce solutions and packages for around 5000 SMEs in the UK, and through commercial acquisitions and partnering, a further 65,000 customers world-wide. What's more we've invested heavily in our business to ensure you get the service and support you need to implement change and innovation in yours.

Maintaining our feel for what SME customers expect is the cornerstone of our service. Despite our solid growth and expansion we've deliberately made sure our wholly or majority-owned subsidiaries are free standing and independent - just like you.

TOMORROW'S CONSUMER

You don't need us to tell you that the world is changing. The next generation of consumers and business managers will not think twice about ordering generic goods and services online via mobile phone, digital TV or PC.

The buying experience is changing. You can already bank with a supermarket and buy your office supplies from a bank. eCommerce is loosening the ties that bind us so that customer loyalty will be tested as never before. This is what the 'big boys' fear the most and where SMEs can grow their business.

The Internet will empower people to switch providers at a click of the mouse.

while tomorrow's software tools will enable you to compile and apply customer data with astonishing precision.

What's more, because these applications will be web-based or virtual, you won't need a multinational budget to afford them. By choosing freecom.net as your web partner, you can rent a sophisticated eCommerce solution for a nominal fee. Compare this to the tens of thousands of pounds it will cost to develop and maintain a system of your own.

COMPETE WITH THE 'BIG BOYS'

[www.webelectricals.co.uk]

THE BRIEF:

With the help of freecom.net, WebElectricals launched an Internet-based electrical store offering consumers up to 40% off High Street prices.

Husband and wife team, Irfan and Fosoun Nevzat, approached freecom.net in March 1999 to help launch the company. freecom.net provided eCommerce functionality and secure hosting facilities for the WebElectricals site. In just three months the new web store went live online for business.

TARGET CUSTOMER:

The cash rich/time poor consumer who doesn't want to spend weekends queuing for assistance and information in traditional high street stores.

QUOTE:

"Internet shopping provides a viable alternative for these customers. They can research their product requirements quickly and easily in time convenient to them and they can purchase just as quickly, easily and securely over the Internet."

"But in order to do online retailing right, it's got to be your primary not secondary focus. eCommerce is where the small business can really begin to give the High Street a run for its money."

Irfan Nevzat, co-founder WebElectricals

BUSINESS TO BUSINESS AND eCOMMERCE

Generating new sales in only half the story. eCommerce is about empowerment. It's about letting you focus on what you do best i.e. your core business. Why spend good money and untold hours on operational as opposed to strategic decisions?

From ordering office supplies to processing payroll, repetitive back office functions are being transformed by eCommerce. Traditionally tendering, purchasing and monitoring is time and labour intensive. Diverting valuable resources to operational function and back office functions is frequently at the cost of focusing on your core business.

freecom.net believes eCommerce will make life easier by taking over many back office operations. Many will be outsourced and monitored by virtual intermediaries, helping you to unlock the potential of the core business. It may sound a little before it's time but the resulting savings in direct and indirect costs will go straight to the bottom line.

Innovative online companies are already emerging that aggregate company orders across an array of business-to-business services. In short, the way you purchase as a business will be transformed. We don't mean to harp on but why purchase as a minor player when you could be buying as a virtual multinational?

It's an exciting time to be doing business. The rules of the game are being re-written - and in your favour. If you want to find out how you can do more business on your terms then see our advertisement on the facing page. Isn't it about time you told us how we can help you?

MAKING YOUR BUSINESS AN eBUSINESS

No matter how new, how established, how big or how small, any business can safely harness the power of the Internet. It offers vast commercial opportunities, whatever the sector, wherever the location - whether for a large corporation or for the small new business being run from a back bedroom at home.

Businesses starting out today have the ability to reach an audience that a new business could only have dreamt about reaching just a few years ago. An antiques shop in Cheshire can sell a Chippendale to China, a dress designer from Durham can provide designs to a fashion house in Paris and an accountant in Leeds can do the books for a brewery in Basildon, all by having a presence on the Internet. Size means nothing on the Web, new businesses can appear on-screen alongside old established firms or international conglomerates.

However, not all new companies understand the importance or the value of taking their business on-line. The government and the EC recently issued an appeal to UK small business to "wake up to the challenge" of e-commerce and are continually pushing this message and raising awareness of it's importance for the individual business and the economy in general. New and existing small businesses are under growing pressure to take action or risk loosing out, not just on the electronic future, but missing out to the extent of not having a future at all for their business.

Many smaller firms have found it difficult to get plugged in to the medium that is changing the way the world does business. According to a survey done by Telewest Business Communications 82 per cent of small and medium sized businesses do not yet use the Internet to buy or sell and 58 per cent say they are "mystified" by the Web.

Starting a business is challenging enough and if the Web mystifies many, the prospect of also making that business an e-business could be extremely daunting. Just developing an initial understanding and getting connected could be a complicated and expensive affair, before even thinking about actually developing a website, advertising it, or trading on-line. This is, however, no longer the case. Companies, such as Telewest Business Communications, have seen the value in opening up the Internet to new and existing customers and helping them grow by offering a free service to take their business on-line.

There is a need for an all-in-one Internet and e-commerce service for new and old businesses alike. Biz-Explore, the service provided by Telewest, has been designed to help companies get on-line quickly, simply and without any fuss. The idea is to provide the new business with the tools to use the Internet for their own needs and above all help cut out the costs and any risk of setting up on-line. It is a total e-commerce solution that takes customers through a simple step by step approach to trading on-line.

Telewest offer the first tier of services completely free of charge, these include free Internet access and a basic domain name such as www.creative-cakes.bizexplore.co.uk and a specially designed on-line business card that will be registered with 20 Internet Search Engines and within the Biz-Explore Directory. This means that if a user wanted to search the directory for, say, a hairdressers in Cardiff, they need only input this information and the businesses with a Biz-Explore Business Card fitting that description will be listed on screen for the potential customer to choose from.

Also available at no charge are an unlimited number of email addresses and an 0845 phone number that would also be advertised on the on-line business card and allow those interested to call at the cost of a local call. It also provides a number of free business and communications tools such as an address book and contact manager, a postcode finder and advanced web services - unlimited web space, bookmark update and web statistics tool.

As with any new user of the Internet or new business starting out there can be endless jargon to try and comprehend. Telewest Business Communications have thought of this and within the initial tier of services they provide for free they include a free guide to e-commerce. This contains a simple to follow tutorial to help master the Internet and a glossary of jargon-busting telecoms and Internet words and phrases. It also includes a demonstration of all the business enhancing features of the Telewest Biz-Explore service.

Telewest have designed this service to grow with a business as its needs grow, offering a whole range of additions and enhanced services to support that growth.

On-line shopping has made a huge impact on the way companies sell their products and services, it offers new businesses the potential to trade and interact with customers in a completely new and different way. This is where a business may want to grow its web presence from the on-line business card to the on-line store. Instead of just gaining information, visitors to the "store" can actually shop on-line. They can check out products, services and prices and, if they want to buy, collect them in a virtual "shopping basket".

Stores, offering the display of up to 50 products, in time can be grown to Superstores for a more diverse range of products or services. A Superstore allows as many as 25 departments containing up to 100 products. Whatever type of store suits the new or developing business technical skills or professional advice are not needed. With the Telewest service buying, setting up and designing the store is all done over the Internet using a simple to use point-and-click process.

Another response generating tool that can be purchased with the Telewest Biz-Explore service is what they call "Biz-Call". This is an extremely clever device using what is known as a hyperphone link, it allows the potential customer to click on the Biz-Call button to initiate a call back. They are offered the chance to specify when they want to receive that call - immediately, in 10 minutes or even later in the day.

For a new business, having an extra service such as Biz-Call shows efficiency and reliability to the potential new customer as it ensures they are never left in a queue and that they can be contacted at their convenience.

It is also designed to be flexible for the business using it. The service can be individually programmed to call a single number, call different numbers at different times of the day, or be unavailable and still capture messages. If responses are required to go to a different person who is continually on the move, the service is even able to follow someone from one number to another. That first time customer will not be allowed to get away!

Biz-Call is just one of many features that are or will be available to businesses taking advantage of the Internet and taking their business on-line. New businesses have the advantage of being able to build on-line development in to their start-up plans and, hopefully, with services such as that offered by Telewest, they can afford not to miss the electronic boat.

modem can join this network by using a standard phone line. The speed of this global network means that, depending on traffic, it can be just as quick for a user in Glasgow to access a computer in Sydney as one in Manchester. It makes it easier and cheaper to do business with companies in the supply chain, as well as with customers and potential customers on the other side of the world.

One of the clearest examples of the Internet's business potential is the rapid development of e-commerce. E-commerce revenues in the UK are expected to reach £10 billion this year – up three times on the 1998 figure. E-commerce allows the smallest companies to sit alongside vast corporations. Your presence on the Internet can be as effective and profitable for your business as a multi-national's presence can be for it.

Thousands of companies now use the Internet for sales and marketing. With your own Web site, you can not only tell the world about your products or services, but also accept orders or requests for information automatically and for 24 hours a day, seven days a week. You can even build up useful market information by tracking visitors to your site. In fact, building a Web site is now becoming an intrinsic part of marketing activity, like producing a price list or company brochure. There's a danger that companies who ignore its potential will increasingly lose market-share to those who have got involved.

Many British retailers are already running sites that let their customers buy directly over the Internet, although the DTI study also revealed that there is still a high level of untapped potential for on-line business, especially in the SME market. There are numerous other opportunities for e-commerce, such as electronic publishing of newspapers and magazines, electronic mail-order, which lets customers browse on-line catalogues, and customer help-desks where customers can leave questions via e-mail.

The Internet is a public network that anyone can access, so the issue of security is important. While this was a concern in the past, most modern browsers now have sophisticated levels of security built in so that no unauthorised person can read, forge or intercept an on-line transaction. The number of UK banks now offering on-line banking confirms their satisfaction with Internet security.

The year ahead will see the introduction of new security measures like TrustUK hallmark, a joint government–industry initiative to allay consumer concerns about the security of e-commerce. You can expect these kind of security-focussed initiatives to encourage growth in on-line commerce in the future.

The Government will pass the Electronic Communications Bill in 2000. This not only demonstrates a commitment to take security issues seriously, but is also a symbol that the Internet has really come of age in the UK.

You can also advertise on the Web by placing banner advertising on other people's Web pages, which can be targeted at those who could be interested in your particular product or service.

Just like your phone number, your e-mail address uniquely identifies you from the millions of other users on the Internet and lets them send e-mail to you. As with any marketing tool, it is wise to talk to someone who understands the medium and how best your company can use it. Your ISI Local Support Centre will be able to help you.

IMPROVING COMMUNICATIONS

Networks

There are valuable benefits to be derived from putting a network into an office. This can be nothing more that two or more computers joined together by a cable. Running network software on each machine lets them communicate with each other and linked computers mean that users can share peripherals such as a printer or fax. They can also have common access to files, such as spreadsheets and word-processed documents or a company database.

A network allows people to share information more readily and therefore allows companies to work faster, more efficiently, communicate better and gain greater security (by being able to back up day files centrally). With the addition of a camera and microphones at each geographical location and the means to send the sound and pictures between them, this can be expanded to accommodate video conferencing.

EVER DREAMED OF OWNING YOUR OWN BUSINESS? DISCOVER A FAST GROWING, SUCCESSFUL AND LUCRATIVE OPPORTUNITY :

TransNet Communications is a fast developing worldwide network marketing company with its sights firmly set on rapid growth in the multi-billion pound communications industry

The reality of employment today and in the future is increased redundancies, outsourcing, global recession and pension erosion. With 18 million unemployed in Europe and part-time workers outnumbering full-timers, how can we be sure of job security? Owning one's own business usually means, amongst other things, serious capital investment, premises, employees, stock and bad debts.

The ideal business would therefore be one in which none of these are required, where there is no risk and which is part of the fastest growing industry in the world. More importantly, a business where one can see the potential for an immediate income. Network marketing is a 50-year-old industry, involving 21 million people in 125 countries, responsible for £45 billion annually and it is an industry, which produces many millionaires each year. It is a dynamic method of product distribution utilising "word of mouth" advertising and personal recommendation.

Henk Keilman, one of Europe's pioneering and most successful telecommunications entrepreneurs, has the ideal business. Highly accomplished and well respected in the industry, Henk has successfully spearheaded five companies one of which he sold in 1998 for a staggering $250 million. Possessing a remarkable ability to accurately identify emerging trends and create opportunities for those associated with him, Henk immediately set about starting a new company - TransNet Communications. His vision - to establish the first pan-European telecommunication and technology Network Marketing company.

Says Henk "It is no secret that telecomms and communication prod-

Henk Keilman

Paula Pritchard

sharing information with other consumers about the products and services they use themselves, they can build a business of their own.

TNC has already established itself in the UK, Netherlands, Belgium, Germany, Austria Sweden and its latest market Denmark was opened in March 2000. Further European expansion is planned over the next eighteen months. TNC has attracted in excess of 75,000 customers and employs over 80 people who are based in its headquarters situated in the business district of Amsterdam.

ucts such as the Internet are the massive growth markets of the modern era. Without doubt this is the market arena to be involved in as we move into the 21st century. Market research shows that this trend is here to stay and like any growth market, the enormous demand for communication products and services outstrips supply." Indeed in 1997 there were 160 million Internet users worldwide, this is now increased more than fourfold.

TNC specialises in the provision of low cost telephony services, the Internet, GSM mobile communications and innovative communication technology products that are sold through an ever-growing network of Independent Distributors. These Distributors have an opportunity to benefit from what is considered the most lucrative Marketing Plan in the industry whilst at the same time they are able to take advantage of the deregulation of public utilities worldwide and the explosion of the information superhighway. By

In May, Henk Keilman announced that the company had attracted substantial funding from a group of private investors and three venture capital firms. Henk Keilman commented at the time "The European telecommunications market offers great opportunities for companies that understand that market and have adequate financial backing. With the addition of our new investors we are in an excellent position to support our plans for pan-European growth".

There are no barriers to anyone becoming an Independent Distributor in terms of the number of hours they put into the business, or by the standard of their education, their cultural background or whether or not they have had previous experience in the telecommunication and technology industry. The opportunity is open to anyone and everyone to achieve their own goals and aspirations and gain

Elaine Fishberg

financial independence, whilst having fun and enjoyment on the way.

On joining, a new Distributor receives a Welcome Pack which contains all the information needed to start their business, though they are encouraged to purchase the Telephony Business Programme which has a number of additional benefits to "fast start" their business. This includes a training programme, a manual, a diskette featuring the company presentation as well as a three pages TNC business website, transnetonline.com, Pop3email addresses. Telephony Marketing Materials and smart portfolio case containing a stock of high quality brochures, a corporate video, an audio tape about the business opportunity and a mobile phone and accessories voucher or free landline use voucher and last but not least free TNC Genie for six (6)months! There is a parallel Internet Business Programme for those interested in developing an Internet based business.

TNC Marketing Plan works as well for people wanting a part-time additional income as for people seeking a new career with significant remuneration.

In either case, the residual income potential of getting paid again and

again in fact indefinitely for the same business is highly appealing.

Discover how easy TNC products are to use and how much money they will save you!

Get the inside story on how TNC's proven results could work for you!

Paula Pritchard, who has reached the top position of International Marketing Director, and has an impressive background in Network marketing with over 20 years experience, helps present the programme and the business opportunity by giving presentations throughout the TransNet markets. Paula Pritchard comments "I want to share with other people this ideal business that I am in. With the training I show people how to activate their position, how to start right and develop their TNC business. They in turn will duplicate by teaching their people how to do the same, and so on. It is a constant duplication which of course is what networking is all about."

A final word from Henk Keilman, "We are equipped with the leadership, the drive, the experience and the resources to make a difference to the lives of our distributors and our customers through technology and communication. The future belongs to TransNet and to those who share our vision."

TransNet Communications B.V.
www.transnet.nl
For further details, please contact :
Maido Garay
TransNet Communications
2 Queen Caroline Street
London
W 6 9 DX
Direct Phone : +44 (0) 20 8323 8153
Direct Fax : + 44(0) 20 8323 8326
Email : Mgaray@transnet.nl

You're about to become the MD, the secretary, the mail boy, and the finance director.

And there's no holiday.

Rewarding, yes, but no one said starting your own business would be easy. Fortunately BT can be a lot more for you than just a phone company. We have created a website with plenty of advice to help you cope. Check it out at bt.com/getstarted. Not only will you find out how the right communications can help you get ahead, but also advice on law, tax, marketing, even recruitment. In fact all the support you need to make your venture a little less like hard work.

bt.com/getstarted Click on it for a start.
Freefone 0800 234 500

BT *Stay in touch*

Electronic mail

Electronic mail (or e-mail) lets you write a message on one computer and send it to a person on another computer, possibly attaching a document or files at the same time.

The message can be sent internally between computers arranged into a network or it can be sent externally over the phone line to a computer anywhere in the world, often over a global network like the Internet. If you already have an internal network, it is comparatively easy to link it to the phone network so your business can, from your computers, send and receive e-mail from all over the world. This is already very common in companies based in several geographical locations.

A distinct attraction of e-mail is that it is inexpensive and the cost is the same regardless of distance. It costs the same to send a message to Washington Tyne and Wear as it does to Washington DC because your connection is charged at local telephone rates. It is also fast. An e-mail can often reach its recipient in minutes, or at most within a few hours, even for those going to someone on the other side of the world.

E-mail is also convenient and flexible. Recipients don't have to be there to receive messages. They will be stored until needed and sending communications to large numbers of people is straightforward, with most software offering mailing-list features. You can also send computer files such as spreadsheets or project plans which can be worked on by the recipient. Many e-mail programmes also offer facilities that include security functions.

Intranet

An Intranet is a specialised kind of network. Based on Internet technology, an Intranet acts for many companies as an internal communication tool, like an electronic noticeboard. One of the most powerful incentives for taking the plunge and getting an Intranet up-and-running is that your competitors may already be utilising its potential.

INTRODUCTION

Today's workplace is very different from five years ago — remote or home working is now commonplace. The reliance on IT systems by the small business owner has never been greater and is growing constantly. Therefore, it is essential to choose the right equipment to allow you to optimise how and where you work.

The modern office needs reliable technology capable of utilising the latest advancements to optimise the effectiveness of the users — notebooks provide the solution.

Notebooks have been transformed over the last few years and their specifications now rival traditional desktop PCs. Demand from SoHo users is at an all-time high and continues to grow; 30% year on year.

UMAX has worked very hard to bring ActionBook prices down to enable everyone to benefit from mobile computing — it has never been more affordable! At the same time UMAX have also given the user advanced specifications, only normally seen in desktop PC's.

SO, WHAT ARE THE ADVANTAGES OF MOBILE COMPUTING?

Firstly, the main and obvious advantage with being portable is the ability to work anywhere. With today's laptops weighing less than 3Kg, they can be easily carried and used anywhere – on the train, at home, or at the office.

Today's laptops are true desktop replacements; they have the ability to do everything that a desktop PC can do. In the past, laptop users had been limited by processor power when compared to a desktop PC — this is no longer the case.

In addition, the expansion capabilities of a laptop used to be limited and certain upgrades weren't available. As technology has improved over the last couple of years, mainly through miniaturisation, these limitations have been overcome. Virtually every major IT component manufacturer has introduced the equivalent products available for both desktop PC's and laptops. This has resulted in the laptop achieving the same levels of performance as a PC. In all laptops today the processor, HDD and memory are equivalent to a desktop PC, the only difference being the size.

In previous years, one disadvantage with a laptop used to be poor screen quality. This meant that for prolonged viewing the laptop had to be plugged into an external monitor, which took away the whole portability of the laptop. Today's laptops have the most advanced screens available, available in sizes up to 14.1" and resolutions of up to 1024 × 768 (XGA). This very high quality TFT design results in the image being just as sharp as a conventional desktop monitor, or in many cases, even better!

THE GROWTH OF THE NOTEBOOK

Latest research from Intel, the biggest processor manufacturer in the world, shows by the year 2003 four out of five computers sold will be laptops — that makes them one of the fastest growing product groups in the IT market today. So, it appears the days are numbered for the desktop PC as we know it.

One of the main reasons for this huge growth is convenience, users don't want bulky boxes taking up room on their desk and they also need flexibility in where they can work. A laptop combined with a mobile phone, to access email and the Internet, results in the ability to work anywhere.

THE UMAX RANGE

With the Internet becoming a part of everyone's life, it is very important for today's laptops to have a built-in modem. The whole UMAX laptop range has built-in 56k modems, which is essential in today's office environment for rapid access to the Internet and email.

Laptops today also have excellent expansion capabilities. The UMAX range has PCMCIA expansion slots, which are the equivalent of the desktop PC's PCI slots. The size of credit cards, these allow easy connection of network cards, enhanced sound cards and a whole host of peripheral items, such as scanners.

Some UMAX models also have one touch access buttons, or 'hot keys', to the Internet and email, which can be programmed to your favourite communications software.

With the performance of UMAX laptops comparable to most desktop systems, small businesses often use them as true desktop replacements. Unplugging the printer, scanner and ethernet connection every morning and night used to be an arduous job, however, using a port replicator makes it very simple and quick – with only one connection, the user can plug all external devices into the back of the laptop.

All UMAX laptops are supplied with a full-sized Windows 98 keyboard as standard, with the additional convenience of being able to connect an external keyboard or mouse via the PS2 port.

PROJECTORS

An ideal extension to the portability of a notebook is a projector — these lightweight, modern systems enable high quality presentations to customers, suppliers and can be used for a whole host of other uses such as training and marketing. Connecting to your notebook is as easy as connecting an external monitor — via one cable that plugs into the back.

The projector market is also experiencing a huge growth in demand with substantial price reductions. The latest Polaroid range is now available from under £2400.

In summary, the laptop PC is the perfect solution for today's small office. It has all the functionality a desktop PC, yet the mobile convenience and flexibility that is needed in today's office environment. The difference in price between a desktop PC and laptop is narrowing all the time and this is fuelling the huge growth in the laptop PC market. The desktop system as we know it today is fast dying — make way for the new PC.

For full details of the UMAX and Polaroid ranges contact IMC Plc tel: 01344 871329

Fax

Fax machines still have an importance in business today, despite the spread of e-mail. They can send documents quickly to recipients who don't have e-mail facilities and can send documents which can't be easily converted to a digital format, for example documents which have originated on paper.

Video and data conferencing

Video conferencing is a technology that enables meetings to be held without having to get everyone together in the same room. A video link with a simultaneous audiolink allows teams and individuals to see as well as hear one another, wherever they are in the world. The great majority of video conferencing systems now offer data conferencing at the same time.

Data conferencing gives the same people the ability to exchange, transfer and work collaboratively on a range of documents and other applications, either alongside video or just using an audiolink. It is now possible to work on files such as spreadsheets, examine remote objects, annotate 3D graphics or even share videoclips without regard to the distance between them. It is this data sharing element which makes conferencing such a potentially vital business tool.

FUTURE DEVELOPMENTS

No one really knows exactly how the Internet, e-mail, video conferencing and the array of information technology applications will develop. However, it is known that companies of all sizes and in all sectors, from finance to manufacturing, are moving on-line on a daily basis.

In the space of just a few years, the Internet has become the most exciting medium for commerce and business communications. Banks now offer banking services on-line. Retailers sell everything from books to groceries, from cheap travel to ice cream. The Internet offers one of the biggest commercial opportunities available.

As more and more people go on-line the potential is vast. With the growing numbers on the Net, the capacity of the network is sometimes tested as service providers catch up with phenomenal increases in demand. But delivery and transmission systems will improve: optical fibres, for example, which carry up to 500 million times more information than current conventional copper wiring promise faster access.

Increasing profits and competitiveness are the critical factors for any business. Doing business electronically is frequently cheaper, quicker, more responsive and more collaborative, improving profits and performance. Given the current size, future growth prospects and attractive demographics of the new media, can any company afford not to investigate the possibilities?

USEFUL CONTACTS AND ADDRESSES

If you are thinking of introducing new technologies into your workplace your first point of call should be your ISI Local Support Centre. Local Support Centres are being set up all around the UK in partnership with Business Links in England and the equivalent organisations in Scotland, Wales and Northern Ireland. You can try out, first hand, technologies like e-mail and the Internet. The emphasis is on helping you make immediate and effective use of technology with guidance tailored to your individual business demands.

Ring the ISI Business Infoline on 0845 715 2000 to find out where your nearest ISI Local Support centre is. The ISI Web site is at: *www.isi.gov.uk*, e-mail: *info@isi.gov.uk*

England

For broad ranging advice, support and help with establishing your priorities, contact your local Business Link. Call the National Business Link line on 0845 756 7765 – they'll put you in touch with your nearest office. Visit the Web site at: *www.businesslink.co.uk*

Northern Ireland

The Industrial Research and Technology Unit (IRTU) can make you aware of the business benefits of using electronic communications and offer impartial advice.

Call the Superhighway Helpline on 0800 515319, e-mail: *superhighway.irtu@nics.gov.uk* or visit the Web site: *www.nics.gov. uk/irtu*

Scotland

Your Local Enterprise Company or Highlands & Islands Enterprise can give you practical guidance, project support and impartial advice.

Lowlands: Sue Kearns at the Scottish office; tel: 0141 242 5527; e-mail: *Sue.Kearns@so049.scotoff.gov.uk*

Wales

Business Connect will direct you to the particular service you need on specific information-based matters and in support of business activity more generally call Business Connect on 0845 796 9798. Visit the Web site at: *www.bc-wales.org.uk*

Other sources of information

BACT (Business Advisory Committee); tel: 020 7634 8773; Web site at: *www.acts.org.uk*

Checklist: Managing IT

- [ ] Contact ISI for information on IT or visit ISI Local Support Centre.
- [ ] Assess your needs before purchasing equipment, particularly with regard to how quickly you will need to receive and send material.
- [ ] Consider the type of computer and how big a memory you will require for your business needs.
- [ ] Spend time visiting other company Web sites to assess if your company would benefit from having a presence on the Internet.
- [ ] Consider advertising your products by placing banner advertising on other people's Web pages.
- [ ] Consider ways in which to use communication tools such as networks and e-mail and whether it is cost-effective.

Appendices

APPENDIX I: THE COSTS OF DIFFERENT METHODS OF RAISING FINANCE

Type of finance	Description	Size of facility
Proprietor's own resources	Savings or personal borrowings	Dependent upon what investors can afford
Private investors	Savings or personal borrowings contributed by family, friends, business partners or acquaintances	No limit. If private investors seek tax relief under the Enterprise Investment Scheme (EIS) there is a limit of £150,000 per person per annum that is eligible
Bank overdraft and short-term loans	Short-term funding that should generally be used to cover short-term business needs. Can be withdrawn at any time	Depends upon the ability of the company to repay and the security available
Business loans from a bank	Unlike mortgages these have a defined term, usually between two and seven years	Usually from £5,000 upwards

Cost to the business	Timescale for applications	Terms and conditions
The income the money could have earned if invested elsewhere	Immediate	None
The interest or dividends that must be paid to investors Legal costs of producing a shareholders' agreement	May take a few weeks or months, depending upon the progress of negotiations	There is usually a shareholders' agreement and possibly amendments to the Articles of Association, which both govern the rights of the investors and the management. They may also restrict some management action such as limiting remuneration and borrowing powers
There is generally an arrangement fee, payable in advance, of around 1.25 per cent for new lending and 0.75 per cent for renewals. In addition there is a fee to cover the completion of any security Interest rates for new businesses vary between 2 and 6 per cent above bank base rates	Usually only a few days but may extend to several weeks depending upon any demands for property valuations or additional information, life insurance policies and legal process	The bank usually requires a debenture conferring a fixed and floating charge over the assets of the business. May also require directors' guarantees. Will usually want regular accounts
There is generally an arrangement fee, payable in advance, of around 1.5 per cent Legal and possibly accountancy costs	Probably a couple of weeks to a couple of months. The bank will want to understand the expected cash flows from the business and will seek information to support this	A debenture giving a fixed and floating charge over the assets of the business to the bank

Type of finance	Description	Size of facility
Commercial mortgages	Available from banks, finance houses and insurance companies. Secured specifically on property assets Available for up to 20 years	Dependent upon the value of the property put up as security and upon the expected amount of cash flow from the business that will be available to pay interest and repay capital
Long-term loans	Usually provided by banks, insurance companies etc	Probably a minimum of £250,000
Bills of exchange	Usually used to finance a particular trade transaction, these are like cheques drawn on a bank but payable at a particular date and subject to certain conditions e.g. delivery of the goods. The recipient can get a bank to lend against one	Usually over £100,000. The amount depends upon the strength of the issuing and receiving company, since a default by either could invalidate the bill

Cost to the business	Timescale for applications	Terms and conditions
Commercial investigation, survey and legal costs are usually borne by the borrower and may amount to up to 2 per cent of the amount borrowed. In addition there may be an arrangement fee of up to 1.25 per cent Interest is charged at rates from 2 to 4 per cent above bank base rates: rates fixed for up to 5 years may be available	Several weeks, giving time for property valuation, internal approval procedures and a review of the expected cash flows from the business	Mortgage document will charge property to the lender. Other supporting security may sometimes be requested
Lower rates of interest than overdraft. May be available at fixed rates, in which case the rate depends upon market expectations of future movements in interest rates Valuation and legal costs together with some cost for the lender's commercial investigation	Two to three months. Can be longer for a large facility	A debenture will give the lender a fixed and floating charge over all the assets of the business
Discounts charged are equivalent to between 1.5 and 4 per cent over the three month inter bank rate There are no set up costs	The initial facility may take a couple of weeks to establish	There will be an upper limit to the size of the bill that may be discounted. There may also be conditions relating to the type of transaction or customer financed in this way. The company effectively takes the risk on default on a bill of exchange

Type of finance	Description	Size of facility
Acceptance credits	Like a bill of exchange but with the addition of backing by a bank	Usually over £250,000
Factoring	A factoring house takes over the sales ledger for a company, an administration fee, and also advances up to 80 per cent of debtors when they are invoiced	There is usually a minimum annual turnover of £250,000
Invoice discounting	Similar to factoring but the finance house does not manage the sales ledger. It advances money against specific invoices, leaving it to the borrower to collect the monies	Up to 80 per cent of the value of agreed debts. Some discounters may also limit a facility to, say, 50 per cent of the total value of trade debtors
Hire purchase and lease purchase	Purchase of equipment, paid for by the finance house, which transfers ownership to the borrower with the final instalment	Usually less than £100,000 per item
Leasing	Generally available for two to seven years to finance plant and equipment. There may be an option to buy the equipment at the end of the term	Can range from hundreds of pounds to millions

Cost to the business	Timescale for applications	Terms and conditions
Acceptance commission is 0.5 to 2 per cent There may be a commitment fee, payable if the facility is not used	As for bills of exchange	There will be an upper limit to the size of bill that may be discounted. There may also be conditions relating to the type of transaction or customer financed in this way
Typically 2 to 4 per cent over finance house base rates (higher than bank base rate) plus a fee ranging from 0.75 to 3 per cent to manage the sales ledger There is usually a set-up fee of around 0.25 per cent of the opening debtors	Timescale depends upon the financial strength of the company, its trade, the number and nature of the company's customers and how much investigation is required. Can usually be done within a month	Can be arranged with no recourse against the borrower if the debtor does not pay but this costs more and a lower percentage of the debt is usually available for finance. Some debtors may not be accepted
Typically 2 to 4 per cent over finance house base rates (higher than bank base rate)	As for factoring	Can be arranged with no recourse against the borrower if the debtor does not pay but this costs more and a lower percentage of the debt is usually available for finance. Some debtors may not be accepted
Depending upon the covenant of the borrower, usually 2 to 5 per cent over finance house base rate	A few days or a week or two depending upon the size of facility and the standing of the borrower	The equipment belongs to the finance house and reverts to them if the borrower defaults; all payments up to that point are lost to the borrower. Equipment must usually be insured by the borrower
Between 3 and 6 per cent over finance house base rate. Fixed interest rates are sometimes available	For lower cost items such as cars, leasing may take only a few days to arrange but for large scale leasing it can take several weeks	Default may lead to repossession of the property by the leasing company. There may also be other business or even directors' guarantees to secure the leasing

Type of finance	Description	Size of facility
Contract hire	Regular hire payments that leave the ownership of the asset hired with the hire company	Can range from a few pounds to millions (eg for large computer installations)
Sale and leaseback	Sale of property or a significant item of machinery to a leasing company – it is immediately leased back	The size of facility can range from a few thousand pounds to millions. The market value of the asset defines the upper limit
Venture capital	Venture capital organisations will invest in shares and loans to a company. They will usually take only a minority stake and may form investment syndicates	There are limited numbers of institutions providing finance of less than £500,000 but there is no upper limit
Venture capital trusts	A special form of venture capital company that bears some restrictions to its operation in return for tax advantages to its investors	Limited to £1m invested in any one company

Cost to the business	Timescale for applications	Terms and conditions
From 2 to 5 per cent above bank base rates	From a few days to a few months for large transactions	There will usually be a minimum period for the hire contract and a lower rental available after that has expired
As for leasing There are also valuation costs and legal expenses on the sale and leasing agreement There may be a risk of a capital gains tax liability	This sort of transaction is usually more complex than ordinary leasing and will therefore take a couple of months or even more to complete	Standard leasing terms
Venture capital organisations will seek returns ranging from 20 to 40 per cent on _equity_ investments. They will take this from dividends, interest and expected capital gains. Since entrepreneurs often seek returns of this scale they are not as high as they seem Legal and accountancy costs will be incurred and there will usually be a charge to cover the costs of the venture capital company	Investments rarely take less than six weeks to arrange	A formal agreement will cover matters such as: prevention of the proprietor from engaging in other business activities without permission, level of borrowing permitted, right for the vc house to be consulted on capital expenditure, levels of directors' remuneration and dividends, what happens if the business performance does not meet targets etc Some institutions want to be able to realise their investment in three to seven years and structure their terms to encourage this
As for venture capital	As for venture capital	As for venture capital

Type of finance	Description	Size of facility
Trade credit	This arises from using the time available before a supplier's invoice must be paid	Depends upon the size of the debts owed
Supplier discounts	Many suppliers will offer discounts for early settlement of their invoices	Depends upon the size of the purchase
Local authority grants	Some local authorities, particularly in poorer areas, will offer grants to assist local businesses e.g. building improvement or marketing assistance	Generally small scale – typically £5,000 to £10,000 maximum
Grants to assist business development and training	There are several schemes available through local Training and Enterprise Councils or Business Link as well as City Challenge for certain areas	Generally up to about £5,000
Landlords rent-free periods	Many landlords will allow new tenants in unlet developments to occupy property free of rent	The period may range from a few months to a couple of years
Consumer credit	It could be said that providing finance to the customers of a retail or mail order business is effectively financing the business	Generally up to £100

(Reproduced by kind permission of Robson Rhodes.)

Cost to the business	Timescale for applications	Terms and conditions
Delayed payment may lead to higher prices, reduced credit or a refusal to trade	n/a	As for venture capital
The cost of this financing is whatever interest could be earned on the money if the supplier was paid later	n/a	n/a
None	Generally a few weeks	The work must be carried out
None, although the funding may be available only on a matching of the company's investment	Generally a week or two but a consultant's report may be necessary	The company must carry out the training or formulate the business plan that is funded. The TEC may insist upon the use of its own or recommended consultants to carry out the work
The rent-free period is often balanced by a higher rent in the future	This can take days or weeks: as long as it takes to negotiate a lease	No specific conditions although the benefit is often not transferrable if the tenant assigns the lease
None	Typically a few days	In some cases the finance house may seek the guarantee of the company for each customer

APPENDIX II:
FURTHER READING FROM KOGAN PAGE

Kogan Page publish a wide variety of helpful titles for people in business. A full list of titles is available by writing to the publisher at the address given on the back cover, by calling on 020 7278 0433 or by visiting Web site: www.kogan-page.co.uk

Leaflets from government offices provide a further source of information, either from the government department concerned or from the Stationery Office.

Business Communication

CBI Corporate Communications Handbook (1998), eds Timothy
  Foster and Adam Jolly
Doing Business on the Internet (1998), Simon Collin
How to be a Better Communicator (1996), Sandy McMillan
Marketing Communications 2nd edition (1998), Paul Smith
Sales Promotions 2nd edition (1998), Julian Cummins

Start-ups, Business Plans and New Directions

The Business Plan Workbook 3rd edition (1998), Colin Barrow, Paul
  Barrow and Robert Brown
Forming a Limited Company 6th edition (1998), Patricia Clayton
Great Ideas for Making Money (1994), Niki Chesworth
Money Mail Moves Abroad (1998), Margaret Stone
*Net That Job! Using the World Wide Web to Develop Your Career and
  Find Work* (1998), Irene Krechowiecka
Working for Yourself 20th edition (2000), Godfrey Golzen
E-Business Start-Up Guide (2000), Philip Treleaven

Law and Company Secretarial

*An A–Z of Employment Law: A Complete Reference Source for
  Managers* 2nd edition (1997)

The Company Secretary's Handbook: A Guide to the Duties and Responsibilities 2nd edition (1998), Helen Ashton
Law for the Small Business 9th edition (1998), Patricia Clayton

Finance, Accounting and Bookkeeping

Accounting for Non-Accountants 4th edition (1999), Graham Mott
Do Your Own Bookkeeping (1988), Max Pullen
Financial Management for the Small Business 4th edition (1998), Colin Barrow
Self Assessment for the Small Business and Self-Employed (1998), Niki Chesworth
Understand Your Accounts 4th edition (1999), A St John Price

Franchising

Guide to Buying Your First Franchise 3rd edition (1999), Greg Clarke
Taking Up a Franchise 14th edition (2000), Colin Barrow and Godfrey Golzen

Import and Export

CBI European Business Handbook 5th edition (1999), ed Adam Jolly
The EMU Fact Book (1998), Niki Chesworth and Susie Pine-Coffin
The Export Handbook: In Association with the British Chambers of Commerce (1998), ed Harry Twells
Getting Started in Export (1998), Roger Bennett
Getting Started in Importing (1998), John Wilson

Management

How to Be an Even Better Manager: A Complete A-Z of Proven Techniques and Essential Skills ... Reveals the Secrets of Successful Managers 4th edition (1994), Michael Armstrong
International Dictionary of Management 5th edition (1995), eds Hano Johannsen and G Terry Page
Introduction to Modern Management (1998), Tony Dawson
Transform Your Management Style! (1998), Hilary Walmsley

Sales, Marketing and Advertising

Customer Driven Marketing: The Ideal Way to Increased Profits Through Marketing, Sales and Service Improvement (1997), John Frazier-Robinson

Do Your Own Market Research 3rd edition (1998), Paul Hague and Peter Jackson

European Direct Marketing Association 3rd edition (1999), eds Adam Baines and Sheila Lloyd

Handbook of International Direct Marketing: In Association with the 101 Ways to Boost Customer Satisfaction (1997), Timothy R V Foster

A Handbook of Marketing and PR for the Small Business (1998), Moi Ali

How to Sell More: A Guide for the Small Business 2nd edition (1997), Neil Johnson

101 Ways to Get Great Publicity (1992), Timothy R V Foster

A Marketing Action Plan for the Growing Business (1999), Shailendra Vyakarnam and John Leppard

Measuring Customer Satisfaction (1993), Richard F Gerson

Selling by Telephone, 2nd edition (1998), Chris de Winter

Successful Marketing for the Small Business: The Daily Telegraph Guide, 4th edition (1998), Dave Petten

Successful Marketing for Small Businesses 4th edition (1998), Dave Patten

Working From Home

Running a Home Based Business revised edition (1998), Diane Baker

Your Home Office: A Practical Guide to Using the Technology Successfully 3rd edition (1998), Peter Chatterton

APPENDIX III:
USEFUL CONTACTS

GOVERNMENT

The Adjudicator's Office

(For complaints against rulings by Customs and Excise)
Haymarket House, 28 Haymarket, London SW1Y 4SP.
Tel. 020 7930 2292.
Web: www.open.gov.uk/adjoff/aodemo1.htm

Business Links

Signpost Line: 08457 567765/freephone 0800 500200.

CCTA Government Information Service

A gateway to all Government Department Web sites:
www.open.gov.uk

Central Office of Information

Web: www.coi.gov.uk

Customs and Excise

New King's Beam House, 22 Upper Ground, London SE1 9JP.
Tel. 020 7620 1313.
Web: www.open.gov.uk/customs

The Data Protection Registrar

Wycliffe House, Wilmslow, Cheshire, SK9 5AF. Tel. 01625 535777.
Web: www.dpr.gov.uk

Department for Education and Employment

Sanctuary Buildings, Great Smith Street, London SW1P 3BT.
Tel. 020 7925 5000.
Web: www.dfee.gov.uk

Department of the Environment, Transport and the Regions

Eland House, Bressenden Place, London SW1E 5DU.
Tel. 020 7944 3000
Web: www.detr.gov.uk

Department of Trade and Industry

Enquiries: 1 Victoria Street, London SW1H 0ET. Tel. 020 7215 5000.
Small Firms and Business Link Division: Level 2, DTI, St Mary's
House, c/o Department for Education and Employment,
Moorfoot, Sheffield S1 4PQ. Tel. 0114 270 1356.
Web: www.dti.gov.uk

Exports Credits Guarantee Department (ECGD)

PO Box 2200, 2 Exchange Tower, Harbour Exchange Square,
London E14 9GS. Tel. 020 7512 7421.
Web: www.open.gov.uk/ecgd

Her Majesty's Treasury

The Public Enquiries Unit, Room 110/2, Treasury Chambers,
Parliament Street, London SW1P 3AG. Tel. 020 7270 4558.
Web: www.hm-treasury.gov.uk

Inland Revenue

The Inland Revenue has a number of helplines for enquiries, a
listing of which can be found on its website at
www.inlandrevenue.gov.uk

Office of Fair Trading

Field House, Breams Buildings, London EC4A 1PR.
Tel. 020 7211 8000.
Web: www.oft.gov.uk

Office for National Statistics

1 Drummond Gate, London SW1V 2QQ. Tel. 020 7533 6207.
Web: www.ons.gov.uk

Rural Development Commission

141 Castle Street, Salisbury SP1 3TP. Tel. 01722 336255.
Web: www.argonet.co.uk

Training and Enterprise Councils (TECs) and Local Enterprise Companies

List obtained from: Small Firms and Business Link Division,
Level 2, Department of Trade and Industry, St Mary's House,
c/o DfEE Moorfoot, Sheffield S1 4PQ. Tel. 0114 270 1356.
Web: www.tec.co.uk

GOVERNMENT OFFICES FOR THE REGIONS

Four departments (Employment, Trade and Industry,
Environment and Transport) have been organised into integrated
offices known as Government Offices (GOs) for the Regions.

Government Office for the East

Building A, Westbrook Centre, Milton Road, Cambridge CB4 1YG.
Tel. 01223 346700.
Web: www.go-east.gov.uk

Government Office for the East Midlands

The Belgrave Centre, Stanley Place, Talbot Street, Nottingham
NG1 5GG. Tel. 0115 971 9971.
Web: www.go-em.gov.uk

Government Office for London

157–161 Millbank, London SW1P 4RK. Tel. 020 7217 3222.
Web: www.open.gov.uk/glondon

Government Office for the North East

Wellbar House, Gallowgate, Newcastle Upon Tyne NE1 4TX.
Tel. 0191 201 3300.

Government Office for the North West

Sunley Tower, Piccadilly Plaza, Manchester M1 4BE.
Tel. 0161 952 4000.
Web: www.go.nw.gov.uk

Government Office, for the South East

Bridge House, 1 Walnut Tree Close, Guildford GU1 4GQ.
Tel. 01483 882 255.
Web: www.go-se.gov.uk

Government Offices for the South West

The Pithay, Bristol BS1 2PB. Tel. 0117 927 2666.
Web: www.gosw.gov.uk/gosw/
Mast House, Shepherds Wharf, 24 Sutton Road, Plymouth
PL4 OHJ. Tel. 01752 221 891.

Government Office for the West Midlands

77 Paradise Circus, Queensway, Birmingham B1 2DT.
Tel. 0121 212 5050.
Web: www.go-wm.gov.uk

Government Office for Yorkshire and Humberside

25 Queen Street, Leeds LS1 2TW. Tel. 0113 244 3171.
Web: www.goyh.gov.uk

Government Office for Northern Ireland

Department of Economic Development (DED)

Netherleigh, Massey Avenue, Belfast BT4 2TP. Tel. 028 9052 9900.
Web: www.nics.gov.uk/ni-direct/ded/

Government Office for Scotland

Scotland Office

1 Melville Crescent, Edinburgh EH3. Tel. 020 7270 6754.
Web: www.scotland.gov.uk

Government Office for Wales

Welsh Office

Industry Department, Crown Building, Cathays Park, Cardiff
CF1 3NQ. Tel. 029 2082 5111.
Web: www.wales.gov.uk

START-UP ADVICE

England and Wales

Local Enterprise Agencies

Business in the Community, 44 Baker Street, London W1M 1DH.
Tel. 020 7224 1600.
Web: www.bitc.org.uk

The National Assembly for Wales

Industry and Training Department, Crown Buildings, Cathays Park, Cardiff CF1 3NQ. Tel. 029 2082 5111.
Web: www.wales.gov.uk

Welsh Development Agency

Principality House, Friary, Cardiff, South Glamorgan CF1 4AE. Tel. 0845 775577.
Web: www.wda.co.uk

Scotland

Scottish Business in the Community

30 Hanover Street, Edinburgh EH2 2DR. Tel. 0131 220 3001.

Scottish Enterprise

120 Bothwell Street, Glasgow G2 7JP. Tel. 0141 248 2700.
Web: www.scotant.co.uk

The Office of the Scottish Executive

Education and Industry Department, Meridian Court, Cadogan Street, Glasgow G2 6AT. Tel. 0141 248 2855.
Web: www.scotland.gov.uk

Highlands and Islands Enterprise

Bridge House, 20 Bridge Street, Inverness IV1 1QR.
Tel. 01463 234171.
Web: www.hie.co.uk

Northern Ireland

Industrial Development Board for Northern Ireland

IDB House, 64 Chichester Street, Belfast BT1 4JX. Tel. 028 9023 3233.
Web: www.aexandre.nics.gov.uk/idb

Local Enterprise Development Unit (LEDU)

LEDU House, Upper Galway, Belfast BT8 6TB. Tel. 028 9049 1031.
Web: www.ledu-ni.gov.uk

NATIONAL ASSOCIATIONS REPRESENTING SMALL FIRMS

Association of British Chambers of Commerce

9 Tufton Street, London SW1P 3QB. Tel. 020 7565 2000.
Web: www.britishchambers.org.uk

Association of Independent Business

Independence House, 26 Addison Place, London W11 4RJ.
Tel. 020 7371 1299.

British Franchise Association

Thames View, Newton Road, Henley on Thames, Oxfordshire
RG9 1HG. Tel. 01491 578049.
Web: www.british-franchise.org.uk

Confederation of British Industry (CBI)

Centre Point, 103 New Oxford Street, London WC1A 1DU.
Tel. 020 7379 7400.
Web: www.cbi.org.uk

Federation of Small Businesses Ltd

32 Orchard Road, Lytham St Annes, Lancs FY8 1NY.
Tel. 01253 72091.
Web: www.fsb.org.uk

The Forum of Private Business Ltd

Ruskin Chambers, Drury Lane, Knutsford, Cheshire WA16 6HA.
Tel. 01565 634467.
Web: www.fpb.co.uk

The Industrial Society

Peter Runge House, 3 Carlton House Terrace, London SW1Y
5DG. Tel. 020 7839 4300.
Web: www.indsoc.co.uk

Smaller Firms Council (CBI)

Centre Point, 103 New Oxford Street, London WC1A 1DU.
Tel. 020 7379 7400.
Web: www.cbi.org.uk

FORMING A COMPANY

The Patent Office

Cardiff Road, Newport, Gwent NP9 1RH. Tel. 01633 814000.
Web: www.patent.gov.uk

Registrar of Companies

Companies Registration Office, Crown Way, Maindy, Cardiff
CF4 3UZ. Tel. 029 2038 8588.
Web: www.companies-house.gov.uk

For Scotland: 37 Castle Terrace, Edinburgh EH2 3DJ.
Tel. 0131 535 5800.

For London: Companies Registration Office, 55 City Road,
London EC1Y 1BB. Tel. 020 7253 9393.

Companies Limited/Rapid Refunds

376 Euston Road, London NW1 3BL. Tel. 020 7383 2323
Web: www.limited-companies.co.uk
To buy an off-the-shelf company.

Lawyers for your business

Law Society, 113 Chancery Lane, London WC2A 1PL.
Tel. 020 7320 5764.
Web: www.lfyb.lawsociety.org.uk

Industrial Common Ownership Movement (ICOM)

Vassalli House, 20 Central Road, Leeds LS1 6DE. Tel. 0113 246 1737.
Advice on setting up worker co-operatives.

The Institute of Business Advisers

PO Box 8, Harrogate, North Yorkshire HG2 8XB. Tel. 01423
879208.
Web: www.iba.org.uk

The Institute of Directors

116 Pall Mall, London SW1Y 5ED. Tel. 020 7839 1233.
Web: www.iod.co.uk

BANKS

Barclays Bank plc Small Business Services

PO Box 120, Longwood Close, Westwood Business Park,
Coventry CV4 8JN. Tel. 01203 694242.
Web: www.barclays.co.uk

HSBC plc Business Unit

6th Floor, Watlin Court, 44–57 Cannon Street, London EC4M 5SQ.
Tel. 020 7260 8711.
Web: www.banking.hsbc.co.uk

Lloyds Bank plc, Small Business Advice

PO Box 112, Canons House, Canons Way, Bristol BS99 7LB.
Tel. 0117 943 3433.
Web: www.lloydstsb.co.uk

National Westminster Bank plc, Small Businesses Service

Level 10 Drapers Gardens, 12 Throgmorton Avenue, London
EC2N 2DL. Tel. 020 7920 5555.
Web: www.natwest.co.uk

RAISING CAPITAL

Association of British Credit Unions Ltd

Holyoake House, Hanover Street, Manchester M60 0AS.
Tel. 0161 832 3694.

British Venture Capital Association

Essex House, 12–13 Essex Street, London WC2R 3AA.
Tel. 020 7240 3846.
Web: www.bveg.co.uk

British Insurance and Investment Brokers Association

BIIBA House, 14 Bevis Marks, London EC3A 7NT.
Tel. 020 7623 9043.

European Grants Ltd

94 Alfred Gelder Street, Hull HU1 2AL. Tel. 01482 211912.
Web: www.europeangrants.com

Factors and Discounters Association

Boston House, The Little Green, Richmond, Surrey TW9 1QE.
Tel. 020 8332 9955.
Web: www.factors.org.uk

Finance and Leasing Association

Imperial House, 15–19 Kings Way, London WC2B 6UN.
Tel. 020 7836 6511.
Web: www.fig-org.uk

Institute of Patentees and Investors

Suite 505a, Triumph House, 189 Regent Street, London
W1R 7WF. Tel. 020 7434 1818.

Local Investment Networking Co (LINC)

London Enterprise Agency, 4 Snow Hill, London EC1A 2BS.
Tel. 020 7236 3000.

The Prince's Youth Business Trust

18 Park Square East, London NW1 4LH. Tel. 020 7543 1234.
Web: www.princes-trust.org.uk

3I plc

9 Waterloo Road, London SE1 8XP. Tel. 020 7928 3131.
Web: www.3i.com/

Venture Capital Report Ltd

Magdalen Centre, Oxford Science Park, Oxford OX4 4GA.
Tel. 01865 784411.
Web: www.vcr1978.com

PREMISES

English Partnership

St George's House, Kingsway, Team Valley, Gateshead, Tyne and
Wear NE11 0NA. Tel. 0191 487 8941.
Web: www.englishpartnerships.co.uk

Estates Today

Web: www.estatestoday.co.uk
Online commercial estate agent.

Royal Institution of Chartered Surveyors

12 Great George Street, Parliament Square, London SW1P 3AD.
Tel. 020 7222 7000.
Web: www.rics.org

MARKETING AND SALES

The Advertising Association

Abford House, 15 Wilton Road, London SW1V 1NJ.
Tel. 020 7828 2771.
Web: www.adassfoc.org.uk

British Safety Council

70 Chancellor's Road, London W6 9RS. Tel. 020 8741 1231.
Web: www.britishsafetycouncil.org

British Standards Institution

389 Chiswick High Road, London W4 4AL. Tel. 020 8996 9000.
Web: www.bsi.org.uk

Chartered Institute of Marketing

Moor Hall, Cookham, Maidenhead, Berkshire SL6 9QH.
Tel. 01628 457 500.
Web: www.cim.co.uk

Direct Marketing Association UK Ltd

Haymarket House, 1 Oxendon Street, London SW1Y 4EE.
Tel. 020 7321 2525.
Web: www.dma.org.uk/

Institute of Direct Marketing

1 Park Road, Teddington, Middlesex TW11 0AR.
Tel. 020 8977 5705.
Web: www.theidm.com

Institute of Public Relations

The Old Trading House, 15 Northburgh Street, London
EC1V 0PR. Tel. 020 7253 5151.
Web: www.ipr.org.uk

Market Research Society

15 Northburgh Street, London EC1V 0AH. Tel. 020 7490 4911.
Web: www.mrs.org.uk

Marketing Society

St George's House, 3–5 Pepys Road, London SW20 8NJ.
Tel. 020 8879 3464.
Web: www.marketing-society.org.uk

MANAGING FINANCE

Chartered Accountants Directory

Datacomp, 4 Houldsworth Square, Reddish, Stockport, Cheshire SK5 7AF. Tel. 0161 442 5233.
Web: www.chartered-accountants.co.uk

Chartered Association of Certified Accountants

29 Lincoln's Inn Fields, London WC2. Tel. 020 7242 6855.
Web: www.acca.co.uk

Chartered Institute of Taxation

12 Upper Belgrave Street, London SW1X 8BB. Tel. 020 7235 2562.
Web: www.tax.org.uk

Institute of Chartered Accountants in England and Wales

PO Box 433, Chartered Accountants Hall, Moorgate Place, London EC2P 2BJ. Tel. 020 7920 8100.
Web: www.icaew.co.uk

Institute of Chartered Accountants of Scotland

27 Queen Street, Edinburgh EH2 1LA. Tel. 0131 225 5673.
Web: www.cas.org-uk

Institute of Company Accountants

40 Tyndales Road, Clifton, Bristol BS8 1PL. Tel. 0117 973 8261.

The International Association of Book-keepers

Burford House, London Road, Sevenoaks, Kent TN13 1AS.
Tel. 01732 458080.
Web: www.iab.org.uk

LABOUR RELATIONS AND PERSONNEL MANAGEMENT

Advisory, Conciliation and Arbitration Service (ACAS)

Brandon House, 180 Borough High Street, London SE1 1LW.
Tel. 020 7210 3000.
Web: www.acas.org.uk

Health and Safety Executive

Rose Court, 2 Southwark Bridge, London SE1 GHS.
Tel. 020 7717 6000.

Institute of Personnel and Development

IPD House, 35 Camp Road, Wimbledon, London SW19 4UX.
Tel. 020 8971 9000.
Web: www.ipd.co.uk

The Institute of Management

Small Firms Information Service, Management House,
Cottingham Road, Corby, Northants NN17 7IT. Tel. 01536 204222.
Web: www.inst-mgt.org.uk

The Institute of Management Consultants

5th Floor, 32–33 Hatton Garden, London EC1N 8DL.
Tel. 020 8971 9000.
Web: www.imc.co.uk

EXPORT

Association of British Chambers of Commerce

Export Marketing Research Scheme, 4 Westwood House,
Westwood Business Park, Coventry CV4 8HS. Tel. 024 7669 4484.
Web: www.britishchambers.org.uk/exportzone

British Exporters Association

Broadway House, Tothill Street, London SW1H 9NQ.
Tel. 020 7222 5419.
Web: www.bexa.co.uk

British International Freight Association

Redfern House, Browells Lane, Feltham, Middlesex TW13 7EP.
Tel 020 8844 2266.
Web: www.bifa.co.org

Commission of the European Communities

Jean Monet House, 8 Storey's Gate, London SW1P 3AT.
Tel. 020 7973 1992.

Department of Trade and Industry

Export Control Enquiry Unit, Kingsgate House, 66–74 Victoria
Street, London SW1E 6SW. Tel. 020 7215 5444.
Web: www.dti.gov.uk

European Commission

European Information Centres, 8 Storey's Gate, London
SW1P 3AT. Tel. 020 7973 1992.

Export Credits Guarantee Department

2 Exchange Tower, PO Box 2200, Harbour Exchange Square,
London E14 9GS. Tel. 020 7512 7000.
Web: www.open.gov.uk/ecgd

Institute of Export

64 Clifton Street, London EC2A 4HB. Tel. 020 7247 9812.
Web: www.export.org.uk

London Chamber of Commerce and Industry

33 Queen Street, London EC4R 1AP. Tel. 020 7248 444.
Web: www.londonchamber.co.uk

Simpler Trade Procedures Board

Venture House, 29 Glasshouse Street, London W1R 5RG.
Tel. 020 7287 3525.

Technical Help for Exporters

British Standards Institution, 389 Chiswick High Road, London
W4 4AL. Tel. 020 8996 9000.
Web: www.bsi.org.uk

Trade Indemnity plc

12–34 Great Eastern Street, London EC2A 3AX. Tel. 020 7739 4311.

TradeUK

Web: www.tradeuk.com
Online advice on export issues and e-commerce.

INFORMATION AND COMMUNICATION TECHNOLOGIES

British Telecom

Web: www.britishtelecom.co.uk
Advice on communications and information technologies for
business.

Information Society Initiative

For IT advice and support centres.
Web: www.isi.gov.uk

Nominet

To register Internet name.
Web: www.nic.uk

Exploit

Web: www.exploit.com

SubmitIt

Web: www.submitit.com
These companies will submit your Web site address to online
search engines.

Internet Link Exchange

Web: www.linkexchange.com
Exchange advertising banner with other sites.

Liszt

Web: www.liszt.com
Description of most mailing lists and joining details.

Technologies for Training

Web: www.tft.co.uk
Gateway to IT help with links to numerous organisations
working in IT.

WebCounter

Web: www.digits.com
Adds visitor counter to your Web site.

SECTOR INFORMATION

Construction
Federation of Master Builders

14–15 Great James Street, London WC1N 3DP. Tel. 020 7242 7583.
Web: www.fmb.org.uk

Crafts
The Crafts Council

44a Pentonville Road, London N1 9BY. Tel. 020 7278 7700.
Web: www.craftscouncil.org.uk

Design
Design Council

34 Bow Street, London WC2E. Tel. 020 7420 5200.
Web: www.design-council.org.uk

Interior Designers and Decorators Association

1–4 Chelsea Harbour Design Centre, Lots Road, London
SW10 0XE. Tel. 020 7349 0800.
Web: www.idda.co.uk

Estate Agents
The National Association of Estate Agents

Arbon House, 21 Jury Street, Warwick CV34 4EH.
Tel. 01926 496800.
Web: www.propertylive.co.uk

Farming

Agricultural Development Advisory Service

Oxford Spires, The Boulevard, Kidlington, Oxon OX5 1NZ.
Tel. 01865 842742.
Web: www.adas.co.uk

Agricultural Mortgage Corporation Ltd

AMC House, Chantry Street, Andover, Hampshire SP10 1DD.
Tel. 01264 334344.

Gardening/Landscape architecture

The Landscape Institute

6–7 Barnard Mews, London SW11 1QU. Tel. 020 7738 9166.
Web: www.l-i.org.uk

Royal Horticultural Soceity

14–15 Belgrave Square, London SW1X 8PS. Tel. 020 7245 6943.
Web: www.horticulture.demon.co.uk

Hospitality

Hotel and Catering International Management Association

191 Trinity Road, London SW17 7HN. Tel 020 8672 4251.
Web: www.hcima.org.uk

Brewers and Licensed Retailers Association

42 Portman Square, London W1H 0BB. Tel. 020 7486 4831.
Web: www.blra.co.uk

IT

Association of Computer Professionals

204 Barnett Wood Lane, Ashtead, Surrey KT21 2DB.
Tel. 01372 273442.

British Computer Society

1 Sanford Street, Swindon, Wiltshire SN1 1HJ. Tel. 01793 417417.
Web: www.bcs.org.uk

Management consultancy

Institute of Management Consultants

5th Floor, 32–33 Hatton Garden, London EC1N 8DL.
Tel.020 7242 2140.
Web: www.imc.co.uk

Retail

National Association of Shopkeepers

Lynch House, 91 Mansfield Street, Nottingham NG1 3FN.
Tel. 0115 947 5046.

Tourism

English Tourist Board

Development Advisory Services Unit, Thames Tower, Blacks
Road, Hammersmith, London W6 9EL. Tel. 020 8846 9000.
Web: www.visitbritain.com

Scottish Tourist Board

2 Ravelston Terrace, Edinburgh EH4 3EU. Tel. 0131 332 2433.
Web: www.holiday.scotland.nat

Wales Tourist Board

Brunel House, 2 Fitzalan Road, Cardiff CF2 1UY. Tel. 029 2049 9909.
Web: www.visitwales.com

SPECIALIST LIBRARIES

Business Statistics Office

Government Buildings, Cardiff Road, Newport, Gwent
NP9 1XG. Tel. 01633 815696.
Web; www.ons.gov.uk

Chartered Institute of Marketing Library

Moor Hall, Cookham, Maidenhead, Berkshire SL6 9QH.
Tel. 01628 427 500.

Department of Trade and Industry Library

Information and Library Centre, 1 Victoria Street, London
SW1H 0ET. Tel. 020 7215 5006/7.

Export Market Information Centre Library

Kingsgate House, 66–74 Victoria Street, London SW1E 6SW.
Tel. 020 7215 5444.

Frobisher Crescent Library at City University

Barbican, London EC2Y 8HB. Tel. 020 7477 8787.
Web: www.city.ac.uk

Institute of Management Library

Management House, Cottingham Road, Corby, Northants
NN17 1TT. Tel. 01536 204222.

London Business School Library

Sussex Place, Regents Park, London NW1 4SA. Tel. 020 7262 5050.
Web: www.lbs.lon.ac.uk/library/

London Guildhall University

School of Business Studies, 84 Moorgate, London EC2M 6SQ.
Tel. 020 7320 1000.

Monopolies and Mergers Commission Library

New Court, 48 Carey Street, London WC2A 2JT. Tel. 020 7324 1467.

Office of Fair Trading Library

Field House, 15–25 Bream's Buildings, London EC4A 1PR.
Tel. 020 7242 2858.

Business Information Service

British Library, Lloyds Bank Business Line, 25 Southampton
Buildings, London WC2A 1AW. Tel. 020 7412 7454/9799.

WEB SITES OF INTEREST

DTI

Web: www.dti.gov.uk
Good links to government-sponsored schemes.

Electronic Telegraph

Web: www.telegraph.co.uk
Access to full text of Daily Telegraph and directory listing of
British business.

Enterprise Zone

Web: www.enterprise-zone.org.uk
Extremely useful resource with useful links for start-ups.

Financial Times

Web: www.ft.com
Business directory and up-to-date financial information.

Keele University Management Web Resources Database

Web: www.keele.ac.uk
Well resourced database of business and management Web sites
with good links.

Kogan Page

Web: www.kogan-page.co.uk
Extensive list of publications for start-ups and SMEs.

Strathclyde University Business Information Sources on the Internet

Web: www.dis.strath.ac.uk
Thoroughly recommended Web site with extensive listings of
sites and general sources of business information.

WhoWhere

Web: www.whowhere.com
E-mail address, telephone number and street address directory.

Yahoo!

Web: www.yahoo.com
Search engine with extensive business directory.

Yell

Web: www.yell.co.uk
Online version of the Yellow Pages.

Index

273

Index of
Advertisers